Norman Enhorning
Glens Falls, 1972

PIERS PLOWMAN AS A
FOURTEENTH-CENTURY APOCALYPSE

To the memory of
my parents
Hanna Mai Brown (1884–1950)
Samuel Bloomfield (1880–1953)

Piers Plowman

as a

Fourteenth-century Apocalypse

Morton W. Bloomfield

RUTGERS UNIVERSITY PRESS

New Brunswick, New Jersey

Rutgers University, The State University of New Jersey

Library of Congress Catalogue Number: 61–10254

SBN: 8135-0398-1

This book has been published with the assistance of a grant from the Ford Foundation.

PREFACE

THE fundamental purpose of this book is to relate *Piers Plowman*, in both form and content, to its fourteenth-century intellectual milieu. This purpose is not new in Langland scholarship, at least as regards content, but the particular approach here set out has not been attempted before. Recent investigations of the later Middle Ages have turned up fresh materials; and we have had some important recent re-interpretations of medieval thought. It is time, I believe, that the results of such work be used in reassessing one of the most puzzling of all medieval poems. It is now possible to begin to understand the meaning of *Piers Plowman*, even if we cannot as yet answer all the questions it raises. This book is, then, a prolegomenon to the study of *Piers*. Too much yet needs to be known about fourteenth-century England to claim more.

Although the central thesis of this book is rather simple, it is nevertheless a closely integrated one which can be broached at several points and in which several parts depend on a knowledge of the others. It is, therefore, desirable that it be summed up at the beginning and that an outline of the order in which the thesis is presented be given.

My thesis has bearing on both the form and content of *Piers Plowman*, and this double relevance necessitates another division of the argument, which does not, of course, coincide with the natural divisions of the thesis itself.

Briefly, the thesis of this book is that *Piers Plowman* is concerned with the subject of Christian perfection rather than with salvation. The former is the creation of the monastic tradition and is the older and more social Christian world view. This tradition was still alive in the fourteenth century and in England. It is oriented towards the Kingdom of God and eschatology. It finds its natural expression in the apocalyptic frame of mind and in corresponding literary forms. *Piers Plowman* can be best understood as an apocalypse that reflects this older Christian tradition.

v

The book starts and ends with an analysis of parts of the poem itself. Chapter I discusses the art of *Piers Plowman*, in particular the problem of its form. The final part of the book (last part of Chapter IV and Chapter V) is mainly a close analysis of the text of *Piers Plowman* from Passus XVIII to the end, where I think my case can be best substantiated, and the bringing together of my arguments to tie them in with all the previous chapters and especially Chapter I. I start from the form of the poem and end on the same subject. The movement of the argument is as follows: the characteristics of the Christian monastic tradition, especially its apocalyptic and eschatological aspects (Chapter II); evidences of the monastic tradition in general in fourteenth-century England and in *Piers Plowman* (Chapter III); evidences of apocalypticism in the later Middle Ages and in *Piers Plowman* (Chapter IV); and, finally, how the apocalyptic and monastic traditions help to explain the form and content of *Piers Plowman* (Chapters I, IV, and V; Chapter I is mainly concerned with the question of what is the form of *Piers Plowman*). This is the skeleton of the book; for the flesh, one must turn to the book itself, where the case here argued can be evaluated by the reader.

I am not arguing, however, that *Piers* contains only apocalyptic elements, for it clearly has other dimensions. My claim is merely that the apocalyptic is the central concern of the poet and that only from this point of view can his main purposes and aims be understood. This book is fundamentally an essay in intellectual history and its application to the general comprehension of a work of art.

I do not feel it necessary to apologize for dividing *Piers* into its form and content. It is impossible to talk about any work of art without doing so; but since the rise of "new criticism," such division is usually done with a *caveat* that, of course, the work of art as such cannot be dichotomized. This kind of *caveat* seems to me to betray a lack of understanding of what intellectual endeavor implies. The experience of a work of art, if it is a successful one, is no doubt unified, but if appreciation is to progress beyond mere experience, intellectual distinctions must be made. Intellectual distinctions are intellectual, and they exist for the purpose of comprehension. Criticism, if it is to be more than a recall of feeling, is an intellectual discipline and necessarily involves the use of intellectual categories, such as form and content. We must not mistake the categories for the thing itself; they are created to enable us to understand it. Categories exist, not for themselves, but for intellectual comprehension; and to the extent that we are engaged in intellectual activity, we need them.

Even if form and content are indissolubly united in a great work of art, it is still worthwhile in our comprehension of it to separate them. If there are a large number of important works of art in which form and content are not indissolubly united, as undoubtedly there are, we have justification for what we do in the structure of the work itself. In any case, even to talk about form and content wedded together requires an intellectual separation of the two. The practice of critics shows that in order to talk about literary art at all, some distinction between form and content is necessary, even if we avoid these words themselves and choose euphemisms like *tenor* and *vehicle*. Further, until the rise of Coleridgean organic criticism, art was considered the conscious manipulation of subject matter on the basis of formal principles and the conscious use of adornment by the artist. The form and content distinction was present in the mind of the artist himself.[1]

This study does not propose to solve the many particular problems with which *Piers* abounds, and it deals with the larger problems quite generally. If I can, however, make more precise than hitherto Langland's general framework of form and thought, indicate the relations between them, and present the actual artistic problems facing him in terms of his purpose, I think our understanding of *Piers* will be advanced; and students will have a few general principles to guide them in elucidating some of the mysteries of the poem. The reader, then, will find here no answer as to why Piers tore up the pardon from Truth, or why Hawkin the Active Man appears, or why Book has two broad eyes (XVIII, 228); but he may get some help in looking for the meaning of these and other puzzling incidents and episodes in the poem and in judging the interpretations already provided.

Several particular usages I employ in this book require a few words of explanation. I have been troubled with the proper translation of the medieval Latin word *status*, for which there is no exact equivalent in English, although *estate* in its older sense will sometimes do. I have chosen the Latin word, instead of seeking various equivalents in English, in order to keep close to the medieval thinking that could use such a word in what to us are diverse meanings. Its plural is *statūs*. *Heilsgeschichte* is another foreign word that I have been obliged to repeat because of its fixed associations, although I occasionally use *redemptive history* for it.

All unspecified references to Passus and line (or lines) of *Piers Plowman* are understood to be from the B-Text, which I have used as the central form of the poem. Whenever the A- or C-Text is quoted or referred to, I have used the appropriate letter in the note or within parentheses. I have used the Skeat edition throughout since the new edition by Professors Kane, Donaldson, and Mitchell has not yet been completed beyond the A-Text. For my purpose, which is not for the most part a close textual analysis, the general accuracy of Skeat's B-text is sufficient.

My reference to *Piers* throughout as if it were written by William Langland of London and Malvern Hills is largely a matter of convenience. It is not completely established that William Langland is the author, although it is most likely; nor is it absolutely certain that the three versions or texts are by one man, although I believe so. I do not think that my central thesis will be disturbed if another name is substituted for William Langland; the author in any case must have been familiar with London and the area around Malvern, and this book should help to substantiate the view that the whole poem in its various forms (except, of course, for the lines by John But) is by one man.

I am indebted to the conscious and considerate help of various friends and acquaintances in the long preparation and writing of this book and should like to thank them for many kindnesses. Needless to say, they do not all agree with my arguments as here presented. I wish to thank in particular my former colleagues Professors R. D. Altick, R. M. Estrich, Marvin Fox, Franklin M. Ludden, Roy H. Pearce, and F. L. Utley; and Professors William Brandt, John Conley, Robert Kaske, A. L. Kellogg, R. B. Mynors, Arnold Williams, and R. M. Wilson; Drs. R. W. Hunt, W. A. Pantin, Beryl Smalley, and Siegfried Wenzel; and Father William F. Lynch, S.J., and Miss Sarah S. Appleton. My greatest debt is to Mrs. Thyra Hicks, who has been of inestimable help in putting my manuscript into its final form.

My debt is also great to the many scholars from whose published writings I have taken much and to whom my notes try to make acknowledgment. The staffs of various libraries have been of great aid to me, in particular those of The Ohio State University, Columbia University, Harvard University, Yale University, the University of Chicago, the Library of Congress, the British Museum, the Bodleian, the Bibliothèque Nationale, Paris, and the Cambridge University Library.

I am grateful to the Guggenheim Memorial Foundation, to the American Council of Learned Societies, and to the Graduate School of The Ohio State University for various financial aids, which have lightened the burden of preparing this book and which have speeded its completion.

Occasionally I have plagiarized sentences and phrases of my own authorship from articles already published in *Anglia, Traditio, Franciscan Studies,* and the *Journal of English and Germanic Philology.*

MORTON W. BLOOMFIELD

Cambridge, Massachusetts
July, 1961

CONTENTS

PIERS PLOWMAN AS A
FOURTEENTH-CENTURY APOCALYPSE

CHAPTER I

The Form of *Piers Plowman*

THAT William Langland intended *Piers Plowman* to be a work of art is obvious from the form in which he cast it. He created characters, fashioned dialogue for them, and provided a narrative, even if at times the action seems bogged down in endless talk. But things do happen and do move, and there is a conclusion which, if puzzling, is nevertheless a conclusion. What form Langland was consciously using, what language and meter he employed, and what audience he was addressing are as vital and important problems as the problem of what he was saying. As an artist, even a not entirely successful one, he must have chosen his forms and language with some purpose and care. They must stand in some relation to what he was trying to say. This chapter deals somewhat tentatively with these problems of rhetoric and art; subsequent chapters deal with what he was trying to say.

Piers Plowman ends, as it begins, with a quest. At the conclusion of the poem, the seeker is Conscience, who, unlike the questing Will at the beginning, knows what and whom he is seeking. Whether or not he finds Piers Plowman, the reader is not told, but he may at least assume that Piers can, and some day will, be found. As a good Christian, the author certainly must have believed this. He has shown that Piers in the later part of the poem is the human manifestation of Christ—either as Jesus or as an ideal head of the Church, His continuing vicar—for it is only through Him that perfection may be found. Conscience and Will are in search of spiritual knowledge that will transform society and the self. The poem deals with the search not the finding; and although the quest has not been in vain, the goal is yet to be attained. More is known at the end than at the beginning—that there is a guide and principles to follow, that there are forces within men and within history working for Christian perfection —but the journey is not yet complete. *Piers* is a work whose artistic and moral claims on the reader reinforce each other. What is sought is a way to seek.

This study regards Christian perfection as the goal of Will, but it has been customary in the past forty years to speak of the poem, when it is recognized as more than a valuable social document, as being concerned with the problem of salvation. In the very important discussion between the dreamer and Lady Holy Church in Passus I, after the description of the field full of folk and the fable of the rats have been detailed in the Prologue, Will raises the question, "How I may save my soule" (I, 84), and is given a brief answer with instructions to teach Holy Church's lesson to unlearned men (I, 134). It is true that this question and answer, and the following action of the poem, seem to provide the poem's rationale. In modern times, however, salvation tends to be thought of in individualistic terms. One of the major themes of the poem is that true salvation is not only personal but social. The Gospel preaches a Kingdom, not a conglomeration of individually saved souls; and the Middle Ages, with its strong corporate sense, understood this message. As Etienne Gilson puts it, "The Gospel had not only promised to the just a kind of individual beatitude, but it had announced to them entrance into a kingdom, that is to say a society, of the just, united by the bonds of their common beatitude. The preaching of Christ had been early understood as the promise of a perfect social life and the constitution of this society had been seen as the final purpose of His incarnation."[1]

It is more appropriate, then, as this analysis will bear out, to say that the subject matter of *Piers* is Christian perfection, which is a broader term than salvation and which includes it. Valuable as many recent studies of the meaning of the poem have been, there has been a tendency to submerge the social, and elevate the individualistic, religious element in it. Fundamentally *Piers Plowman* is about social regeneration; and in this, the poem is in the main stream of the Judeo-Christian tradition.

Christian perfection is a well-known subject of Christian thought and endeavor, and it normally presupposes the existence of grades or levels. Salvation is an all or nothing proposition; but the poem is, as the section on the three Do's shows, closely concerned with levels of Christian living and with moral distinctions and subtle-

ties. In every way, then, *Piers Plowman* is fundamentally concerned with the problem of Christian perfection.

The poem is divided into four major sections—the Visio and
the Lives of Do-wel, Do-bet, and Do-best, the last three being
known as the Vita. The whole Visio (from the Prologue to
Passus VII) may be regarded as an introduction in which the
dreamer remains the observer. He locates himself and defines his
self-image—a hermit and possibly a monk seeking after Christian
perfection. He describes his contemporary world, which is full of
sin and yet in a confused way longs to be free of sin. In this
introduction, Langland also shows how men fail in their attempt
to find salvation and perfection because they are fooled by Meed
(cupidity) and because, even if cleansed of sin, they cannot find
the way to the Saviour and fall into sin again. Their leaders betray
them. The guide, Piers, who appears in the last few passus of the
Visio, seems to be misled by a false pardon, and all ends in
wrangling and despair. New complexities have opened up, and
new distinctions must be made. Now the dreamer himself must
undertake a pilgrimage and become active instead of passive, a
seeker instead of an observer.[2]

The Vita (Passus VIII–XX) consists of three parts, corresponding
to three grades of perfection. Do-wel is concerned with the ordering of self to the natural world in terms of Christianity and raises
questions about such topics as predestination,[3] the value of learning, and the meaning of nature, natural man, and natural law.
The quest in the first part of Do-wel (VIII–XII) is in general
concerned with a burning fourteenth-century problem—that of
authority. The movement of Will from one authority to another
here dramatizes the problem of the relative authority of learning,
reason, the Bible, and the Church. Possible autobiographical elements in this part of the poem may be present, but if they are
here, they are secondary. After the search for an authority to
answer these questions on perfection is satisfied at least on one
level, by the clarifying speech of Imaginatif[4] in Passus XII, we
are finally led to the knowledge that patient poverty is Do-wel—
the best way to lead the Christian life in the world, the lowest
but by no means unworthy way of Christian perfection, which,
perforce, must embrace the vast majority of Christians. The

conclusion to this section is centered in the figure of Hawkin the Active Man and dramatized in his conversion and repentance.

Do-bet is concerned with the ordering of the self to Christ. The part centers on a discussion of the theological virtues, especially love, and culminates in a vision of the Harrowing of Hell. Do-best, coming back again, as in the Visio, to society and history, is concerned with the ordering of self to the Kingdom of God and to the regenerated society, centered in the cardinal virtues. The true Church is in the throes of "a time of troubles" and is being assailed by Antichrist at a time of crisis. Tribulation and persecution are the fate of the elect throughout the history of the world, and the betrayal of the ideals and doctrines of the Church by its adherents and leaders is the clearest sign of a coming renewal and of a further step towards the Kingdom of God.

How must a Christian live in order to attain as much perfection as possible within the limits of his human nature? What is the meaning of Christian perfection in general, and how can it be applied in Langland's own time? These are the basic questions of the poem and are closely related to the whole crisis of late medieval thought.

Unlike Marsiglio of Padua in his own century, Langland still believed in the Christianization of society and did not attempt to separate society (or the state) from religion. He went back to an older view of society and life to relieve the contending tensions of his age—the competing claims of society and the individual, of grace and free will, of piety and learning, and of this world and the next.

These contending claims, which are the sum and substance of the spiritual crisis of the age, appear throughout *Piers* in dialectical fashion as part of a dialogue in the broadest sense of the word between Will the dreamer and the exterior and interior worlds, the *saeculum* and the *anima*, under the overarching shield of the realm of grace. Langland fails, in part, to satisfy these claims completely and in perfect artistic form because his aim is to show the spiritual confusion of his own times. Spiritual confusion demands to some extent artistic confusion.

Today we have been taught to beware of reading autobiography into a work of art so as not to minimize the artifice and craft of the artist, although in some sense every work of art has some

biographical significance however indirect; nevertheless, autobiography occupies a special role in a poem about the quest for
perfection. One does not write such a poem in the first place unless
one is committed personally and strongly to the subject; moreover,
such a quest is not only for perfection but for a way in which the
quest may be artistically presented. The artistic problem is closely
related to the historical problem, and the historical problem is
partly Langland's personal problem. Had Langland merely been
presenting an ideal society so as to criticize contemporary society,
he might have been able to find the right artistic form; but he is
presenting the *search* for the ideal society in terms of the dilemmas
of his time. His answer, therefore, is bound up with history, contemporary history and his own history, which is not complete until
the end of time. Langland does believe that man can do something
about the problem and indeed foreshadows his final answer; but,
in effect, only history can give him the answer he is working for
and of which he is convinced. *Piers Plowman* reflects in a very
special way the dilemmas of its author.

All this is not necessarily to say that Langland and the dreamer
are identical. But there is some of the one in the other. Evaluating
the "I" of the poem is important in its interpretation, but certainly the "I" and the author are related to each other.[5] Will is
both William Langland and every Christian man. In brief, the
dreamer is "both species and individual at the same time."[6]

Langland was well aware that he was a craftsman who had to
work in the traditions of a craft possessed of styles and forms. Such
awareness was not a hindrance to his creativity and originality, but
the very presupposition of his art. The traditions provided the
conditions of his art, and he could no more have conceived of
himself as a rebel against them than he could have imagined
nuclear physics. His task was to use them in the fittest way so as
to produce what he had to produce with decorum. He was as
free within these confines as a religious thinker could be free
within the limiting dogmas of Catholicism. Medieval theology
shows a wide variety of attitudes and beliefs and many a clash of
opinion; and medieval art similarly within its boundaries presents
a wide range of works of different types and illustrating different
points of view, some successful and some not. The limits gave

strength to both theologian and artist, and within them all kinds of things were possible.

In what formal tradition of genre was *Piers Plowman* conceived? What kind of work was it, and in what form did the author choose to express himself? Actually, it seems that Langland never could decide what form he was using, and from beginning to end, part of the difficulty of *Piers* to its readers is its confusion and even clash of genres. Just as Langland could never come to rest in his search for perfection, so he could never find the one genre in which to express himself. In other literary works there is a mixing of genre—indeed it is a characteristic of much medieval literature, but a deliberate one—but in *Piers* it seems that the mingling is more extensive than in most and is intimately related to the quest for perfection that is the basic subject of the poem. And it is not entirely deliberate on the poet's part.

This is not the place to enter into a discussion of the importance of genre as one of the literary boundaries for the artist. Some have denied the validity of considering genre in assessing art; but without any reference to other periods, it is obvious that the medieval writer was very conscious of the kind of form in which he chose to present his artistic vision and that it is against the customary lines of this form that an author's innovations and uniqueness can best be understood. With a certain form went certain expectations which the writer felt he must at least satisfy.

Genre analysis is not a scientific subject. What is one man's genre may be another man's theme or motif. Some genres are artificially created by modern critics even when they have gone beyond the romantic notion that rhetoric implies insincerity. One must, however, accept as genres only literary forms defined as such before the time of the composition of the work being considered; for some forms are esoteric and others are so broad that they lose the distinguishing marks of a genre—a literary type that has a certain general organization and arouses certain definite expectations in its readers and listeners.

This problem of definition comes to the fore in connection with the quest around which *Piers Plowman* is mainly organized. The quest has been a most popular unifying principle in literature in all ages, but in the later Middle Ages it reached its apogee. "Then indeed," says R. W. Southern, "it meets us on all sides—in the

Arthurian Romances, in allegories of love, in descriptions of the ascent of the soul towards God. The imagery of movement seemed at this time to lay hold on the imagination, and it invaded secular as well as religious literature."[7] The quest is the literary counterpart of the new or revived twelfth-century conative attitude towards life, of the general Christian image of life as a pilgrimage, of actual travel, which increased as a result of the Crusades and greater wealth, and of what may be termed the idea of the Crusade itself, which seized all Europe.[8] But Mr. Southern's opinion, that it is a theme or dominant image rather than a genre, is probably correct. It is certainly the commanding image of *Piers*.

A simple answer to the question of the genre of *Piers Plowman* would be to say that it is an apocalypse. The classic Judeo-Christian apocalypse is cast in dream form, or consists of several dreams, is a revelation from some superior authority, is eschatologically oriented, and constitutes a criticism of, and warning for, contemporary society. In the Old Testament and Apocrypha, we may see such literary forms in Daniel and Second Esdras and in early Christian literature in Revelation, the *Shepherd of Hermas*, and in the *Visio sancti Pauli*, to take only a few examples.[9] The form of the apocalypse owes something to the late classical aretalogy, a narration of the theophany of a god among men with emphasis on his miracles for the furtherance of his cult. But its actual origins are obscure, and the matter need not be pursued further.

These apocalypses and others were known to the Middle Ages, and there is even a parody of one, in the *Apocalypsis Goliae* of the twelfth century, possibly by Walter Map but certainly connected with the British Isles. It is fundamentally a satire on the Church, and the superior guide is Pythagoras. It is closely modeled on the Revelation of St. John.

In many ways *Piers Plowman* seems to fit the category of apocalypse, yet there are certain fundamental differences. The emphasis on the quest is foreign to the apocalypse as we know it. There is no single guide in *Piers*, but rather a search for guides, although Holy Church and Conscience have a certain authority. The use of personifications is not a characteristic of the apocalypse, and there is a strong vein of irony in the figure of Will that is not consonant with the apocalypse. Although *Piers* does criticize contemporary society, is in dream form, and is eschatologically oriented, these characteristics of the apocalypse can be accounted for otherwise.

The chief objection to taking the form of *Piers* to be an apocalypse is that it is doubtful whether such a literary form existed. I agree with Father H. Musurillo when he writes, "The form known as 'apocalypse' creates a problem, and perhaps no useful purpose is served in making the term a technical one applicable both to the Revelation of St. John and the so-called Shepherd of Hermas."[10] He says that the *Shepherd* is rather "allegorical fiction disguised as a primitive Christian prophecy."

The problem of the genre of *Piers Plowman* is thus complex, but in some sense it can be said to be formally an apocalypse. The apocalypse as it appeared in the Bible and early Christian literature and in the occasional late parody of it may have prepared the way for *Piers* and made it possible in a very fundamental sense. However, the particular shifting organization of *Piers* can be understood only in terms of other and more common high medieval literary forms. In a basic sense, it is an apocalypse, but because we cannot clearly accept this form of literature as an established genre, we had better see it in another light.

It appears that *Piers Plowman* is based on three literary genres: the allegorical dream narrative; the dialogue, *consolatio*, or debate; and the encyclopedic (or Menippean) satire.[11] And it is influenced by three religious genres (or forms): the complaint, the commentary, and the sermon. These genres are not mutually exclusive, and some are related. The *consolatio* in its classic medieval form is also a dream vision; the religious complaint owes something to classical satire and to the diatribe; and no doubt the sermon and complaint are difficult at times to keep apart. It is still true that in the Middle Ages these six forms were distinct in tradition, had a definite organization, and were designed to satisfy certain expectations in an audience.

The term genre as applied to the religious literary forms that Langland used requires qualification, because customarily they are not considered genres. Perhaps the term *form* is a more satisfactory word, since it is hard to think of a sermon—in spite of its normally having a definite form and arousing definite expectations in its audience—as being on the same level, say, as an allegorical narrative. Yet in some ways these religious forms are genres, and I believe they exercised a definite influence on Langland when he faced his literary problems. However, they must be treated somewhat differently from the purely literary genres, and must not be considered as fundamental to his purpose as the traditional genres.

The difficulties of genre classification arise primarily in the first two literary forms. Both the narrative (which is usually a quest or battle) and the debate can be looked upon as different types of literary dream vision—one moving through time, the other essentially out of time. Each form will be treated separately. Written accounts of real life dreams in the Middle Ages seem frequently to have conformed to the literary conventions and were probably partially the source of such literary forms.[12] The background to the medieval literary dream is very complex—based partly on literary sources in late antiquity and in the Bible and partly on real life.

The root of the dream as a literary convention was no doubt the divine oracle and revelation. This too was probably both real and conventional. In classical times the dream was largely used in literature as a vehicle of divine revelation or for reports from the next world. Personification, which is also very old, began to enter literary dreams in late antiquity. The full combination of personifications with dream as a literary genre did not, however, take place until the twelfth century, when we find both the narrative and the *consolatio* types.[13]

By Langland's time, the use of a dream to introduce a literary, historical, or philosophical work was well established; and although the dreamer is in some ways the author, one can base autobiographical deductions on this fact only with caution. Langland certainly chose the dream form with deliberate intent, because he believed it could convey in proper fashion what he wanted to say. It is quite clear that the dream was a favorite literary device because it bespoke a revelation, a higher form of truth. It was not adopted because, as many scholars have thought, it was a means of criticizing contemporary society behind a convenient veil or because it afforded "sufficient remoteness from life to make the introduction of allegorical figures possible."[14] Quite the opposite, for a literary dream was "not a mere subjective happening caused by the play of an excited imagination and devoid of meaning, but objective reality."[15] A dream was or could be a vision, and the poet in reporting visions was only fulfilling his traditional role as seer.

It was a means not of giving less but of giving more reality to what he said. Dream theory in antiquity and the Middle Ages recognized, of course, that there were false or misleading dreams, and much ingenuity was expended in attempting to set up criteria for distinguishing the true from the false.

Some false dreams were the result of "fumositee" caused by over-eating, drink, or sickness.[16] A true dream had to be free of all suspicion of physiological causes. Morning dreams, after the head was cleared of the effects of food and drink, were the only dreams that could be true dreams, revelations. This is why medieval poets dream in the morning, that is, after midnight. "Dreams at night are the devil's delight and dreams in the morning are the angel's warning."[17] Not all morning dreams were necessarily true, and some men no doubt questioned all of them. But this was hard to do, for the Bible itself had given examples of true dreams; and most medieval men who thought about the subject at all, even if inclined to limit very severely the number of true dreams, must have allowed that some were true. In any case, as a literary device, the dream must be understood as a vehicle for the delivery of truth, although not necessarily of divine origin.

We cannot blame or defend Langland's lack of order because of his use of the dream form, as J. W. Mackail[18] does, or explain the disappearance of the dog in Chaucer's *Book of the Duchess* on the same ground. Dreams had to be taken seriously even in the pre-Freudian era, at least before the seventeenth century. As late as Pope's *Rape of the Lock*, burlesque and parody though it was, Belinda receives a true warning in a morning dream. Will is a somewhat uncouth and naïve prophet, but, like the character Dante in *The Divine Comedy*, a prophet for all that. This literary device implied, at the least, high seriousness (or assumed high seriousness) if not a divine message. In Langland's case, if the subject matter is considered and allowance is made for merely conventional uses of the dream framework by the fourteenth century, the dream must have been related to the idea of prophecy and revelation.

Visions[19] were often associated not only with a higher truth but with actual descriptions of the next world.[20] They were, especially in the early Middle Ages, markedly eschatological and frequently highly critical of this world. The vision could be and was used to portray social and religious finalities which directly or indirectly condemned this world. Impressive to medieval Christians were the dreams of the prophetic books of the Old Testament—some rebuking, some consoling, some foretelling the future, some clear and some obscure. In Daniel, Ezekiel, Isaiah, and the rest, were visions of a compelling power and majesty. In Zechariah, for instance, we find agricultural and pastoral imagery that may even have suggested the figure of Piers to Langland. The tradition of dreams as a mode of revelation and instruction was carried over into the New Testament and early Christian writers and became a recognized method of social and moral criticism in terms of God's judgment. Christian visions were probably both "real" and conventional, having a basis in religious experience and in literary history. Sometimes these eschatological dreams were used for narrowly political ends or general political advice, the last probably inspired by Macrobius' Commentary on Cicero's Dream of Scipio from the *De republica*, which had made this purpose very well known.[21]

Although in the discussion of dreams so far real dreams as reported by dreamers and conventional dreams as presented in literature have not always been kept clear, this mingling reflects the fact that even in earliest times the two were closely related. Although not in its mature form until the twelfth century, the literary dream was probably created in late antiquity as a specific feature for certain kinds of narrative or debate and may be seen in Boethius' *De consolatione philosophiae* and the *Visio sancti Pauli*. Earlier it had been used in parts of literary works such as the *Aeneid*. The Bible is full of visions, many of an apocalyptic nature. In the early Middle Ages monks were especially apt to receive visions of various sorts, often of palpable intention and purpose. It was therefore very easy for the twelfth century to conceive of the vision as a vehicle for literary revelations of a satiric or eschatological and even philosophical nature, and the dream begins then to appear in sermons and in literature in ever increasing number. A little later even secular romance is found in the form of a vision, whereby the improbable and the fictional could be made to appear probable and true.

Though originally a separate literary mode or trope, personifications are closely allied to high medieval dream visions. Although

present in earlier dream visions like that of Boethius, personifications began to enter the literary dream form (and others)
extensively in the twelfth century. The majority of the allegorical
figures in *Piers* are either moral or psychological. There are a few,
like Kind and Elde, who are physical, and a few, like Holy
Church and Fortune, who do not readily fall into any category,
although perhaps they may be considered religious or philosophical.

Of these various kinds of personification, the psychological is the
most recent. Prudentius' *Psychomachia* of the fifth century, although not presented in the form of a dream, has the virtues and
vices fighting it out with one another. Roughly contemporary with
this moral battle, Martianus Capella in the *Marriage of Mercury to
Philology* gives a story with philosophical and rhetorical personifications. Personifications of natural and occasionally of psychological forces occur earlier in classical times. But it was the rediscovery
of self in the twelfth century that gave vitality to psychological
allegory. A. P. Rossiter puts it thus, "It [the allegorical tendency]
appears as nothing less than an instrument in the process of the
evolution of self-awareness."[22] Although the popularity of psychological personification is due to more than the rise of self-consciousness, it is certainly true that this discovery of self is a major cause
of the later medieval expansion of this type of allegory. It may be
conceived of as a first groping literary method of exploring the
self or as the proper method of psychologizing a faculty concept of
the human mind and of an objective approach to the self.

Of all the types of vision we have been briefly touching upon
here, the two of immediate concern are the religious personification
narrative and the personification *consolatio*-debate. In general the
allegorical romance was centered around a battle or quest or a
combination of the two; and when, as was frequently the case, the
romance was religious, it was concerned with the battle against
temptation and the pilgrimage of man to his final end. The other
major subject of the allegorical romance was love, which found
its highest expression in the *Roman de la Rose*. Inasmuch as the
influence of this work was peripheral, it does not, however, have
a direct bearing on this discussion.

By looking at a few major religious allegorical romances— all
French— which preceded *Piers Plowman* and in some cases may
have influenced Langland, it is possible to see better the poem's

major characteristics and the tradition in which it is at least partially set. Dorothy L. Owen has shown the many particular points of similarity between most of these French romances and *Piers*.²³ The interest here, however, is in the broader points of similarity and difference. There can be little question that *Piers* is in large measure in this same tradition, even though one cannot speak unequivocally of influence in any particular case.

In all these romances the poet himself appears as a character, and in most of them he is the chief actor and spectator. He is always the motivating force for the action. As an artistic device, he gives the work its center, not as a "point of view" as in much modern fiction, but as the objective pole around which the events take place. In the *Romans de carité*, for instance, which is much like *Piers*, the poet searches throughout the world for charity. He moves largely in a "real" world, not a world of personifications. Rome, Europe, France, and Palestine are the places where he searches, and the various classes and occupations are weighed and found wanting. Only in heaven can true charity be found. Here the quest is an excuse for moralizing and preaching.²⁴ On the other hand, in the *Voie de Paradis* we have a straight pilgrimage of man through various personifications. Grace takes the hero to the House of Love, and then, in spite of Temptation, he finds the House of Contrition and moves on through the Castle of Confession, but before he can arrive at the House of Penitence he is attacked by the sins. After getting there finally through the help of the virtues, Penitence tells him he must mount an eight-step ladder. His journey is then continued until he successfully climbs to the throne of God. The *Tournoiement de l'Antecrist* is partially a quest but mainly a battle between the followers of Antichrist and of the King of Heaven. Here the poet is largely a spectator and witness of the events.

In *Piers*, Will is "both in and out of the game," a spectator and an actor in almost evenly divided roles. In the Visio and Do-best, the beginning and the end of the poem, he is chiefly a spectator, whereas in Do-wel and Do-bet, the middle part, he is primarily a seeker. Yet, curiously enough, there is more action in the first and last sections and more talk in between. During the whole poem Will is a seeker, but in Do-wel and Do-bet he moves about very little and is largely engrossed in long conversations, though not of the kind we find in Guillaume de Deguileville's *Le Pèlerinage*, where there are also some long speeches but mainly on doctrine. Will is personally involved in his conversations, and the answers he receives are ambiguous. We get the sense in *Piers* of both detachment and attachment, and as the poem progresses, even in the last scene of Do-best, Will becomes more and more involved until his soul and the outside world move in a kind of parallel action. The movement is from detachment to involvement, until at the end the attacks of Antichrist upon the Church are a kind of correlative to the progress of death within him. Unlike the more mechanical relationship between the hero and his experiences in the French allegories, a dialectical relationship is established between the world and the questing hero, and this is admirably suited to the search for perfection that characterizes *Piers*.

The personifications in these French romances are for the most part not psychological, but moral, theological, and natural. In *Piers* we find a large number of personified psychological figures, although we cannot say they form the majority. Conscience, Kind Wit, and Reason in the poem are not personal or subjective, as in the modern psychological approach to the self, but objective though inward. They reflect an older type of psychological interest, antedating the intensity of men like Bernard of Clairvaux and Richard of St. Victor, as well as later mystics. Thus Langland's psychological personifications neither ignore the psyche completely nor make it the center of existence but are somewhere between the two extremes.

In all these romances, including *Piers*, there is little of the purely decorative description that was to become popular in the later Middle Ages. The pleasure of pageantry was mostly expressed in the allegorical love romances, not in the religious romances. Although the latter may be wearisome, they are not so because of overelaborate and overrich decorative detail. Description in this genre is strictly functional in terms of the religious purpose of these visions.

Of these French allegories only the *Roman de la Rose* and Robert Grosseteste's *Chasteau d'Amour* can definitely be proved to have been known in England in the fourteenth century. But that the form was well known, there can be no doubt. It is no easier to prove that Langland knew particular English religious allegorical romances than it is to prove that he knew French ones. Most of the English examples were written after *Piers*; however, a few early ones will bear looking at a little more closely. These works provide solid evidence that the allegorical romance, usually in vision form, was well established in England in the fourteenth century.

The *Chasteau d'Amour*, which because of its language, Anglo-Norman, must be separated somewhat from English examples of this genre, provides a kind of bridge between the French and English allegories. It has a number of features that distinguish it from the other French examples. There is, for instance, no really central character. Throughout, only the poet speaks in his own voice. Although he frequently attracts attention to himself by his comments, he occupies no role in the development of the action. Grosseteste tells us calmly and dramatically, by means of real and allegorical figures, of the centrality of Jesus in human history. It is *Heilsgeschichte* (redemptive history) which concentrates on Jesus—the necessity of His incarnation, His character, and His defeat of Satan. In essence it is a paean of praise to the majesty of Jesus. It is not merely a narrative but also an exposition. It approaches the story of salvation and redemption from the outside. With the *Chasteau d'Amour* we get an objectivity, an approach from beyond, and an impersonal picture of man's religious history from the Creation to the Ascension. It is not centered on the story of Everyman. There are battles here but not with the self; and there is no quest at all.

Inasmuch as this allegory was translated into Middle English several times in the last half of the fourteenth century, it could, even assuming Langland knew no French, have been available to him. His work shows signs of its influence, and it helps to explain some of the divergences of *Piers* from the normal tradition. Langland also is fundamentally interested in redemptive history rather than in individual salvation; and although his hero is extremely important in the development of the poem, he makes the "objective" facts of history the central concern of the poem through the interplay of Will (Langland and Everyman) and the exterior world under grace. Langland had a poetic precedent for this point of view in the *Chasteau d'Amour*.

Howard Meroney has recently called attention to the similarities in the last two passus of *Piers* with the *Abbey of the Holy Ghost*, one of the rare fourteenth-century English allegorical romances.[25] I do not find the similarities as striking as he does, yet it is clear that *Piers* and the *Abbey* have something in common. The *Abbey* is a rather descriptive and static allegory and only barely qualifies as a narrative. Both works, however, show an awareness of the "monastic philosophy" to be discussed later, and both generalize it to apply to all men. The *Abbey* is much briefer and less arresting in its artistic power. It is based upon the efforts of the Holy Ghost, the traditional protector of monks, to drive out the evils, personified as four daughters, which infect an abbey that has just been built by allegorical figures like Righteousness and Purity, Meekness and Poverty, Obedience and Mercy. Interestingly enough, the site of this Abbey is Conscience, and it is implied that conscience is a kind of interior abbey. This is an older monastic conception of the conscience, which Langland himself uses, especially in Do-best.[26] It, however, is a matter of content rather than form. As an allegory-narrative, weak as the narrative part may be, the *Abbey* offers an interesting contemporary parallel to *Piers* in its use of an attack on a castle and in its wide use of religious and psychological personifications.

These French and English religious allegorical romances, except perhaps for the *Romans de carité*, have little satire in them except in a very general sense—divine or cosmic satire of man in his insignificance rebelling against God. This is also true of the *Parlement of the Three Ages*, which has frequently been mentioned as a source or at least a model for Langland. The *Parlement* is a short allegorical work on the variety and mutability of human existence, with the threat of old age and death always overshadowing it. It too has little action within the dream and little direct satire. On the other hand, *Wynnere and Wastoure*, another allegory frequently mentioned in connection with *Piers*, is a "topical narrative allegory,"[27] full of satire on contemporary England, organized around the symbolism of two armies drawn up in battle array. As Neville Coghill thinks, Langland may well have been indebted to this work for combining topical and moral satire with the conventions of the dream allegorical romance, although the idea may also have come to him from sermons or the complaint.

Of all the English allegorical romances, *Wynnere and Wastoure* is the closest approximation in intent and structure, if not in detail, to *Piers*.

It is easy to see the general structure of all these allegories in *Piers*. The dream form, the quest, the eschatological concerns, the use of personifications, and the allegorical battle are the main structural features which Langland owes, although perhaps not exclusively, to this genre. The very movement of the narrative, depending on a central character, however differently Langland managed it, is indebted to the allegorical romance. An audience reading or hearing a religious allegorical romance would expect these elements, and Langland does not disappoint them. These allegories are all didactic too, in one way or another, and a few are satiric in the social sense of the word. *Piers* is in this tradition, but Langland has his own feeling for the form. He breaks up the poem in Gothic fashion into a series of dreams, a variant form that is rare if not unique in this literary type; but it is characteristic of his originality. Langland manifests a sense of humor, which is uncommon in the genre.

Will, too, is not merely a passive character, or a pole around which the action develops; he has a historical dimension. He is William Langland of Malvern and London, a clerk in minor orders who has high hopes but who is mostly a failure, and the reader is never allowed to forget it. But at the same time he is every questing Christian, like the hero of *Pilgrim's Progress*. The later work is, in this regard, more like the allegorical romances than Langland's, for Bunyan's masterpiece is also a-historical. *Piers*, on the other hand, in keeping with its emphasis on the quest for perfection and the hindrances to it in this world, presents us with the failure of Christian society through the failure of Will himself. There is an interplay of significance between Will and the *saeculum*. Will is the bridge, to put it another way, between the soul and the world. This use of the central character, which partly stems from other literary genres, is the means by which Langland made the religious allegorical narrative serve his purposes, serious, ironic, and comic, at the cost of even its strong impersonality and clarity of aim and form.[28]

Almost as important in understanding the structural intent of *Piers* is the *consolatio*-debate woven into the heart of the poem.

The debate or *altercatio* or *conflictus* is an old form and can be found in classical times when it was sometimes called *syncrisis*, but it is characteristically between allegorical figures on the same level, as for instance fortune and virtue, a cook and a baker.[29] They are what Stephen Gilman calls horizontal debates, but with Boethius we get a new type, the dream vertical debate, "a dialogue between a narrator and an allegorical personage who comes to him on the basis of admitted infallibility."[30] One speaker has "didactic superiority" over the other. This device may have been suggested to him by Judeo-Christian apocalypses. Both types persisted throughout the Middle Ages, but Langland's work falls, for the most part, into the vertical type, although there is, as in Passus XVIII, where the four daughters of God debate, and elsewhere, some horizontal dialogue.

After the Prologue in the first scene, for instance, Holy Church meets Will. Holy Church here seems to be the equivalent of Philosophy in Boethius' *De consolatione*. Will, like the speaker in that famous work, wishes to be consoled. After some valuable comments, many of which are to be taken up later in the poem, Holy Church disappears never to reappear. Langland seems to drop both the figure and the form, and Will becomes a rather passive observer in the rest of the Visio. At the beginning of the Vita and throughout its first part, Do-wel, Will becomes once more the active seeker, and the poem settles into the vertical debate form again.[31] Here, other figures, Study, Imaginatif, Conscience, Nature, and others take up Holy Church's task and instruct Will, perhaps sometimes ironically. This search for authority continues more or less throughout the Vita, although it is most prominent in Do-wel. Not all these personifications speak to Will, and the main one, Piers, never does.

Langland seems to be struggling to find an authoritative answer to the question of salvation and perfection, and by the multitude of his instructors, Langland in a sense admits his failure. Just as the uncertain employment of various genres reveals a basic uncertainty in his mind, Langland cannot make his structure uniformly vertical or decide on a final and definitive teacher. This does not imply that he did not put Holy Church in a special category as spiritual adviser; but the very fact that she disappears after such a short time and Will feels forced to look for other authorities implies a certain difficulty with her advice. Perhaps it was because he felt that the voice of the true Church was so hard to hear in his time that he makes of her a minor character in his search for spiritual instruction. What she does say to Will is, however, of great importance.

Perhaps out of this difficulty of finding *consolatio* and an answer to his questions arises the fact that Langland's best piece of debate is a horizontal one—between the four daughters of God in the Harrowing of Hell scene (Passus XVIII), where the action and the words are dramatically welded together. Here, there is no problem of authority, and the whole debate takes place on the divine level and from a divine perspective.

The vertical dialogue is not necessarily static. Certainly in *Piers* the succession of vertical dialogues is itself proof of movement and life, and some are lively and dynamic indeed, with a vigorous interchange of opinion and humor. Will is by no means the acquiescent figure who receives but does not give.

There is no need to list or summarize the large number of medieval debates, many in Latin, since for our purposes Boethius' *De consolatione* is enough. Not all debates are of course of the *consolatio* variety, but it is this type that is behind much of *Piers*. The popularity of the *De consolatione* is unquestionable, and certainly Langland must have known it. The vertical dialogue combines very neatly with narrative, and in some medieval debates of this type, there is a sense of movement in both conversation and action, as in *Piers* itself. The weakness of this genre from the point of view of aesthetic considerations—a weakness Langland does not altogether rise above—is a tendency to bog down in endless talk. Langland, too, tends to use this genre in somewhat confused fashion, changing his instructors and on several occasions shifting to the horizontal type, just as he tends to mix different genres in his attempt to express himself.

The problem of the apocalypse arises again in connection with Boethius' *De consolatione*, for some scholars have called it an apocalypse.[32] It has also been considered a Menippean or encyclopedic satire. The difficulty of genre analysis is very marked in this work, and it is not easy to settle the matter. To those who believe in the existence of an apocalypse genre, no doubt the *De consolatione* could be made to fit in this category, although the dream form and the superior guide are really the only features which it has in common with the usual apocalypse. I prefer to see it as a *consolatio*-debate, which has an established existence as a literary type, although it may owe something to other forms and some apocalypses.

Both of these vision genres—the religious allegorical romance and the vertical *consolatio*-debate—use personifications freely. Personification may be used for various purposes, depending on the general aims of the form or genre in which it appears. Narrative is essentially concerned with, although not necessarily limited to, the sequential and the unique. It is the literary counterpart to the movement of history itself. Dialogue is essentially dramatic and is the literary counterpart to the clash of wills and opinions in life.[33] Personification fulfills a different function in each mode.

In narrative, personification is a means of getting beyond the particular to the universal; it is a way of directly adding meaning to the sense-bound course of events. It attempts to transcend the limitation of fact and detail—the unique which is of the very nature of art—in order to reach significance without falling into pure symbolism. Like *aevum*, that scholastic category between time (which has a beginning and an end) and eternity (which has no beginning or end), personification is a *via media* between the particular and the universal, fit for the angels who are between men and God. Its popularity in romance in the later Middle Ages is due not only to its value in portraying states of the soul objectively, as C. S. Lewis has urged, but also to its usefulness in economically conveying meaning. It also throws emphasis on action. It is what the personification does that requires interpretation.

In dialogue, too, personification can convey, with a directness not matched by concrete description, meaning and psychological states. Here prosopopoeia is less essential to the movements or clash of opinion and will than it is, in romance, to the sequence of events. Nevertheless it is very valuable in portraying, as in vertical debates, authority and, as in horizontal debates, different faculties of scholastic psychology or different social or physical states or theological categories. It enables the writer to concentrate on the dramatic quality of his work. He need not waste energy or time on background explanation or description but can plunge into the heart of his subject. He can thus avoid unnecessary *amplificatio*, to use a rhetorical term.

Within his various genres, Langland made full use of the potentialities of prosopopoeia, a literary mode not limited to the vision genres just discussed. He employed it to convey meaning and authority, and to portray the psychology of Will (and Everyman), and to present the abstractions he wished to emphasize. Simply and directly, he could give us God, nature, and man as he and the Middle Ages conceived them.

The third literary genre manifest in *Piers* is the encyclopedic satire or anatomy, which is just as common in the Middle Ages as the vision genres and like them has its forbears in classical times, perhaps most notably in Lucian's romances. A figure, somewhat foolish or at the least ingenuous, is chosen to pass through various, often ridiculous situations for the purpose of satire on current events, foibles, or sins. Sometimes the hero is successful in spite of himself and wins out over more powerful forces, a victory that produces an ironical situation. More frequently the *ingénu* sustains the buffets of the world and conquers by sheer persistence. In antiquity this satirical genre, called Menippean, was often written in alternating prose and poetry (*prosimetrum*), although little of the type has been preserved; later, prose alone served the variety of functions the genre was called on to perform. By strict artistic standards, the literary form seems loose and indeed merely a bag to stuff anything into; it is encyclopedic in nature. It has had a long history in Western civilization and is by no means dead today. Examples of the genre from a formal point of view show a remarkable similarity, and the chief differences seem to lie in the role given the hero. We have, on the one extreme, encyclopedic satires like *Gulliver's Travels*, wherein the chief character plays a very important part and, on the other, those like *Gargantua and Pantagruel*, wherein he plays a minimal role. In Rabelais' work the "I" has a very minor role except in the prefaces and yet appears now and then, notably in the last two books.

Twelfth-century England produced two good specimens of the encyclopedic satire, both written in Latin. Nigel Wireker, a monk of Christ Church, Canterbury, wrote in elegiacs his *Speculum stultorum*, with a donkey-hero like the one in Apuleius' *Meta-*

morphoses. Burnel, seeking a longer tail, gets into a series of improbable adventures wherein medicine as taught at Salerno, monks, merchants, law, and the University of Paris are all ridiculed. The monk-author was not particularly enamoured of the new orders of his day, especially the Cistercians, and they come under his most vigorous lashings. It is a true mixture of satire and adventure, in which the hero plays an important part.

John de Hanville's *Architrenius*[34] is cast in the same mold, but his hero is a weeping seeker for Truth. He visits the palace of Venus, the house of Gluttony, and the University and sees the Mount of Ambition and Hill of Presumption. A final visit in Thule, the abode of the philosophers, still gives him no peace. At the last he is married to Moderation at Lady Nature's suggestion and presumably finds peace and an end to his longing for an answer. The rich and gluttonous, the learned and place-seekers, the clergy and monks, cupidity and philosophy, are all satirized. The hero, Architrenius, the archmourner, is much less involved in his narrative than Burnel, but he is by no means a passive figure.

It is clear that *Piers Plowman* also participates in this literary tradition. The wandering Will in search of perfection perceives and enters into relation with various aspects of life; and if in the end he is perhaps not satisfied, he knows that Piers Plowman has or is the answer to his searching question. The poem is also a grab bag of satire, and all of contemporary England is tested and mostly found wanting. Satire on contemporary life is, of course, only part of Langland's purpose, but it is a large part. Besides, the dreamer-hero is naïve and at times a fool, although, as is usual with Langland, only at times is this genre-role stressed.[35] At other times he is a rather neutral character.

Will begins his poem by telling us that he puts on the garb of a hermit "unholy of works," a phrase which may mean merely that as a new hermit, he is not yet holy or that he is, as a hermit, more sinful than is normal.[36] Langland was no doubt aware of the *gyrovagus*—the fourth type of monk as defined by Benedict of Nursia: the careless, selfish, wandering monk who, free of religious discipline, made a livelihood by his profession; and he is no doubt here hinting at this possibility in Will.[37] He points up the problem of the *gyrovagus* a few lines further on in the poem (line 28 of the Prologue) after he states that Will has clothed himself as a

hermit "unholy of works." Here Langland praises good "ancres
and heremits that holden hem in here selles," who do not covet to
"kairen aboute" in the country, unlike Will himself. Nor is this
motif confined to the first few lines of the poem, for beginning
with line 53 he gives a picture of a "heap of hermits" going to
Walsingham with their wenches because of their hatred of work.
"Anarchic eremeticism" was a real problem of the later Middle
Ages. To the older religious orders the friars must have seemed
gyrovagi. Langland probably regarded them as such, but he did
not regard his literary counterpart as a friar, for he put the mendicants into a special category of obloquy that would be too much
for his main character, in spite of his weaknesses, to bear. Will
is not even a pure monkish *gyrovagus*, but he does have some of
his traits.[38] Wandering religious in various forms ("now is Relig-
ioun a ryder · a rowmer bi stretes," X, 306) are continually
satirized throughout the poem, a category in which Will himself
may be placed. He too is a wandering religious.

Although Will in the *Visio* is largely a passive creature, an
observer, he is also a seeker, possibly a rascally *gyrovagus*, but one
who raises important and fundamental questions. After Langland's
description of the fair field full of folk in the Prologue, which in
the B- and C-Texts contains the famous fable of the rats with its
probable contemporary political significance, we find in Passus I
a long vertical dialogue with Lady Holy Church that sets out
clearly the object of Will's search and really gives him the answers
later to be made detailed and fully clear.[39] Here, however, we are
interested in the character of Will as it is revealed in the dialogue.
Lady Holy Church, like most of Will's mentors, punctuates her
advice and information with admonition. Will asks rather obvious
questions, leading ones in fact, which enable his mentor to ex-
patiate on various subjects of importance to the poem but which
do not do his intelligence much honor. He is the real *ingénu* here,
made to assume the traditional role in order to lead into the heart
of Langland's subject. Will arouses his teacher's anger in lines
138 ff. by raising the psychological question that is an abiding
issue of the poem. By what psychological power in his body can
he know the truth of Christian living? He is told it is a "kynde
knowyng," a natural knowledge implanted by God the Father;
love is the doctor of life and the gate of heaven.[40]

Will still wants details, and in Passus II Lady Holy Church directs him to Meed, who is about to be married to False; Lady Holy Church thereupon leaves him with a warning. Then follows the whole story of Meed, ending in the King's court, where the King finally accepts Reason and Conscience as his counselors. Will then wakes and (in the C-Text), himself "clothed as a lollere,"[41] meets Conscience and Reason. He is upbraided by them in a famous passage (VI, 1–108) that seems autobiographical and that certainly has often been taken to be such. Here a partially humorous interchange takes place between these two royal advisers and Will. Reason scolds him for his useless life, and Will tries to defend his role as a clerk in minor orders who lives off the good will of his patrons. He talks back to Conscience, too, but at the end, in words of moving seriousness, he speaks of his hopes that finally all will be well.

In B none of this occurs, but the scene immediately moves back into another dream of the field full of folk, Reason's sermon, and the Confession of the Seven Deadly Sins. The converted determine then to seek truth, but they need a guide; and he appears in the form of Piers. Then comes the scene of the plowing of the half-acre and the visitation of Hunger. The Visio closes with the Pardon Scene, but at the end the hero participates in the action again by looking over the shoulder of the priest and Piers to read the pardon. The quarrel awakens him; he becomes serious as he ponders on what he has seen and speaks directly to his audience.

With the Vita, Will becomes much more active, although the movement of events for the most part slows down. His further adventures cannot be followed now in detail, but he seeks for the meaning of Do-wel, Do-bet, and Do-best, the grades of Christian perfection. He is confused and frequently rebuffed by his would-be mentors and those he thrusts into this role. He speaks at the beginning of Passus XI of his seduction, in spite of Elde's (old age's) warnings, by Concupiscencia-carnis, Coueytise-of-eyes, and Pride of parfyte lyvynge (based on I John 2:16), and of how Fortune even closes the door of her cabin on him. He is worthless, and only his pleas and begging can finally soften her. In Passus XII, Imaginatif gets him out of his intellectual difficulties,[42] and Do-wel moves into its final section in which Will meets Patience and Conscience and the minstrel Hawkin the Active Man, who is spotted with sin and yet tries to do well.[43] Hawkin is in some way the double of Will himself, the sinner on the road to salvation, the worldly man "unholy of works."

In Do-bet, Will is again castigated and scorned, notably by Anima, but not so frequently as in Do-wel. In Do-best, he becomes again more of a pure spectator, but this reversion and the serious tone of the final section do not prevent him from experiencing one of the most farcical episodes in the poem. In the final apocalyptic scene when Unity is being attacked by Antichrist and his hordes, Elde, fighting with Life, suddenly sees Will and goes after him, speeding over his head to make him bald, beating him to loosen his teeth, and making him sexually impotent. Thus Will, who started in the vigor of his manhood, ends in weakness and old age, while Unity (Holy Church) is being assailed so violently that Conscience has to set out to find Piers again.[44] We can hardly say that Will comes out of Langland's poem with much honor. He is at times the *ingénu,* the fool, the earnest seeker, and a butt, and as such is characteristic of the hero of the anatomy. Looking at the matter from the point of view of Christian perfection, however, we may perhaps say that only the fool, the innocent, the naïve, can find the truth of Christian living if it is to be found at all. Langland touches a deep spring here—that of the outcast, the lost, the seeker, who displays *sancta rusticitas.*[45]

Some of this self-deprecation in the figure of Will may of course be due to an expansion of the *trepidatio* motif or the "affected modesty" *topos,* as Curtius calls it.[46] It was traditional since antiquity for the speaker or author—or perhaps more properly the literary counterpart of the author—to affect a modesty and fearfulness in broaching or developing his subject. The *accessus* or prologue to many a medieval work affords many examples of this literary device. It was considered proper to the *captatio benevolentiae* of the audience and effective in producing a receptive and favorable attitude. However, in general this modesty does not extend beyond the prologue, whereas in the character of Will, it is a recurrent feature.

Thus in the chief character and in the diversity of his satire, we find the elements of the encyclopedic satire. This genre, along with the dream religious allegory and the *consolatio*-debate, gives the

literary tradition in which *Piers* is set, making possible an understanding of Langland's over-all literary aims.

When considering the religious literary forms behind *Piers*, one
is dealing with traditions much more nebulous than the literary
and rhetorical genres we have just been discussing. Such religious
forms do not go back to a rich classical tradition and were not
thought of as literature in the Middle Ages. It is the thesis of this
book that the "monastic philosophy" or form of thought best
accounts for the forms and the ideas of *Piers Plowman*. This
"monastic philosophy" will be discussed later. But here it is
necessary to say that there were certain religious literary forms, or
genres, which were especially characteristic of the monastic philosophy. Two of the three—complaint and commentary—are among
these monastic genres, and the third, the sermon, if not as with
the others almost uniquely monastic, at least was very common
in the monasteries.

Monasticism favored, even if it did not create, special literary
forms—history and chronicle, complaint, lives of the saints, biblical
exegesis, meditations, and prayers. Medieval Latin literature up
to the mid-thirteenth century is full of these types of literary
endeavor, and they are usually the work of monks or men closely
associated with monasteries. After this date new forms became
dominant, owing to the revival of the classics, the rise of vernacular literatures and the bourgeoisie, and the supersession of
monastic philosophy by scholasticism, which favored other forms
like the *summa* and the *questio* to present its teachings. The older
monastic forms did not, of course, disappear, but for the most
part they lost their vitality. The sermon, however, was transformed
by the friars and continued to exist and even flourish. Its popularity rose rather than declined because of the use of the vernacular
and its new close concern with everyday life.

The complaint, the first of the three religious forms discernible
in the background of *Piers*, is a favorite form of medieval satire
based largely on the contempt of the world theme, which, in its
particular early medieval manifestation, is of Christian and monastic origin. At its most characteristic, the complaint lists the sorrows
and sufferings of life and either directly or indirectly argues for
the repudiation of the world and the acceptance of the next world
as the only reality. The use of the term *complaint* to describe this

form is taken from John Peter, who builds his book upon a distinction between satire and complaint.[47] Peter sees in the Middle Ages a predominance of the latter, which lacks the personal quality and the individual detail, although it repeats some of the matter, of the classical satire. The complaint or elements of it are found in European literature until the seventeenth century, but its great period is the earlier Middle Ages, especially the eleventh and twelfth centuries. Its purity of form begins to be adulterated in the later Middle Ages and the Renaissance.

The monastic and indeed the Christian view of man is ambiguous in its polarity; for if the world is contemptible as an evil temptation and as a transitory state, it is also admirable as the work of the Creator. Man is tarnished and stained, but underneath is the image of God, which can be uncovered. In the first half of the Middle Ages, the stress was on the temptations of the devil in and through the world and on the necessary corollary in the religious life—contempt of the world. The pettiness and puniness of man rather than his glory and dignity were what intrigued monastic thinkers and writers. This attitude gave rise to a literary genre of which we find numerous examples but which culminated in Innocent III's *De contemptu mundi*, a most influential work written when the full tide of monastic philosophy was beginning to recede.

Satire is a most complicated literary mode, and in its background lie the tradition of the Latin satirists and an even more ancient tradition, that of the curse and the power of the word. But the center of Christian satire is the monastic contempt of the world with its long catalogue of the sorrows and sufferings of our transient existence. The sins stressed were those of pride, avarice, and lust. It is out of this center that we must trace the literary origin of much of the satirical element in works such as *Piers Plowman*. Donald R. Howard has made an interesting analysis of *Piers* from the point of view of the *de contemptu* tradition which shows how much Langland's satire and point of view are indebted to it.[48] The words of I John 2:16, "For all that is in the world, the lust of the flesh, and the lust of the eyes, and the pride of life, is not of the Father, but is of the world," were surely in Langland's mind as they were in the tradition.[49] I do not want to exaggerate, for besides the gloom of the complaint there is humor as well as the complex moods proper to the other genres in the poem. To indicate fully and properly what Langland's satire owes to the complaint and its *contemptus mundi* theme is beyond the scope of this book, and Donald Howard has already done excellent pioneer work in the matter; but both in detail and in general there is enough evidence to substantiate my claim. The complaint of course is not a narrative but rather a long meditation on the woes of the world, and in placing *Piers* in this tradition we must allow for this fundamental difference in organization.

The commentary is the second medieval religious form which has left a strong impress on *Piers.* The *lectio divina*, the obligatory reading of the Bible undertaken by monks, as well as the interpretations of and quotations from the Bible in the liturgy, would make that book and its meaning central not only to the literary but to the religious experience of those in monastic orders. Exegesis and hermeneutics are the essence of the study of the Bible. In fact the commentary on the Old Testament—the use of quotation and interpretation—is to be found in the New Testament itself. At all times biblical interpretation has been the central concern of Christians. Sometimes, especially in the earlier Middle Ages, explanations tended to be somewhat far fetched, and sometimes the "significance" overshadowed the text itself.

Although the so-called four levels of meaning—the literal, allegorical, tropological, and anagogical—were often referred to and less frequently applied, a dimensional approach to the Bible was characteristic of the early Middle Ages and never did die out, especially in sermons.[50] In the matter of typology—the concept of texts prefiguring Christ in the Old Testament—there could be no question whatsoever at any time for Christians. But these texts were relatively few and in general widely accepted as referring to Jesus. As for the rest of the Bible, interpretations did and could vary—and some enthusiastic homilists did, at times, border on the fantastic. But from the twelfth century on, in spite of occasional exceptions the emphasis was on the literal meaning of the text, the literal including the normal rhetorical modes of interpretation. A suspicion of over-elaborate symbolic interpretations of the Bible is characteristic of many critical and influential thinkers of the later Middle Ages. Yet the commentary approach, in spite of its increasing emphasis on the plain meaning of the text, was widespread throughout the Middle Ages. Nor was it confined to the Bible, although biblical exegesis is the type par excellence.

From the point of view of formal analysis, the commentary or gloss is a literary form whose principle of organization is determined by another work outside it to which it is subordinate. The commentary assumes that the text upon which it is based, whether it be the Bible or Virgil's *Aeneid*, is worth explaining, that its words contain important meanings, and that it is known at least generally to the audience. There is a lack of progression within the commentary, for the progression is in the work commented on—that is, extrinsic to itself. It expands from a fixed point—the lemma, the phrase, sentence, or sentences which are to form the exegetical unit— and then returns to the next fixed point outside itself in the work being explained. There is no necessary connection *within the commentary* between one comment and the next, although there often may be one. A commentary consists of separate sections, units of explanation, one piled on the other, the clue to the order to be found only in the work from which it takes its being. The artistic form of the commentary must exist, if it exists at all, within each unit and not in the whole, unless we take both the text and the commentary as one, in many cases most difficult to do. Even in the latter case, we seem to move from a point and return to another. It is like reading a book which is seven-eighths footnotes.

This method of commentary was characteristic of the earlier part of the Middle Ages up to the thirteenth century and is still present in the exegetical works of a man like Grosseteste.[51] This lemma method was generally but not universally superseded by the chapter method, where the unit commented on was either the whole work or its chapters (or sections), as seen, for instance, in Thomas Aquinas' Commentary on Aristotle's *De anima*. With much larger units as the base, the commentary makes a less disjointed impression and appears instead as a group of essays, closely or vaguely related, as the case may be. The earlier method, which is illustrated somewhat in *Piers*, was characteristic of monkish exegesis and is in keeping with what appears to be Langland's basic approach.

The commentary as a form is to be found in *Piers Plowman* in the movement of its long arguments and in the suddenness of some of its transitions. In the narrow sense of the word there is a good deal of actual glossing in the poem, for it is a tissue of quotations; but this may be considered a stylistic rather than a genre element, and need be of no concern at the moment. Of more consequence is the movement of Langland's thought and to some extent his action. The over-all effect of much of the poem is akin to that of the commentary seen in the shifting from one block or argument and action to another. Now all narrative moves from scene to scene, but some of the suddenness of the transitions is due not to the dream form, as some have thought, but rather to the influence of the commentary.

Even more in the long arguments, especially in the Vita, we get the effect, often marked off by actual quotations and paraphrases of quotations, of a running commentary on a text. Sometimes these blocks are themselves well organized, sometimes not. The over-all effect, however, is frequently one of confusion. It is like reading a commentary on an unknown text. The *cento* character of *Piers*, its massive employment of quotations, its apparent disorganization, owe something to the commentary form, which no doubt was in Langland's mind.[52] The wave-like movement of *Piers*—its swelling out from a point, so to speak—also reminds one of the commentary. It is indeed hard to be precise in this matter, but there are the marks of the commentary in the literary form of *Piers*, which in part account for its apparent looseness of form.

The last religious literary form to be distinguished in *Piers* is the sermon, which has enough points of similarity with the commentary to be called an expanded and well-organized single gloss. Since historically, from its most ancient form in the Midrashim, the sermon arose from a haggadic explanation of a biblical text, one cannot easily separate the influence of the commentary from that of the sermon. To compound the difficulty, the complaint is also close to the sermon in its satiric thrust. The sermon influence on *Piers* has been well analyzed, although mainly from the point of view of its content rather than form, in G. R. Owst's fine study of the late medieval English sermon.[53] Owst has an excellent section on the relation of satire and complaint to the sermon, which may be profitably read for an understanding of part of the form and content of *Piers*.

In Langland's use of personifications, biblical quotations, and *exempla,* and in his attacks on various classes, one may clearly perceive the influence of the sermon. From the twelfth century on, beginning with Bernard of Clairvaux and Hugh of St. Victor, there occurs the frequent use in sermons of allegorical narrative with personifications and of the pilgrimage motif. The universal appeal of the literary and real-life pilgrimage and the directness of allegorical personification made both these devices popular with preachers.[54] In fact it is the sermon that first introduced social satire into allegorical narrative and in a sense made possible a work such as *Piers.*

The type of sermon that comes closest to Langland's work or parts of it is what Roger Higden calls the *sermo ad diversos status hominum* or, more shortly, the *sermo ad status,* which is directed at one or more, frequently several, classes or groups.[55] In fact, parts of *Piers,* such as Passus IX, 107–206, on marriage or XIV, 49–96, on patience, may be lifted out of context to do as short sermons. Both Reason and Scripture deliver sermons. The tricks of the trade, noted so well by Owst, are scattered throughout the work, and if one cannot go as far as Owst does in saying that the poem is "nothing more or less than the quintessence of English medieval preaching,"[56] one can nevertheless agree that the sermon form (and content as well) was a potent force in its creation.

The sermon itself, from its earliest Jewish form to its fifteenth-century manifestations, underwent considerable changes in detail and emphasis, not the least of which were due to the activity of the friars in the later Middle Ages. Although early monkish sermons can be distinguished from the early fraternal sermons, by the fourteenth century the influence of the friars had made itself felt in the sermon, by whoever composed or delivered, in its increased liveliness, homeliness, and concreteness. I do not think, therefore, that an investigation of the type of sermon used as a model by Langland would serve any purpose here. The monastic sermon was not particularly his model, but the average sermon of the fourteenth century provided him with the exemplars he worked from. It will serve the purpose of the study to treat the sermon as a single form, based on a text usually biblical and progressing in usual fashion through theme, protheme, dilatation, *exemplum,* peroration or application, and closing formula. Langland, like most preachers, used this academic schema with considerable freedom.

It is essentially in its other formal characteristics—the plentiful use of quotations, the love of everyday detail, the use of moral personifications, the satire directed at classes and groups in society, and so forth—that the influence of the sermon must be sought. The sermon is a dominant mode of the literary background of *Piers*, and a knowledge of its structure and conventions is essential in uncovering the literary forebears of the poem.

These six forms—three literary and three religious—are the genres in which Langland chose to work and with which he attempted to give structure to his poem. To them we may add the somewhat dubious literary form of the apocalypse. They were already to some extent intertwined before Langland's time, although I know of no writer who attempted to use them all. It is possible that Langland did not think of them all as separate, but in intellectual analysis they may be separated so as to see more clearly their impact on the poem. This study of them is not intended to be an interpretation of Langland's actual creative process—a hopeless task anyway—but a normative study of the basic literary forms in the background of *Piers*, forms that may have to be separated artificially. That each of them existed and has its own tradition, we cannot deny; they are not the creation of modern scholars but actual medieval literary forms. Yet it is most unlikely that Langland himself sat down and took these six, one after the other, and mixed them up into his potion.

Rather, Langland was probably well aware of all these traditions; and in attempting to present his concern with perfection in the apocalyptic and prophetic frame of mind that was his, he could not properly solve his formal problem. The confusion of genre in *Piers* is a reflection of his concern with the quest for perfection. Langland combines in extraordinary degree a detachment and humor along with an intense involvement and unhappiness. He stood for a moderation—a balance between being a spectator and an actor—which he never could quite achieve.

All this is in Langland's style. Like most issues connected with the poem, the style of *Piers Plowman* presents a problem of considerable magnitude. Ostensibly it is written in the alliterative tradition, and certainly the chief poetic binding device is alliteration, yet the total effect of the poem is strikingly different from that of the ornate repetitive parallel style most other monuments of the "alliterative revival" display.[57] Unlike their authors, Langland does not use an aristocratic "baronial" style; nor does his poem echo the heroic Old English alliterative line and vocabulary. In short, Langland is not, like perhaps the author of *Gawain and the Green Knight,* writing in high, but rather in middle, style, if one may accept these stylistic distinctions as laid down by Augustine and others, which were based on Cicero and the Roman rhetoricians.[58] The *genus temperatum* could well describe Langland's style in the alliterative tradition.

The conclusion that *Piers Plowman* is written in the middle or moderate style is actually forced on us. The subject matter alone would eliminate the low or humble style, which for the most part could be used only in writing of erotic matters and of humble life or in simple religious instructions. The absence of long apostrophes and elaborate descriptions and ornamentation and the nature of the diction would seem to eliminate the high style.

The problem of the three literary styles in the later Middle Ages is not simple, because estimating the literary effect of the older stages of a language is not easy. England, with the struggle between English and French, had a complicating element. It is dubious whether a high style in English was at all thought possible until the last half of the fourteenth century. In any case French style had certainly differentiated itself by the thirteenth century and possibly earlier.

The tradition for a middle style was probably not well established by Langland's time, but everything we know of the work and a close analysis of its language, not merely the negative reasons given above, argue that *Piers* is written in this style. The vocabulary is not simple, imagery of an intellectual sort is present, and high ornamentation is absent. The contrast between the language and style of *Sir Gawain* and those of *Piers* is instructive in this matter.

There is no clash of style in *Piers* that could be used for special effects. Its tone and diction are remarkably stable; only occasionally does one find a heightening of effect, as in the last two Passus and here and there elsewhere. The heightening is obtained by a speeding-up of the action or by the sudden force of pathos or sincerity rather than by any analyzable change in diction or ornamentation. The stability of the author is found in his style; his uncertainty in his clash of genre.

As J. A. Burrow says, Langland can be accused of *circumcogitatio* but hardly of *circumlocutio* or *gratuitous poeticism*. When he is narrating or when he is describing someone or some scene, his poetry moves briskly along, even though he indulges in word play or parallel clauses. The slowing down which is apparent, especially in the long speeches in the Vita, is largely due to Langland's difficulty in saying exactly what he means or to our inability to catch the scholastic or medieval mode of argument and allusion. The long-windedness of extensive sections of the poem arises from the long-windedness of Langland's thought or has this effect because of a lack of sympathy with the details of his argumentation.

It is possible that the very choice of the alliterative meter, as W. L. Renwick and H. Orton has suggested, "is indeed symbolic of opposition to the society and politics of which Chaucer was an apparently contented part."[59] Langland, who lived in London, at least for part of his life, as his knowledge proves, even if we doubt the veracity of the autobiographical passages, must surely have been aware that this meter was not used over a vast part of the country. It is hard to think that deliberate choice did not enter into the selection of his verse form. And the choice may have been dictated by his disapproval of the current standards of the world about him. He may thus have harked back perhaps for his poetic meter to his youthful memories of baronial entertainment in Shropshire, Herefordshire, or Worcestershire. Yet all this is speculative. We cannot penetrate his mind to this extent.

Looking at the poetry more closely, one must be immediately impressed by Langland's frequent use of quotations, mostly Latin, either worked into or merely deposited in the texture. "No work, whether literary production or dogmatic treatise, is so interlarded with Latin Scriptural quotations and Patristic *excerpta*—sometimes thrown in with utter disregard of rhetorical structure or easy comprehension of the sense, sometimes neatly incorporated into the flow of thought, now given in full, now forming a fragmentary tag—as the *Piers Plowman*."[60] Sometimes we find true macaronic lines, half English, half Latin, and sometimes whole lines of quotation inserted into the flow of the verse and sometimes whole lines or tags quoted in what is in effect an aside. As in theological writings, Langland often uses quotations to settle a dispute; he assumes a knowledge of the exegetical tradition.[61] *Piers Plowman* is impregnated with the Bible and the writings of the Fathers, but more especially the Bible.[62] It has been said of Bernard of Clairvaux that he speaks Bible as one might speak French or English.[63] Langland speaks Bible too; phrases, echoes, and paraphrases crop out everywhere. His whole mind is steeped in the Bible; it is a real language to him.

This use of biblical (and Patristic) citation, besides giving Langland the authority he seeks for, reveals a remarkable sense of the power of language, which we see as well in his love of word play and puns. Acrostic and macaronic poetry are no longer much in fashion, yet they convey a respect for the magic power of language which is still not lost. Thought, serious thought, must always struggle against its medium, words. In using several languages or in writing acrostics, a poet is indicating his desire to pass beyond the limitations of his medium and at the same time indicating his belief, possibly subconscious, in the magic power, in a literal sense, of language.

This is all very general, and to apply it particularly to Langland and the problems he was struggling with would take up a great deal of space. The confusion of genres, the endless revisions of *Piers*, the struggle within the poem, are, however, all reflected in Langland's very choice of words and his dissatisfaction with one language. His movement from Lady Church to Conscience, to Reason, to the friars, to Dame Study, to Imaginatif, and all the others is a seeking for authority, for an answer to his own and his age's crisis; and this quest is duplicated in his reaching out for words that one language alone cannot satisfactorily supply, in his love of word play, and in his turning again and again to the Bible.

Part of his trouble is due to the inadequacies of English in Langland's own time. He was concerned with theological ideas, and "the fact that he quoted his authorities in Latin and not in English," not to speak of his choice of the content, "indicates that he regarded his poem as belonging rather to the theological than to the devotional type of religious literature."[64] English in the fourteenth century did not have an established learned vocabulary. In this, it was similar to Hindi or modern Hebrew. Latin provided the scientific and learned language, and the vernacular writers were as yet only groping towards a solution in their own terms. Chaucer and Gower might seem to be exceptions, but they were not struggling with theology and religious genres, as Langland was. This difficulty is not always recognized by modern scholars in dealing with Langland's diction.[65] We can see it in the wide-ranging meaning carried by many of his technical words, like *inwit, conscience,* and *kind wit.* Latin, and more rarely French, provided Langland with the *mot juste* time and again.

But this is not the main reason for his use of Latin citations. The way Langland uses them shows they represented at one and the same time his desire for authority, his reaching after the absolute, and his way of dealing with intellectual perplexities. Above all, they were normal concomitants of the religious literary forms to which he was indebted. Langland's problem is not the struggle with the inexpressible, as a mystic might struggle, but the struggle to answer a very precise question—how to live the Christian life in society. The difficulty lies, not in the nature of what is to be communicated, but in the multiplicity of conflicting answers.

I do not wish to give the impression that Langland's style is tortured and ungainly. It is, on the contrary, relatively smooth and quick moving, even though there is a certain amount of after-thought and modification, such as is still characteristic of colloquial English and a certain negligence with regard to person, for frequently the language moves from second to third person, or vice versa.

In spite of the rhythm and alliteration, at times Langland's verse reads remarkably like blank verse. It is a segmented but smooth style,[66] and its quality comes out very clearly when the complexities and tortuosities of his near contemporary Richard Rolle's Latin or English are compared with Langland's. It is difficult to find passages similar enough to make a fair comparison, yet there is an intensity in Rolle that Langland does not have. Rolle's violent sensuousness is lacking, and in its place one gets a coolness of development broken by occasional phrases or clauses in apposition and longer units interrupted by Latin quotations. It is the style, not of a fourteenth-century mystic, but of a puzzled man who is both detached and terribly involved in his problem, who is both spectator and actor. It is vivid with apt metaphors, appropriate pictures and images, and delight in word play.[67] There is an intellectual rather than a sensuous perplexity in his long lines. Langland's problem is not, as with Rolle, essentially how to communicate, but what to communicate in the face of too many answers.

Langland's social and intellectual orientation may also be seen in his love of puns, half-puns, repetitions, and word play in general. They presuppose an audience, a certain society, and they reveal an intellectual perplexity and at the same time a fascination with that perplexity. This notable characteristic of his style has been studied by B. F. Huppé, and since his article has appeared, students of the poem have been very much aware of it.[68] Each careful reading of the poem uncovers more puns, and further discoveries in Langland's use of various forms of word play may well be expected.

Langland's balance, on the other hand, may be seen in the tendency for the rhetorical unit of his line to correspond with the semantic unit. It would be too much to say his lines are end-stopped, for he writes in rather long sentences (if we may accept in general Skeat's punctuation) with parallel and parenthetical clauses; but the end of a line tends to be the end of a clause or at least a thought unit. When Langland does use, as on rare occasions he does (for example, in VI, 202–203, XI, 143–144 and 292–293), a violent enjambment dividing a syntactic unit in two, we are brought up short. In general his sentences are paratactic; he favors the extensive use of *and*. Here is a typical sentence:

> Saul, for he sacrifised · sorwe hym be-tydde,
> And his sones al-so · for that synne myscheued,
> And many mo other men · that were no Leuites,
> That with *archa-dei* ȝeden · in reuerence and in worschippe,
> And leyden honde ther-on to liften it vp · and loren hir lif
>   after.
>
> (XII, 117–122)

Or, again, two sentences:

> Lyf and Deth in this derknesse · her one fordoth her other;
> Shal no wiȝte wite witterly · who shal haue the maystre,

Er Sondey aboute sonne-rysynge · and sank with that til
    erthe.
Some seyde that he was goddes sone · that so fair deyde,
    Vere filius dei erat iste, etc.
And somme saide he was a wicche · good is that we assaye,
Where he be ded or nouȝte ded · doun er he be taken.

                            (XVIII, 65–70)

These excerpts give us typical Langland without the occasional
striking image or metaphor and without the humor and irony that
frequently play about his line. The colloquialism is marked in
the appositions and repetition, especially by pronouns, and the
general parataxis.

Langland's style is temperate, balanced, and clear, but its temperateness, balance, and clarity serve to reveal his fundamental
intellectual complexity. His style, reconstructed from his poem,
perfectly mirrors the movement of his mind.[69] Following the tradition of the sermon, of exegesis, and of complaint, apparently tem-
pered by scholastic literary forms, Langland uses texts as pillars of
support both within and without the texture of his work.[70] He
reaches out after truth, the whole truth, which in abstract form the
Bible and the Fathers give him, and hopes for the great bargain
which God's grace can bring to him.

And ȝut, ich hope, as he · that ofte haueth chaffared,
That ay hath lost and lost · and atte laste hym happed
He bouhte such a bargayn · he was the bet euere,
And sette hus lost at a lef · at the laste ende,
Such a wynnynge hym warth · thorw wordes of hus grace:
    Simile est regnum celorum thesauro abscondito
    in agro & cetera:
    Mulier que inuenit dragman unam, et cetera;
So hope ich to haue · of hym that is al-myghty
A gobet of hus grace · and bygynne a tyme,
That all tymes of my tyme · to profit shal turne

                          (C, VI, 94–101)

A word or two about the stylistic effect of Langland's use of
personifications may not be amiss. Their frequency can be accounted for by their presence in the genres discernible in *Piers*, but

more must be involved. They must have corresponded to some inner artistic need of Langland and must be seen, at least partially, in this light. Personifications are essentially clarifying concepts, and they seemed to appeal to Langland because they afforded an objective and cool method of direct exposition. They are evidence of Langland's balance and temperateness and round out the presentation of his thought. Yet the endless dialogue and sometimes strife between various personifications and between them and Will reflect the other side of the coin, the perplexity and uncertainty of the seeker. His choice of genres and his style reveal a fundamental internal crisis that he cannot completely solve and at the same time demonstrate his admiration for moderation and clarity. His is the style of a moderate, clear-headed, but perplexed man.

Langland's use of personifications is the most potent force in the poem making for the strong sense of timelessness and spacelessness which it creates in the reader. Reading *Piers* gives one a feeling of being unlocalized and atemporal, in spite of Langland's strong concrete sense of human existence. We are in no particular time or place, yet Langland's lines are full of naturalistic detail and homely images. Personification is always a matter of nouns that are *per se* general; in personification the adjective and verb carry the particulars. Prosopopoeia thus is especially suited for portraying both the undifferentiated universal and the detailed concrete. Sharp lines separate one scene from another, but the background of depth seems missing. The scenes of *Piers*, vivid as they are, seem to move in an undifferentiated medium that makes the familiar strange. The concrete element seems to be at war with itself. The foreground is sharp; the background is vague.

One must be cautious in comparing works of literature with contemporary or near-contemporary works of art. Yet this sense of an empty stage on which the action of Langland's poem takes place is not unlike the bare or empty backgrounds in the paintings of Simone Martini or, to take an example closer in time, the Wilton diptych of the National Gallery. Against an empty background, or one in which space and depth are merely suggested, one sees in these paintings extremely naturalistic features. In the foreground, very real people and things are presented in an empty medium. Space and depth stop at the foreground; the background, without any or only the slightest suggestion of perspective, is out of time and space. Another splendid example is afforded by the Avignon *Pietà*, which is much later (1460) but is recognized by art historians as *retardataire*. Here, in moving detail, the naturalistic agony of the figures of the foreground is acted out against a background that is vacant except for the very small picture of the city of Jerusalem and a faint suggestion of a mountain. All these pictures suggest the combination of representationalism and non-representationalism so characteristic of *Piers*, a combination much enhanced by the way Langland uses his personifications and also by his selective use of detail.

For whom was Langland writing? J. A. Burrow argues that his audience consisted, not of the aristocracy or landed gentry, as was probably the case with the other poems of the "alliterative revival," but of clerics and the new, educated lay class.[71] He gives convincing reasons for the argument. The evidence from wills and the contents of the codices in which *Piers* is found when it does not take up all the space bear this out. Although, as the autobiographical passages show, Langland was probably a member of what W. A. Pantin calls the "clerical proletariate,"[72] this need not mean that his audience were fringe clergymen in minor orders or wandering semi-goliardic clerics. It was probably otherwise. Unlike other alliterative poems, *Piers* is preserved in a large number of manuscripts—over fifty—and although this evidence is perhaps a little ambiguous, it argues for its popularity among serious-thinking people, religious and lay. It is hard to think of a large, popular audience for the work, in spite of John Ball's reference to *Piers* in his famous letter of 1381. The poem is too difficult and too allusive to have been enjoyed by the common people or by restless, uprooted clerics. The references to *Piers* and the poems influenced by it all argue for a medium-sized, literate, thoughtful audience.

Piers was widely read probably for the same reason that popular mysticism, anti-scholasticism, personal piety, and even heresy flourished in the late fourteenth and fifteenth centuries. The subsequent rapid rise and spread of Protestantism was possible because of the presence of a large number of people who were dissatisfied with the abuses of the Roman Church and its internal divisions and the conflict between ideals and reality, even though many were at first not prepared to go beyond an internal reformation. Yet when the logic of extreme censure and criticism carried the leaders of the Reformation to repudiate Catholicism completely, many Catholics were not prepared to fight for their faith or beliefs. The defenses had crumbled.

Within scholasticism itself we see in the fourteenth, fifteenth, and sixteenth centuries an increasing concern with minutiae, a growing skepticism and a rising emphasis on the will rather than reason. The dominant scholastic schools of the end of the Middle Ages were strongly voluntaristic. Reason, the very basis of scholasticism, was suspect, and we get evidence piled upon evidence of the desire for a new concept of Christian perfection that could be realized in action and life.

Piers attempted to analyze the ills of contemporary society and to redefine the ancient idea of Christian perfection, both desperately needed in the crisis of late medieval life. It was for this reason, no doubt, that *Piers Plowman* had a wide, if not popular, audience and appeal. Now, it is necessary to turn more directly to this notion of Christian perfection to see what it is. Langland's approach was in some ways reactionary, but a reactionary often becomes a revolutionary. Langland held up the monastic ideal of perfection, and it is by tracing the line of monastic philosophy that we can best approach his point of view and "message," his tradition and his revolt.

CHAPTER II

Monasticism and Perfection

THE Christian life is fundamentally the quest for perfection. Of all the manifestations of such life, monasticism is the one that has historically been most closely associated with this search. As an institution, it was founded expressly for the purpose of producing perfect Christians, as far as that is possible to human beings. Its only ideals were salvation and the Kingdom of God, and its founders and theoreticians believed that they had found the way to realizing them. Their point of view—the goals and means whereby their ideals could be reached—may be called monastic philosophy.

"Monastic philosophy" is, however, a vague phrase which means various things. Recently it has been used to characterize the philosophy-theology that was dominant in the West from Gregory the Great to the twelfth century, when it was submerged although not eliminated by scholasticism.[1]

Monasticism was more symbolically oriented and Platonically inspired than its successor. There is not just one monastic philosophy-theology any more than there is just one scholasticism, but the movement does have features and emphases that distinguish it from the later scholasticism, with its more categorical, rationalistic, and Aristotelian qualities. The shift produced a change in method of teaching. The universities became prominent over the monastic schools, and lectures over the *lectiones*; and in literary forms, the *disputatio*, the question, and the *summa* are its characteristic genres, as compared to the *meditatio*, the chronicle, and the commentary.

Important as this shift in the twelfth century is, together with the concept of monastic philosophy-theology it presupposes, the primary concern here is not with "monastic philosophy" in this sense, although it is to some extent contained in the expression as used in this book. I am using the word "philosophy" advisedly;

perhaps the German *Denkform* (form of thought) is more exact. I shall call monastic philosophy-theology, "monastic theology" when there is occasion to refer to it, and for the monastic *Denkform* I shall use the term "philosophy." Monastic philosophy indicates the kind of thinking peculiar to the monastic view of life in general; and this includes various monastic theologies as well as the monastic concept of itself as opposed to other forms of Christian life. I use the term "philosophy" with some reluctance, since the customary use of the word implies a rationalistic bias and a love of categorization that are very different in tone and spirit from the monastic point of view, with its existential attitude and its orientation towards God and the next world. When used to characterize monastic thinking, the term must be understood in a more general sense, as the term is sometimes used in phrases such as a "philosophy of life." In fact, "monastic philosophy" is essentially the Christian world view before the twelfth century.

In the fourteenth century this view involved certain very special attitudes which were created in opposition to a different and very successful type of regular religious life represented for the most part by the friars. Yet these attitudes sometimes found a place for all regulars, even the friars. If only the friars would be true to their rule, they too could be embraced as fellow monastics in the broad sense of the term.

This wide embracing outlook in essence explains Langland's attitude towards the friars. He criticizes them violently, much more violently than any other group. Yet because they are potentially monks and Christians on the highest level of perfection, Langland makes the reform of the friars one of the crucial issues in the reform of the world. Their condition is to Langland the basic problem of his time, as both his perpetual concern with them and the conclusion to his great poem reveal. Their corruption is the pattern of all Christian, and especially ecclesiastical, corruption.

Conscience, in setting out on his last great quest for Piers (XX, 378–384), says that he wishes to find him for two reasons: that Piers may destroy pride and that he may provide a living for the friars who now have to flatter men because of need and therefore oppose him. Without a full awareness of the centrality of the issue of the reform of the friars, and this may be seen only in the light of Langland's monastic philosophy, the desire on the part of Conscience seems like a pathetic anticlimax. If the friars are merely one group in society among many, why Conscience in the great climax and conclusion of the poem should give them this crucial place is inexplicable. But their reform is in a sense the calling back to the road of perfection of the group that have most flagrantly violated their high ideals; they too are monks in a profound sense. Hence this goal of Conscience' quest begins to make sense and all falls into place.[2] How could all this have come about? This book attempts to answer this question. At least one may now, however, see that the vicious attacks on the friars throughout the poem are prompted, not merely by Langland's disapproval of their misdeeds, but by his view of their high calling and their role as regulars or "monks"; for the "monks" are the key to the establishment of the just and loving society, which will make possible the just and loving man. If the highest group can reform itself, all of society can also do so.

Langland was a conservative radical, and his ideal was a society of *status*, with each class or order performing its proper duty. In effect, it is Plato's ideal of the just society transformed by Christianity and in particular by monastic philosophy.

How may we characterize this monastic *Denkform*? It must be borne in mind that the fourteenth century is not the fourth, and that profound changes in the monastic point of view had taken place as a result of a changed world. Monks had accepted to some degree the new things that the womb of time had brought forth. Some monastic legacies to the world were by the fourteenth century so widely accepted that it is only clear to scholars whence they came. Yet persisting throughout all these changes were certain leading ideas that characterize the monkish point of view, even though by Langland's time some of them had become the general possession of the Western World. Although enough monastic forms and ideas persist in *Piers Plowman* to justify the claim that we can best understand the poem by looking at it from this point of view, any particular item in the poem may well be due to fourteenth-century thinking rather than to a monastic tradition, and in some cases one must beware of committing the genetic fallacy of judging things in terms of their origin.

In order to make clear the arguments advanced in the next

chapter, it will be necessary to discuss the origin and content of monastic philosophy and leave *Piers* for a while.

In the first half of the fifteenth century a monk of St. Albans, at the urging of another brother, obtained permission to migrate to Christ Church, Canterbury, because of its musical facilities. He was castigated by Abbot John Whethamstede of St. Albans in an interesting letter:

> Out of the clay of the earth and out of the dust of poverty was this man created, and placed in a Paradise of contemplation, that there he might work according to rules, and to keep watch over it in monastic form; it being granted to him freely to enjoy all claustral delights, and indifferently to eat of every tree of religion, provided only that he should keep one commandment, that is, faithfully abstain from the tree of knowledge, which tendeth to evil. Now a certain one, who was a crafty serpent, seeing this, who had theretofore himself departed from this cloistered heaven [*claustrali caelo*] and who was now enjoying a life at Christ Church more musical than monastic, envied the happy state of this man, and seeking the Paradise from which he had taken his departure, transformed himself into an angel of light, and offered to this flexible brother a threefold apple for him to taste.[3]

And thus he continued, lashing out at the unfortunate brother. This incident affords excellent evidence of the vitality of the monastic philosophy in England as late as the fifteenth century, for the image at the heart of this philosophy is that the cloister is the earthly paradise, from which fact a whole series of conclusions arise. The earthly paradise is the image of the heavenly paradise, and its inhabitants are similarly angels or beatified souls. Earthly paradise is also an image of the pure soul, the paradise within perhaps not happier but at least as happy as the eternal one.

The imagery of paradise in Christian thinking is most complex, and most of it goes back to Patristic speculation on the subject.[4] Paradise, according to Father Jean Daniélou, may be: the earthly paradise of Adam and Eve; heaven, the place of beatitude; a place where the souls of the just await resurrection (most developed in the early centuries and in the Middle Ages; after Gregory the

Great, relatively unimportant); the Church, the Ecclesia (and its highest part, the martyrs, virgins, and monks); the soul; and finally the *paradisus regnum*, the new paradise, the new Jerusalem on earth that will be established with the coming of the King. In the works of Ephraem the Syrian in the fourth century, paradise is at one and the same time the summit, the circle, and the center of the universe. The central view of Patristic thought, according to Father Daniélou, is the correspondence between spheres of different realities: the primitive state, the two Testaments, the Church, mysticism and eschatology, and, one might add, the universe; and paradise is a unifying image for these spheres. One must pass through fire and water and be divested spiritually of one's clothes to re-enter paradise, retracing Adam's steps. Baptism, as its early iconography shows, is the first step towards the return, just as entry into a monastic order was conceived of as a new and second baptism.

The harmonious unity of this picture of the universe gradually crumbled in the West during the Middle Ages; but various elements of it, helped by the theorizing of the Pseudo-Dionysius, persisted, and in no milieu so thoroughly as in monasticism.[5] Paradise is a garden, with well-defined boundaries. Hell is a desert with no boundaries at all. The purpose of life is to be dead to the claims of the world, the realm of Satan, and to return to one's source, one's paradise; and the Church, especially the monastery, is the road to paradise and at the same time a foretaste and pattern of it. The monk is pre-eminently the athlete, the soldier, the pilgrim of God.[6]

To the Middle Ages, this profound picture was delivered, somewhat modified and changed by Augustine and Gregory the Great. It became the basis of the dominant view of the world as reflected in monastic theology and philosophy,[7] until finally it was submerged by scholasticism, which represented a new approach to the world and to theology. By the fourteenth century it had been considerably modified and no longer formed the dominant mode of thought. But even in modified form it persisted, not only in monastic milieus, although mainly there, but elsewhere. The reaction against scholasticism in the fourteenth and fifteenth centuries did not primarily mean a return to monastic theology but rather a development of lay piety and devotion and a flowering of mysticism; for the fourteenth century was one of the greatest centuries in the history of mysticism. This anti-intellectualism[8] manifested itself in various other ways too—in a return to the Bible, in the raising of the problem of authority,[9] in unusual intellectual positions such as the theologism of Bradwardine,[10] and in various heresies, and so forth. Although to some, especially monastics, the monastic philosophy, which had never been abandoned, became a new source of strength; the rise of scholasticism had changed its emphases and approach.

The monastic philosophy was worked out fundamentally in the fourth and fifth centuries in the East as monasticism itself came into being. The ideal of perfection was strongly urged in Christianity from its beginning, and this ideal carried along with it the concept of grades of attainment, expressed in various images and by various terms. Sometimes we find the triad of beginner, progressor, and perfect; sometimes marriage, widowhood, and virginity (or martyrdom); sometimes in class terms, lay, priests, monks, or lay, preachers, doctors, virgins, martyrs; sometimes in mystical terms, purgative, illuminative, and unitive; sometimes in devotional terms, meditation, prayer, and contemplation; and sometimes in moral terms, civil, purifying, pure, and exemplary virtues. Nor are all these necessarily mutually exclusive. Basic to all is the notion of harmoniously analogical levels which make analogical demands on those Christians in each level. Each Christian must be as perfect as his *status* requires, though not every member of a more perfect *status* or state is necessarily more perfect than a member of a less perfect *status* or state. Indeed, he may be much worse because of his failure to live up to the higher commitments he has undertaken. It may be said that a conscientious member of a more perfect *status* is more perfect than a conscientious member of a less perfect *status*.

In the Old Testament, a large number of Hebrew words occur that are frequently translated into English as "perfect": *gamar,* with basic meaning of to cease, to come to an end; *tamam,* to finish, to complete; *ḳalal,* to bring to the highest peak; *shalem,* to finish, complete, to settle accounts; *maleh,* to fill, to complete. (Only verb forms are listed.) Noah and the Law are both called *tamim* (adjective from *tamam*) in the Bible, where the central concept seems to imply wholeness, simplicity, integrality, completeness. Yet God is never called perfect in the Old Testament. In later pre-Christian Jewish books wherein we may suspect Greek influence, such as Wisdom, we find sentiments, as in 11:21 (20), which imply a strongly developed notion of philosophical perfection and which were quoted again and again in the Middle Ages to justify the assumption of an ordered and perfect universe: "But Thou has arranged all things by measure and number and weight."

In the New Testament, *teleios* and its related forms meaning "perfect," "having attained the end," are used again and again. The command of Jesus to be "perfect, even as your Father which is in heaven is perfect,"[11] is perhaps the most notable expression of the concept. The whole problem of sinful man is posed against this difficult command. As theology developed, this statement gave a biblical basis to the idea of the deification of man that was to play such an important part, especially in Greek theology. Matthew 19:21 links poverty with perfection, and this was to be another rallying concept during the following centuries. The Epistles are full of references to perfection, and in general they refer to the best life possible here, to superiority and completeness.[12] Paul in I Corinthians 7:20 and elsewhere had a conservative ethic of class and vocation and implies that a perfect society is one in which each man performs the social role most suitable for him. The term *teleios* may have been taken from the mystery-religions, although Christianity certainly gave the term a richer and more profound meaning.[13] When the "old" man is cast aside and becomes the "new" man in Christ, a Christian is then perfect; but even in St. Paul there are degrees of perfection. This idea of grades of perfection was to be developed elaborately later. Philo Judaeus, Paul's contemporary, certainly distinguished grades of progression—the beginner, the professor, and the perfect.[14]

In the New Testament the whole concept is ethically and religiously oriented. It conveys a strong sense of compulsion and of drive. The kerygma must be put into action so that the Kingdom of God may come. This emphasis in the New Testament, which is plain to anyone who may read it, has made perfection an important concept in theology and in the history of Christianity. Time and again, the cry has been to return to the apostolic and evangelical life, and the New Testament itself has provided the guiding words.[15] The idea of perfection was never so important in Judaism, although its Pelagianistic views might be supposed to have made it so.[16] Possibly the strong Jewish sense of separation between man and the divine may be responsible. Christianity, on the other hand, in spite of its emphasis on grace and original sin, has always been preoccupied with the concept of perfection, which after contact with Greek and Hellenistic thinking, especially in Alexandria, became a vital issue in theology, and has been a vital issue ever since. As Gregory of Nyssa and others saw, the God who became man also in some sense calls for man to become God.[17]

The problem of perfection raises questions of great perplexity. Does Christian perfection imply a state of sinlessness? How far is it attainable in this life? What role do the precepts and counsels play in the attainment of perfection? If one stresses perfection too much, does not one run into moralism and Pelagianism? These raise issues that cannot be simply answered, as the long history of Christian perfection shows.

The early interest in perfection in Christianity bespeaks an enthusiasm, a drive in those to whom the Master had appeared, and their followers. Life could no longer be the same. Perfection could not be merely a pale metaphysical concept but had to be brought down into everyday life. The hopelessness and despair of the pagan was sin. The message of Christ was joy; and a new man more perfect than the old must be born. The very idea of typology, of the Old Testament as a preparation for and foreshadowing of the New and of a progressive revelation towards the truth, must have fostered the quest for perfection in early Christianity. It was in an apocalyptic and expectant Jewish milieu in ancient Palestine, as now seems clear, that Christianity made its appearance. The Day of the Lord was here or nearly here. The plenitude of time, the fulfillment of the old, had arrived. In their own salvation, the early Christians saw the wondrous workings of the Lord, who at one stroke dispelled the shadow and allowed the sun to shine clear. The change in the economy of the world and of history must be reflected in a new attitude toward self. A new dispensation called for a new man, and newness could be justified only if it were perfect.

Although there are probably more than traces of Greek thinking on the question of perfection in the New Testament, especially in the Epistles, as there are in the later books of the Old Testament and in noncanonical late Jewish writings, it is in Alexandria that the combination of Greek and Hebrew concepts was forged. Philo was most concerned with the question, and some scholars have seen perfection and deification as his central concern.[18] In him, as with some later theologians, the concept of perfection is often assumed rather than argued. In the world of Greek philosophy and Greek categories of thought, perfection as an underlying assumption of much thinking was almost impossible to avoid. Final causes, the *arete* of all beings, the hierarchy of being, and a belief in the objective existence of values and qualities would make it absolutely necessary. In the early Christian Alexandrines, the concept becomes alive and is often actively discussed. The general problem facing Clement and Origen—to offer an intellectually respectable alternative to Stoicism, Judaism, Gnosticism, and Neoplatonism or perhaps to understand as far as possible the Incarnation in philosophical and theological terms—made the problem of perfection virtually impossible to avoid. In regard to perfection, thinkers wished to show that there was a Christian concept of perfection which was existential and systematic.[19]

In Alexandria, too, the concept of perfection came in contact with the pagan ruler cult, with its blend of the oriental sacred king and sun worship. The king as the imitation of god, or even god himself, provided a pagan equivalent to the incarnate God, Jesus, who set the model for all Christians. The perfection concept took on, however, some of the ideas of the world-emperor who would establish for Christians the external social conditions for the perfection of society.[20] These ideas were to prove very fruitful. Just as the ancient Hebrew and Greek concept of perfection, defined in new terms and made a living problem by the advent of Christianity, was combined with apocalyptic and eschatological dreams and ideals, so the pagan concept of the saviour-emperor was transformed. Later in the high Middle Ages a companion to the saviour-emperor appeared, the angelic Pope.[21] These two figures, the heads of the *regnum* and *sacerdotium*, were to lead the world into a final period of bliss. Whenever thinking on perfection in the Middle Ages stressed the historical and social, and the eschatological, always joined with the first two, these ideal figures of emperor and Pope crop up. The King in *Piers Plowman* who is to give a knock to the Abbot of Abingdon and all his issue forever has a long ancestry.[22]

Greek and perhaps early Hebrew thinking on the subject of personal and social perfection tended to throw emphasis on the goal, on rest (the Sabbath is the prototype of all perfection, and of the Kingdom of God), on attainment. Essentially this emphasis sets up a static idea of pattern and norm on which mankind can model itself. As with Euclid's method of hypothetically laying one figure on another to prove equality, we find here a kind of spatial dimensional equality. In the Bible, even in the early books, there is a chronological sense, a belief in the reality of time; and in the Hellenistic era, we find in rabbinic exegesis, in Philo, in the New Testament, and even in Stoicism, a new awareness of time in the concept of perfection as in other ideas. Time (and history) is not an irrelevant factor but of the essence of existence.

More and more stress is put on the progress of perfection. Perfection is a journey, a movement, an ascent. Life is a pilgrimage, a meaningful pilgrimage, and if it is properly lived, a progression towards perfection. In the story of the Exodus, we find the supreme exemplar of the movement towards perfection, and indeed in Philo and Gregory of Nyssa (to take only two of the possible figures of the early Christian period), the stress in the subject of perfection is on movement and progression—on continual purification.[23] "La perfection consiste en un progrès continuel."[24] Origen saw in the deliverance from Egypt a parable of the soul casting off sin and evil. Paul writes in Philippians 3:14 of this spiritual progression, "I press toward the mark for the prize of the high calling of God in Christ Jesus." In short, perfection became a part of mysticism and time.

Of course, the earlier and spatial concept of perfection by no means vanished; but after the early centuries of our era, perfection in the moral sense embraced both time and space, history and ontology—in short, it became dynamic. Perfection is both continual spiritual growth and spiritual attainment; and theologians could stress either or both as they wished. Perfection now had a psychological and historical dimension; but it also contained sharp contradictions, especially in regard to the idea of limitation. The limited alone could, according to classical Greek thought, be perfect; but now infinity and eternity have become attributes of the all loving and just God who is by definition perfection. Can virtue increase to infinity? Is infinite progress possible? Can rest and movement both be perfect? Can mankind struggle for perfection? These are some of the troublesome questions that Christian perfection brought on, which arise when the individual strives to be perfect.[25] They were to be debated over a long period of time, and some of them are still debated.

By the third or fourth century, one may say that the essential definitions and problems of perfection had been worked out or posed, and the rest of the story is a long attempt to synthesize the doctrines already laid out or to put them into practice. A few highlights of this story may not be irrelevant here.

The Greek Fathers were all more or less concerned with perfection, and in general the Greek and Eastern churches have followed that tradition. Their approach was largely by means of the deification and transfiguration concepts. Christ was the Pantocrator, the ruler of the universe, the divine King on whom we must model ourselves. Deification was a mystic participation and a return. "Der Mensch ist gottentsprungen und darum gottsüchtig."[26] The return is progress. Theology is the means to that end. Theology is primarily a guide to mysticism, not a mode of knowing and understanding. The West has, at least since the eleventh century, tended to concentrate on charity and on an *imitatio* of the suffering Christ and His human nature. Theology is rather a mode of knowing and understanding even within the limitations of the human mind. Perfection in Augustine and Gregory was essentially, if not exclusively, a moral goal, even if for the ultimate purpose of reaching heaven. The Platonic conception of knowledge as an assimilation of subject and object, however, lies behind Eastern thought on the matter of perfection and deification. To know and to love are essentially the same. Only God can know God; if man's true purpose here below is to know God, then in the last analysis man must become God. *Theosis* is the goal of all perfection and of Christian living. Through *apatheia* we attain *theosis*.

These Eastern views were transmitted to the West chiefly by the Pseudo-Dionysius and his commentators, beginning with Maximus the Confessor and John Scotus Erigena. The Areopagite occupies a very important place in the history of perfection both in the East and West, first because of the profundity and elegance of his thought, and second because he provided a final rationale for monasticism, which may be also seen in Evagrius, Cassian, Augustine, and Gregory.

Much has been written on the Pseudo-Dionysius, and much more no doubt could and will be written on him.[27] For our purposes it is sufficient to say that he combined the Neoplatonic hierarchy of being with Christianity and Christian perfection. He gave an ontological basis for Christian perfection, rooted in the notion of a universal hierarchy in which all tends analogically to the good. There are in his universe horizontal hierarchies (through time) as well as vertical hierarchies (out of time), and there are hierarchies within hierarchies. The whole universe is both like God and tending towards him. The highest earthly hierarchy is the ecclesiastical hierarchy parallel to the heavenly hierarchy, and the monks are on its highest rung, almost comparable to the highest angels. Monks prefigure and correspond to the heavenly hosts more closely than any other earthly order or class.

The whole universe and everything that is in it is a series of graded and analogical levels, all tending to perfection and, in a sense, to the negation of all negations beyond all perfections. All things actively tend to good. This magnificent scheme combines the various orders of being and existence, including the historic, in a sweep and amplitude that can only make one humble. It became a, if not the, basic concept of medieval cosmic thinking. The world in all its areas is organized into levels of reality.[28]

At first one feels in reading the Epistles and the scanty very early Christian literature that Paul and the earliest Fathers felt that the Christians as a whole, the *verus Israel*, were in the most perfect status by virtue of their having been baptized and having accepted Jesus Christ, the resurrected man-god, as their King. The harshness of early Christian penance implies this concept of themselves, no less than does the very name of Christian, which they applied to themselves.[29] By their title, they indicated that they were servants of the true King or the Messiah (Jesus). With the beginning of the persecutions and the entry into the faith of many who did not have the fervor of the earliest believers, however, it was felt that distinctions must be made within the fold. Martyrdom was soon considered the highest manifestation of Christian perfection.[30] Martyrdom was regarded as a second baptism, and martyrs were believed to go to heaven immediately and to be made the equal of angels. Even when it was recognized, as it soon was by men like Clement of Alexandria, that Christian perfection could be attained in other ways, martyrdom was still considered its peak. Clement allowed a spiritual martyrdom, which could be attained by conforming to Christ's doctrine and by holding the world in contempt. Origen made even more of this concept. Later in Basil the Great and John Chrysostom, when monasticism had been established, the monk appears as a spiritual martyr who showed his contempt of the world by his virginity, his withdrawal, and his poverty, and who followed Christ's doctrine by *ascesis* to recover as far as was possible the image of God in himself by imitating Christ.

With the disappearance of active persecution, at least in the Roman world, and the narrowing of the opportunity for martyrdom, the monks conceived of their vows as taking its place; and from the fifth century on, Christian thought commonly regarded monks as the successors of the martyrs and representatives of the highest grade of Christian perfection, even though theoretically actual martyrs still occupied that station. Instead of a second baptism of blood, as in martyrdom, the profession of monastic vows was looked upon as a second baptism that raised the rebaptized to a new level of perfection by infusing the monk with more grace. The imagery and symbolism of martyrdom were transferred to virgins and monks.[31]

The story of the rise and early history of monasticism in the deserts of Egypt and its spread to all the Roman World and the West, and to Syria and Palestine, where already hermits were to be found, has been well told by others. With the expansion of the institution we also find an expansion of the associated theory of the high role of the monk; this was to be worked into the fabric of the early Christian world view and eventually to become that view. The monks were ideally the foremost exponents of Christian perfection; their dwelling, the cloister, was the most perfect habitation on earth, close to both the earthly and the heavenly paradise, and their purpose was to lead back all Christians and all mankind to true spiritual regeneration, *apocatastasis* and *restauratio*, both a return and a progress.[32] They were like Christ, naked pilgrims on earth with the goal of paradise.

Augustine and Gregory were the most effective of the Fathers in preserving and reorganizing monastic philosophy and theology for the West.[33] In Augustine, we do not find the term monastic philosophy or theology, but in the West what it in effect became was an amalgam of traditional ideas as interpreted by both him and Gregory.

Augustine's importance for the understanding of the whole Middle Ages cannot be overestimated, and in one sense his whole work may be interpreted as an ascension towards God.[34] In particular, however, Augustine made a special impress on monastic philosophy (along with John Cassian, Benedict, and Gregory) that gave it its characteristic Western features, built upon the Eastern substratum.[35] It is this impress which will be my particular concern, although it is not always possible to separate it from his thought in general.

In brief, Augustine, without repudiating the ideals of poverty, chastity, and obedience, gave a social orientation to the monastic ideal which it was never to lose entirely in the West and which indeed became a strong element in its monastic theology and philosophy. Augustine's ideal was a Christian community of love united in the Church, the Ecclesia. "Through Augustine's whole life there runs the search for a communal or social way of Christian life."[36] Cenobitical life is more than a means to perfection; it is its goal, the heavenly city. Monks were to be at the disposal of the whole Church, and their work was to be apostolic and ecclesiastical.[37] The monastic role in the mystical *Corpus Christi* was stressed. Augustine was a great teacher to the monks in the West as well as to the Church generally; and the well-known rule he wrote for nuns not only formed at least the basis of the later Augustine Rule adopted by canons and friars but influenced other rules. In his opusculum *De opere monachorum* he argued that monastic work (agriculture and handicrafts) took as far as possible the curse off labor and dignified it. Karl Burdach believes Augustine was the great force behind the attack on mendicancy in the fourteenth century. Thomas Aquinas apparently did not give agriculture any special pre-eminence. Monasticism is thus again a step back to paradise.

Together with this social bias, Augustine also, curiously enough, stressed that inner probing and spiritual self-consciousness that was to flower only in the later Middle Ages. His famous psychological analysis of the Trinity was to prove most influential. We know the Trinity by faith, but its image in man's mind can be discovered by reason and introspection.

Augustine, along with Ambrose and Jerome, impressed further on Western thought the concept of grades of perfection, which Augustine defined in various ways.[38] He tended to place, in consonance with his high regard for the sacerdotal office, priests or clergy first; and monks or the continent, second; and the faithful, third. At the end of time, priests will be in the field, symbol of the Church bringing in the harvest; monks will be in bed, symbol of peace; and the faithful will be at the mill (the image is based on Matthew 24:40–41 and Luke 17:34–36). Of course some monks were priests. He is not completely consistent, nor does he always use the same terms. At other times the triad of virgins, widows, and married folk is used, a parallelism that assigns the highest role to monks.[39] But, on the whole, Augustine does not make as much of the grades of perfection as do some of his predecessors and successors. This is possibly because his vision was primarily on the barrier separating the two cities rather than on the grades within each commonwealth.

Augustine also developed the Greek idea of deification or recapitulation (*apocatastasis*) in a special way that was to have its bearing on Western ideas of reform.[40] The social emphasis in his monastic ideal also had a strong bearing on the Western idea of reform—an emphasis that was to have momentous importance in our history. In the East, owing to the ideas of Gregory of Nyssa and others, together with the play of political and social forces, moral and social reform ideas were absorbed into mystical purification and spiritual ascent. In the West, however, the situation was different, and in some not insignificant measure this was due to Augustine. These differences may be traced back both to the social emphasis in Augustine and to his concept of deification. Man was a picture of God rather than a divine exemplar. According to Augustine, the barrier between man and God is greater—as it also is between nature and grace. We cannot return to paradise by purification; this idea is too suggestive of Pelagianism. And besides we actually desire more than a return to paradise. We want true immortality, which even the prelapsarian Adam did not possess. He merely would not die if free from sin. Our bodies, too, will be different at the Resurrection. Grace can give gifts to the predestined greater than those possessed by Adam. The aim of reform is not spiritualization, pure and simple, but an order in which spirit and matter both have their place.[41]

G. Ladner has stressed the importance of the Augustinian faculty of memory in his theory of reform. Memory, reflecting the Father, is more than a knowledge of the past; rather it is a faculty which learns from God how to know itself and how to direct its will towards the right kind of love towards God. It is closely bound with time—that is history—past and present and future.[42] We must move under God's grace to become citizens of the City of God, and baptism is our first step on the way. But the model must be a monkish community, which, imitating Christ and the Apostles, would work as priest and cleric in the fields.

Besides emphasizing repeatedly two of the major metaphoric themes of the monastic, and indeed Christian view of life—the pilgrimage of life[43] and the struggle or warfare of the movement towards Christian perfection[44]—Augustine's vision of God's order in the universe helped to reinforce the concept of the world as perfect and rational.[45] The various orders of Being parallel each other, and evil is disorder. Each nature naturally seeks its formal perfection, and man lives in the most orderly fashion when his highest faculty—reason—dominates all other parts. Augustine, following Stoic and Neoplatonic ideas, presents a rational universe with measure, number, and weight, echoing Wisdom 11:21. Weight (*pondus*) is perhaps the most important term—indicating that the universe possesses a gravitational pull, one might say, towards God. But the pull up has to contend with the pull down. Morally man is in harmony with the universe when man is temperate. Like Cicero,[46] Augustine valued as a psychical counterpart to his ontological picture, the balancing virtue of temperance. This picture is essentially the Platonic (and Aristotelian) view of a rational universe with a proper *arete* for everything in it. But it is Plato Christianized, especially in the moral field.

Gregory the Great, a monk himself, presents an even more authoritative picture of the monastic philosophy and theology that set the pattern for the Middle Ages in the West. To Gregory the role of monk was of the essence of the Christian life.[47] In the darkness that was settling over the West even in Gregory's time, his formulations of the monastic philosophy were to provide a beacon and a refuge. Much of what he had to say was traditional; but, as frequently with new combinations of the old, something original emerged. Gregory also lived after Benedict and was one of his ardent admirers and his most famous hagiographer; and Benedict left an impact on his thought and way of life which was never to diminish.

The center of Gregory's thought was the monastic view of life. Mortal man's proper home is paradise (in general, heaven in Gregory), and with God's grace and God's justice he tries to win it through the pilgrimage of life. The precepts of monkish life—solitude and silence, communal life in poverty, mortification, obedience and humility, liturgy (*opus Dei*) and prayer, work and the *lectio divina* (reading of the Bible and Fathers and Saints)—are all emphasized and set in the center of the Christian life. Obedience and humility are especially praised as leading to complete subjection to God and love. They lift a monk directly to perfection.[48] The categories of perfection appear too in his writings. The division into the married, the continent, and the *rectores* (leaders) is one of the ways he formulated the grades of progress towards God.[49]

We struggle with the devil to win freedom from the world of evil desires. To regain our original goal and our original selves we have the help of Jesus, through the Church and the Sacraments; but we must cooperate by holding the world in contempt, by despising earthly goods and values. Gregory stressed again and again the importance of being dead to this world, of being *extra mundum*. His analysis of sin is noteworthy, and it is his reorganization and presentation of the cardinal sins, in the *Moralia*, that became classic for the Middle Ages.[50] The fight with sin is the first and most difficult of all the tasks for the Christian pilgrim. The road of *ascesis* can be traversed only by conquering the sins; but before they can be conquered, they must be known. Although Gregory did not invent them, his map of the sins provided the chart for the good Christian throughout most of the Middle Ages. It was he who established the leadership of Pride in the demonic army; and this is the sin of rebellion, of disorder, of self-love. It is the opposite of obedience, ordered love, of chastity.

Like Augustine, Gregory emphasized the pull of the universe towards God and God's *dispositio* and *dispensatio*, both open and secret, which guaranteed its rationality. *Pondus* is a moral and spiritual as well as physical concept. The physical nature of the universe partially guarantees, in the light of Christianity, its spiritual nature and its perfection. There is a physical basis in the order and movement of the universe for the supernatural ends God has decreed in his *dispensatio* for it. The Gregorian universe is no less rational and orderly and also no less mysterious than the Thomistic one. The purpose of life on one level is to put ourselves into harmony with the universe.[51] The drive of the appetites in all the virtues and vices is a parallel to the force that makes an apple fall from the tree. Love, in its non-ecstatic form, in both Thomas and Gregory, is a kind of gravitational equivalent in the soul. In Gregory, however, as contrasted with Augustine, there are qualitative, not merely directional distinctions in the gravitational forces of the natural and supernatural realms. Gregory has a more complex conception of *pondus* than Augustine. The divine dispensation is a gravitational pull that must be met by the human disposition to work with it to save the souls of the living; but these forces are opposed by earthly pulls and weights that must be overcome to re-establish the proper order of the universe as determined by God.

In general, monastic philosophy is only the Christian life lived to the highest degree and affected by some of the particular qualities obtaining in the cloister.[52] The monastic ideology which became the dominant mode of Western thought until the eleventh and twelfth centuries may perhaps, in order to avoid further chronological treatment and the listing of many names, be summed up in the divisions Kassius Hallinger uses to categorize the basic ideas and ideals of monasticism in the West in the post-Gregorian–pre-Bernardine world.[53] In order to introduce the spiritual world of the beginnings of Cluny, the monastery that was to be of prime importance in the West, Hallinger bases his summation largely on the writings of Abbot Odo of Cluny (*c.* 924–942), especially his long poem *Occupatio*. His list of basic principles form the best introduction to the classic medieval view of monastic philosophy or *Denkform* that I know.

Hallinger divides these principles into four groups.

(1) Monasticism is the realization of the pentecostal Church. The Holy Ghost created an ideal Ecclesia at Pentecost. The path of the spiritual history of the world began with the Creation and was followed by the Fall, the Incarnation, and, as a crowning touch in *Heilsgeschichte*, Pentecost, which was to make possible the fruits of the Incarnation to the world. The highest manifestation of Pentecost is monasticism, which is the tip of the Ecclesia most closely aimed at God and which stands as a model for mankind in its struggle for perfection and salvation. The divine pentecostal fire alone can bind together the split in mankind created by the egotism of original sin.

(2) Monasticism is a passing beyond the world, as Gregory the Great taught. It involves a repudiation of this world for the sake of the next—earthly fame and renown, for heaven. Monks are the witnesses for the next world and the Kingdom of God. Their proper sphere is that of the angels, and they must travel through this world without care. "The true monk must be a stranger on earth."[54] They throw themselves on God, and they condemn utterly this world.

(3) Monasticism is a return to the original state of man. Virginity, poverty, and obedience are the means whereby he returns to paradise. Asceticism, manifested in these means and intensified by an active struggle against sin, by tears, and by prayer, enable the return to be made. This is the goal for all men and especially monks.

(4) Monasticism is an anticipation of the future. The delights of the cloister are a foretaste of paradise, and in the halls and cells of the monastery time stands still and heavenly rest is attained. The monks are the living eschatological element in history. Their communal life reflects that of the angels, and their silence reflects the peace of heaven. The liturgical round represents the praise of the Creator which will be the perpetual work of those in heaven. Monks are especially close to Christ.

The monks with their eschatological vision, closely allied with a strong sense of chronology sharpened by the continual expectation of the end of the world, were naturally drawn towards annals and history. The rise of the chronicle, which originally was an outgrowth of the problem of the date of Easter and the desire to keep a record of the martyrs of the Church, was soon broadened to include the reigns of kings and notable events. Augustine's philosophy of history and his emphasis on memory stimulated the desire to keep a record of occurrences which were landmarks in the progress towards the Day of Judgment.[55] These chronicles grew into full-fledged histories, and by the twelfth century they were considered the special province of monks and monasteries. And this monastic predilection for history continued throughout the Middle Ages, even when scholasticism with its generally systematic and metaphysical approach prevailed. The Bible, the main source of the *lectio divina*, was fundamentally if not exclusively, a historical work; and it was the core, along with the liturgy, of monastic spiritual and intellectual activity.

The chief narrative forms favored by monasticism, besides those relevant portions of the Bible, and history, were the lives of saints and holy men. As far as I know, the influence of the narrative technique of saints' lives, the most popular medieval narrative by far, has never been studied fully.[56] The medieval mind was nourished on these tales and legends, and to the monk, of course, they were a favorite fare. Their influence on later medieval narrative must have been immense.

The twelfth century, which saw great changes in Western civilization, produced two great representatives of monastic philosophy during this period. Bernard of Clairvaux in many ways set the new, or rather later, pattern for monastic philosophy and is notable for his psychological emphasis. He and the Cistercian movement wrought great changes in Western thought and art, and it is not surprising that some scholars tend to see him as the basic influence on Langland.[57] Joachim of Flora, on the other hand, represents the culmination of the older monastic tradition and piety, and is strictly speaking a reactionary. Yet, because of his thoroughness and his intensity, his views became, as often happens, the rallying cry of the radicals in the later Middle Ages. By his intransigence and intellectual consistency, he presented a picture of the universe—the apex and culmination and logical conclusion of monasticism—which appealed immensely to the eschatologically and apocalyptically oriented minds of the later Middle Ages.[58]

Bernard, or to be more exact the Bernardine position, is undoubtedly an influence on *Piers Plowman*, although some of the points of contact may not specifically be Bernard's but rather those of monastic philosophy. Where Langland got some of his ideas must remain, if not forever, at least for a long time, a mystery.

The second division of *Piers Plowman*, Do-wel, is essentially organized around the movement of the mind into itself—a kind of psychological (although not in the Proustian sense) exploration, in which Imaginatif (the *vis imaginativa*) occupies an important place. Passus XII contains Imaginatif's key speech, which clears up the three basic problems that so far had blocked Will's quest—the problems of the value of learning, of salvation and predestination, and of the meaning of nature. (Why Imaginatif—a relatively low psychological faculty—should have been assigned this crucial role is not at all clear, but I hope to partially solve the puzzle.)[59] Throughout the whole poem also, Conscience plays an important part, and it is he who sets out in search of Piers at the end.

In general this psychological orientation in the poem is due directly and indirectly to Bernard, for it was he who psychologized and interiorized the older monastic tradition and emphasized the personal way to God and the importance of conscience, based on the doctrines of Paul. Conscience to Bernard was, however, a mystical faculty.[60] Following perhaps Philo, through Origen, Bernard made conscience the voice of God in the soul. It is more than the rational faculty it was to Thomas and Duns Scotus; it is the chief means of return to God and in a sense the living internal evidence of God.

This intense mystical interpretation of conscience in Bernard is akin to his love for the Song of Songs and his whole view of the spiritual intimacy between God and man—or in particular Christ and man. For Bernard helped the West to see in the details of Jesus' daily life and death the true imitation of God. He helped to bring God down from his pedestal and make him less the cosmic king and more the loving incarnate Supreme Being.

Langland is closer in many ways to the older monastic tradition that Bernard helped to change so profoundly. It is a tradition more socially and less individualistically, more objectively and less subjectively, oriented. Christ as King and Ruler is more important than the suffering Jesus. Human nature ennobled is more important than divine nature humbled. Even conscience in its highest reaches is not quite a mystical but rather an eschatological faculty in *Piers*. One must not, then, overstress the similarities between

Bernard and Langland, for the differences in their view of the world are just as important.

Bernard had to struggle with language to express his new-old ideas and to contain his fervor. One may say of him that his writings, with their repetitions and puns, climaxes and antitheses, express a crisis of language. Yet there is throughout "a sense of decorum, of interior sweetness and of stylistic knowledge free of ostentation," creating a curious and perhaps uneasy balance. Impregnated as he was with the Bible, he turned to it for help in his linguistic problems, as monastic writers in general did. Augustine had set a precedent for him in recognizing biblical rhetoric. P. Dumontier says of Bernard that he speaks Bible as one might speak any language.[61] All this is highly reminiscent of Langland's style. We need not claim that Langland is directly imitating Bernard's language, but because both were influenced by the monastic tradition and because both faced a similar crisis of expression, although sharpened and distinguished by different historical factors, Langland fell naturally into a style somewhat akin to Bernard's, yet lacking his fervor. Nevertheless the style of the English alliterative tradition must be taken into consideration when discussing Langland's diction and poetic. They cannot be totally explained by Bernard's use of language, but the struggle, if not the intensity, is there.

With Joachim of Flora there appears what would be today called a philosophy of history; but it was a philosophy of history that grew out of and incarnated the highest ideals of monastic philosophy. Joachim, however, brought history into the concept of perfection and restoration in his well-known threefold division. Joachim historicized the Greek and monastic idea of deification and increase in perfection.[62] To reach perfection, as far as is possible, one must be a monk; but for the world to be perfect all must be monks, and a new age of monasticism was to be expected. Joachim thought that such an age was inevitable if one understood the true meaning of the Bible.

Arguing on the basis of analogies that he claimed to find between the period of the Old Testament and the period of the New Testament down to his own time, and on certain New Testament texts like Ephesians 4:13 and I Corinthians 13:10, Joachim assumed a new age coming in the future. This "trinity" of ages would correspond to the divine Trinity and would satisfy a desire for order and rationality in history. The period of the Old Testament was primarily the age of the Father; the period from the time of Jesus down to roughly Joachim's time was that of the Son; and the third age, which is a naturally completing period, would be that of the Holy Ghost, under whose aegis the Saracens and Jews would be converted and about which certain general predictions could be made. Each subsequent age follows the pattern of the first age.

The Old Testament, then, is the key to the meaning of history. Joachim estimated that each age lasted, as the Old Testament age did, for forty generations and had a precursor or germinator as well as an initiator or a fructifier. Hence, around 1260, would begin the final age, which would presumably last for about forty generations before the Last Judgment. The birth throes of each age are violent and give rise to Antichrists. Each age, however, is an advance over the preceding one, explains it, and gives a rationale to its pattern. Human history is divine fulfillment. The human race progressively receives a fuller revelation of the meaning of time and historical existence and progressively becomes more perfect. King Uzziah (Ozias) was the precursor of the second age, which was initiated by Zechariah, the father of John the Baptist. Benedict of Nursia was the precursor of the coming age, which would be a spiritual age.

The first age was dominated by the Law, the second by Grace, and the third was to be under dominance of the Spirit and Love. It would be characterized by *viri spirituales* living a monastic form of life, just as the preceding age had been characterized by the clergy and the first by married men. The Church would continue to exist, but the Sacraments would be spiritualized. The role of the papacy in the new age is somewhat dubious, but probably the Church, embracing all the faithful including the Greeks and all mankind, would continue to be presided over by a purified Bishop of Rome. This doctrine, then, gave an explanation of their tribulations to those men who cared to listen and provided them with a hope.

Such in brief is the core of Joachim's theories, which he claimed were based on a spiritual understanding of Scripture. We cannot here elaborate their influence on monks,[63] the left-wing Franciscans (the Spirituals), the other orders, and medieval man in general; but suffice it to say that much Utopian and reformist thinking of the later Middle Ages owes something to Joachim; and to those who were apocalyptically and eschatologically oriented, he was their master. Moreover, he was known all over Western Europe, including England.[64]

In the fourteenth century, to the monks who felt keenly their loss of prestige in the face of the rise of the friars, monastic philosophy (and sometimes the Joachite version) became a defense and a self-justification. Some seized eagerly on a philosophy of history that would give them their old precedence. History, these monks thought, was on their side, and their apocalyptic hopes were raised by the hope of a new age. In general this attitude is more frequently associated with the Spiritual Franciscans, but it was not unknown among the monks, although their general lack of dialectic fervor did not give them the publicity the friars gained. But nonetheless even when they accepted Joachim with reserve or not at all, their hopes were fed by the ancient philosophy of monasticism—which gave the monks the highest status on earth among the *viatores* and made their dwelling places a pattern of heaven.

CHAPTER III

Monastic Philosophy in Fourteenth-Century England and in *Piers Plowman*

SOME years ago, largely in the hope that some more conclusive evidence would turn up, I wrote an article pointing to some very hypothetical evidence linking Langland to the Benedictine Monastery at Whitby.[1] Unfortunately that hope has remained unrealized, and it is quite possible that I was on the wrong track altogether. I want, however, to make it clear that my present argument has nothing to do with that unsubstantiated hypothesis; for I am not here claiming that Langland had any intimate Benedictine connections, and the force of my argument does not turn on what may have been a mere coincidence. I propose to take *Piers Plowman* at its face value as far as autobiographical evidence is concerned and concede that the author probably was a clerk in lower orders.[2]

The primary concern in this book is not with biography but with Langland's intellectual milieu. The point of view and emphases of *Piers Plowman* can best be understood in the light of the monastic or older Christian tradition, a tradition that was by no means dead, as many think, in the fourteenth century and that even earlier than this century was no longer confined to the cloister, even though it was not the dominant mode of thought of the period. This does not, of course, rule out the possibility that Langland had some direct knowledge of monasticism, but to establish this fact is not the purpose of this book.

For what it is worth, the author does show a partiality for monks and monastics in the poem, which at the least makes plausible the supposition that he was aware of the most energetic exponents and basic tenets of monastic philosophy in fourteenth-century England and earlier. It is not necessary to argue for any direct connection, however, to establish Langland's concern with this philosophy.

In any case Langland does not refrain from criticizing the monks. In XV, 313–315, for instance, he advises laymen not to leave their property to monks and canons; in X, 267, he advises abbots and priors (as well as other churchmen) to amend their ways; even more strongly, in X, 291 ff., he reproves monks who leave their cloisters (although at the same time revealing a knowledge of the true meaning of the cloister).[3] Other criticisms of monks can be found, but they are generally from the point of view of a monk; attacks against the *gyrovagi* (wandering monks) and *sarabaites* (monks under no rules), who are castigated in the Benedictine Rule itself, will be pointed out. Thus, Langland was no blind admirer of the monks of his time. Fundamentally, he was concerned with the reform of the religious orders as a key to the reform of the world; but he felt that, though the monks were also sinners, the friars were much worse and the problem of their reform was more urgent.

In general the monks are let off lightly compared with most social and religious groups. Moreover, the poem contains not only direct generous praise of the monks but also a number of passages that must be interpreted in their favor (and these show an appreciable knowledge of their image of themselves). Yet as known from contemporary evidence, the monks needed as much, if not more, reforming than the friars. Admittedly, the sins of the monks were not so visible behind their monastic walls as those of the friars, who moved about quite freely in the world. On one point, Langland would certainly have differed with fourteenth-century monks, without of course necessarily repudiating monastic ideas as such; and this was the matter of secular interference with monastic possessions. Langland at least warns ecclesiastical holders of wealth that secular lords can take over their property and that a saviour-king will very probably take away their possessions. This threat would hardly have met with the favor of monks. This point of view, as well as the autobiographical passages, make it clear that when the B- and C-Texts were written, Langland was no monk.

An examination of some of the portions of the poem devoted to monks and monasticism reveals Langland's knowledge of monastic philosophy. First, Will is probably journeying through the fair field full of folk as a monk. "In habite as a hermite" Will wanders through this world to hear wonders, that is, to receive prophetic revelations. A hermit is frequently a monk and was recognized as such by fourteenth-century men. A hermit was one of the four types of monks listed in the first chapter of the Benedictine Rule. Although to Benedict, "hermit" and "anchorite" were synonyms, in medieval times a hermit was generally thought of as a wandering solitary person devoted to religious purposes, whereas an anchorite was one who had withdrawn from the world to a fixed abode for solitary living.[4] A hermit was primarily devoted to works, whereas an anchorite favored contemplation. One occupation could and did pass into the other, but a distinction was usually made. These modes of life were especially popular in England even as late as the fourteenth century.[5] Will dresses as a hermit because he is seeking what a hermit seeks—perfection.

By the fourteenth century, and even earlier, not all hermits and anchorites were considered, strictly speaking, monks. All that was needed for such a life was episcopal approval. But the historical connection between the two had never been forgotten. In Langland's period all monasteries made provision for recluses and hermits, and many attached themselves to these centers. Some of the friaries also encouraged hermits. Many monks became anchorites and some even hermits, and in general a close connection was maintained between the eremetical and cenobitical lives.[6] It is clear that the goal of both lives was considered the same—*summa perfectio*—with the crown going perhaps to the anchorite.[7] Thus although dressing as a hermit does not prove that Will dressed as a monk, it is most likely that he did so; and when one considers the monastic philosophy in the poem and its centering around the quest for perfection, it is reasonable to think that Langland wanted his hero to be considered at least in some way connected with monasticism.

It is, however, characteristic of the irony with which Langland regards Will that he calls him at the beginning of the poem a hermit "unholy of works" and suggests he is a *gyrovagus*. Langland keeps from the start a deliberately ambiguous attitude towards his chief character Will. This self-irony, or rather ironical tone towards his own representative in the poem, Will, is a characteristic feature of his appearance throughout.[8] In Passus VI, 147 ff., occurs a similar picture of Robert Renne-aboute, the wandering religious, who is unfavorably contrasted with "ancres and here-

mytes that eten no3t but at nones.'' [9] In C, X, 188–281, there is
long passage specifically devoted to contrasting good and bad
hermits. No doubt to fourteenth-century antimendicancy the
wandering bad hermit or *gyrovagus* was frequently equated with
the friar, who was a special *bête noire* to Langland.

The famous Confession of the Seven Cardinal Sins includes an
interesting section on the confession of Wrath (V, 134 ff.). In the
shifting manner typical of Langland's treatment of his personifications, especially of the sins, Wrath describes his adventures among
the friars, nuns, and monks. He meets his downfall among the
last and consequently shuns them, for they order him to fast, and
beat him. Wrath is a common sin of those who live in a closed
community, true enough, but the monks in general know how
to handle it. This unfavorable reception of a deadly sin by any
group is unique in Langland's list and shows very strongly his
sympathy for the monastic life. It is in fact an extraordinary concession. There is also an incidental line praising monks in the confession of Sloth. Sloth promised to hear matins and Mass "as I a
monke were." But too much must not be made of this conventional, and possibly ironic, simile.

One of the major ecclesiastical disputes in the fourteenth century was over the friars and their claims. A side-issue of the quarrel
was whether religious should work or beg. That theoretically they
should be poor was not disputed. By Langland's time the threefold vow of poverty, chastity, and obedience was accepted as man-
datory for the life of regulars. However, there was a bitter quarrel
between monks and friars regarding the nature of poverty. St. Francis had associated poverty with mendicancy, and St. Dominic had
adopted this interpretation. But the older tradition of the monks
had always associated manual labor with the apostolic and religious
life. There are numerous references to this problem of interpretation in the thirteenth and fourteenth centuries,[10] and there is no
doubt where Langland stood. In Passus VI, where the various
classes attempt to plow Piers's half-acre, Langland comes out definitely against mendicancy and favors manual labor. Those who
can work must work. Hunger (vv. 190 ff.) makes a group of
hermits take spades in hand, cut their long habits, and work as
laborers. This obviously has the author's approval and at the same
time reveals his monastic conception of true poverty. He is not

always completely consistent in this matter or completely opposed to friars.[11] He severely criticizes the friars; in fact one may say that they are his chief targets. But at the same time he recognizes the legitimacy of their ideals and the extreme importance of their return to their earlier standards.

A further clue to Langland's attitude towards and possible relationship to monasticism and the monastic philosophy may be found in X, 300–301, in a long speech of Clergy. At this point, discussing the sins of the religious, he finally breaks into an apocalyptic vision (vv. 317 ff.) of a saviour-king. But earlier, in arguing that religious should stay in their cloisters, he makes use of the well-known comparison of the cloister to heaven on earth—"a golden phantasm of the cloister that had never wholly faded from his imagination."[12] This image has a very long history behind it; and the concept is a widespread presupposition of monastic philosophy. Just as the monkish life is a foretaste and pattern of heaven, so his dwelling place, the cloister, is a kind of paradise. The use of this image by Langland, and by Dante, hardly proves that either had monastic connections; but it does show that they both were well aware of one of the commonest elements in the *mystique* of monasticism. It is certainly an image not used very commonly in extra-monastic writings in English.[13]

In a long passage in Passus XV (263 ff.) developing the virtue of patient poverty, Anima tells Will of the early monastic fathers and their sufferings and above all of their willingness to labor with their hands. Anima tries to reconcile two arguments here—that God will take care of those who throw themselves "recklessly" on His providence and that God helps those who help themselves, an important point in Langland's poem. Her historical argument at this point, with its references to Anthony, Egidius, Paul, "primus heremita," Paul of Tarsus, and some of the Disciples, is reminiscent of the historical argument used in fourteenth-century English defenses of monasticism, all variants of an original written before the 1360's at Bury St. Edmunds, to which Mr. Pantin has recently called our attention.[14]

The emphasis on manual labor and the appeal to history to establish the antiquity of monks show a familiarity with monastic apologetic in the face of attacks from seculars and friars. The Monk of Bury St. Edmunds was not original in his appeal to history,[15] but his treatise was an elaborate defense of the monks on many counts, and merits being considered an original work. Langland may well have been acquainted with it, or at least the kind of thinking that produced it. This whole section in Passus XV tends to support my view that Langland was imbued with "monastic philosophy." Passus XII, 146, gives the other side of this argument, for there Langland accuses the friars of their modernity. "If any frere were founde there [at the manger when Jesus was born] ich 3if the fyue shillynges."[16] All this shows that Langland was very well up on the inter-order disputes of his period and was especially aware of monastic apologetic.

Although Langland does not clearly connect Longinus, the Roman soldier who pierced Jesus' side with a spear, with monasticism, he was widely accepted as a monkish hero. Blind, Longinus was supposedly given his sight by contact with the blood of the crucified Jesus. It was believed he was thereupon converted and became a monk. He is recorded in the *Golden Legend* as St. Longinus and was considered the first Christian monk.[17] Langland, in describing the Crucifixion in Passus XVIII, devotes a long passage (vv. 78–91) to Longinus which makes one think of his monastic connection. He appears in lists of monastic saints and was especially venerated by them. Thomas Brinton, Langland's contemporary, says, "Indeed when the hot blood of Christ running down along the lance had touched the eyes of the lancer, he [Longinus] saw clearly, he believed in Christ, he abandoned the army, and instructed in the faith by the apostles he led a monastic life for thirty-eight years. He converted many to the faith by word and deed, and finally he poured forth his blood for Christ through martyrdom."[18] The Benedictine Bishop honored him as a monastic hero, and it may well be that Langland thought of him similarly.

Among the famous Benedictine figures of the fourteenth century we find William Rymington and Adam Easton, Thomas Brinton and Uthred of Boldon.[19] These last two figures impinge on *Piers Plowman*, and one must conclude that their points of view at least were known to the author of *Piers*. These men, along with the first two, would be those to whom, if the hypothesis of this book is correct, Langland must have been sympathetic at least as far as their thought is concerned.

Since the work of Miss E. H. Kellogg and G. R. Owst,[20] it is possible to assume that the "angel of hevene" (Prologue, 128) was Bishop Brinton, who in a sermon (Number 69) used the very same fable of the rats which Langland employs in this apocalyptic passage of the ideal kingdom. It is a position of honor the Bishop holds, and he may have been assimilated to the traditional figure of the angel speaking from on high as in Revelation 15 ff. His sermons, as pointed out in the notes, provide numerous parallels to Langland's thought.

Although there are no definite proofs of Uthred's influence on Langland beyond a few possible echoes, it has been clear since M. E. Marcett's monograph[21] that in the gluttonous master of divinity who sat at the place of honor while dining at Conscience's house (XIII, 21–201) Langland is satirizing William Jordan, a Dominican friar, who was the foremost opponent of Uthred in a bitter theological controversy in the late 1360's. This does not prove that Langland was a follower of Uthred, but at least his great enemy was also Langland's enemy. There may perhaps be other contemporaries satirized in *Piers Plowman*, but so far that distinction has been shown conclusively only for this Dominican friar. Langland must certainly have put him in a special category of obloquy.

In a recent article, I have discussed Langland's use in two places (XII, 31–52, and XVI) of the chastity metaphor when he discusses the three grades of perfection.[22] The second of these cases, the Tree of Perfection in Passus XVI, offers striking evidence of Langland's knowledge of monastic philosophy. In general a knowledge of the marriage-widowed-virginity (chastity-continence-purity) triad corresponding to the three grades of perfection would argue in the same direction, but this comparison is fairly widespread and could perhaps have been used by anyone.[23] However, one particular detail of the description of the Tree was a prime point in monastic apologetic and is stronger, if not conclusive, evidence for my argument.

This detail, found only in the C-Text (XIX, 71 ff.), is the allusion to the virgins (religious) whom the Holy Ghost, the sun of heaven, accompanies. He comforts those who live in contemplation, such as monks and nuns of Holy Church. *Liberum Arbitrium*, who is the speaker at this point, is describing the Tree of Perfection to Will. He speaks of its fruit as comprising married men, widows, and virgins. The last are on the top of the Tree[24] and receive heat from the Holy Ghost, as the topmost fruit does from the sun. Widows and widowers who deny their own natural desires and lead a chaste life are dearer to our Lord than those who live according to nature, following what the flesh wishes and bringing forth fruit—following a life which learned men call the active life.

Traditionally, the religious (sometimes interpreted as including friars and sometimes not) are under the special protection of the Holy Ghost; and this association was a favorite theme of monastic apologists in the later Middle Ages. It is especially characteristic of Joachim of Flora, who often alludes to the three grades of chastity metaphor and the link between virgins (or religious) and the Holy Ghost. This latter idea is, I suspect, not original with Joachim. It certainly grows out of the earlier conception of the Holy Ghost favoring especially good and perfect men; but whether it is as neatly and exactly phrased earlier, I have not been able to discover. In *Concordia* V, 21, Joachim writes, "In primo statu auctorizatus a Deo Patre ordo coniugatorum. In secundo glorificatus est a Filio ordo clericorum. In 3d glorificabitur a spiritu sancto ordo monachorum."[25] Bonaventure, probably picking up the parallelism from Joachim, makes a similar point in *In Hexaemeron*, saying, among other things "... ordo monachalis respondet Spiritui Sancto," probably conceiving this "ordo" as embracing the various orders of the friars.[26] The very same image is used in the same century by the monk of Bury St. Edmunds, who writes that the *ordo coniugatorum* has the image of the Father, the *ordo clericorum* the image of the Son, the *ordo coenobitarum* the image of the Holy Ghost. He attributes the parallelism to a "Januensis in libro questionum de antichristo," whom I have not been able to identify.[27]

The point is that Langland accepts the monastic picture of monasticism and gives it the highest place in *Heilsgeschichte*. If there is to be an age of the Holy Ghost, the monks will take over the world. If not, they at least are specially protected by the active principle of the Godhead. This hardly seems to be an idea that would be ardently supported by anyone without a knowledge of monastic philosophy. Coupled with all the other evidence, it seems to offer strong support for believing that Langland was immersed in the monastic point of view.

Until quite recently, it has been generally accepted that monastic spirituality with the exception of that of the Carthusians, a very individualistic spirituality, was pretty much dead after the twelfth or thirteenth centuries, when it had its last flowering in Bernard, Ailred of Rievaulx, William of St. Thierry, and, if we include the canons, the great Victorines.[28] But thanks to the work of men like Dom Knowles and W. A. Pantin for England, we now know that monastic philosophy and indeed theology was by no means extinct in the fourteenth century. The great spiritual and intellectual forces in the fourteenth century were scholasticism, monastic philosophy, and a widespread individualistic spirituality that sometimes reached the mystical heights. Apocalypticism was primarily an aspect of monastic philosophy. The revival of Augustinianism in this century, "a crucial period in the history of European thought," affected all three.[29] Scholasticism was primarily associated with the friars and the universities, and aroused the suspicions of the other two forces. Yet the reform movement associated with Wyclif and the Lollards in a sense grew out of it, for Wyclif was a great scholastic thinker, though his school was made up of individual lay or lower clerical "pietists."

At present, unfortunately, it is impossible to trace these intellectual currents throughout the fourteenth century in England.[30] Too much material is unedited; too few monographs have been written. It is only out of Langland's own context, difficult as that may be to discover in detail, that the primary interpretation of the poem must come. It is not enough to leaf through Migne's *Patrologia latina* or Thomas Aquinas' *Summa theologica* in order to find parallels to *Piers*. They are not far to seek. They may be used to illustrate points of doctrine and spirituality, or they may, in the face of the lack of more contemporary material, be used as supporting evidence; but in a historical study such as this book attempts to be, one must also try as far as possible to find out what was easily available to Langland, and to explore the temper of his age.

No sure knowledge of Langland's career or interests outside of the poem itself exists. With Chaucer, one knows of the circles within which he moved and many of his friends; one knows of his travels and many details of his biography; but with Langland, the reader moves in an area of few facts and many contradictions. One cannot be sure when Langland is being ironical or perverse. There are no external facts to provide clues. One is forced back to the text again and to his own sense of literary fitness.

Then, there is the problem of transmission and availability. Were various European writers whom we call upon to explain *Piers* known in England in Langland's time? Even if there were English manuscripts available, can one be sure that Langland used them? Possibly Langland used a work in another version than the one we know. The commentaries on the standard works must also be considered. Hardly anyone in the Middle Ages read, without a commentary, Augustine's *City of God*, Boethius' *Consolation*, Cato's *Distichs*, and similar popular intellectual writings —and, of course, the Bible. What commentaries did Langland know?

I do not believe, further, that everything in *Piers* can be explained on the basis of monastic philosophy. I feel that this is its basic intellectual setting, but there are points in the poem which cannot be accounted for in this fashion. The fact that the monastic *Denkform* was by no means dead in the fourteenth century, as is commonly assumed, does not mean that it was the dominant mode of thought or that it had not been affected by scholasticism and individualistic mysticism. Langland was a man of his age and could not think as a man in the fifth or twelfth century thought. On some matters Langland comes closer to the scholastics[31] and on others to popular lay piety; but his general point of view, his chief emphases, his solutions to the crisis of his age, can be best understood in the light of the monastic philosophy or older Christianity.

Recently, some of the vast mass of printed and manuscript registers, archives, and intellectual works of fourteenth-century England have begun to be intensively exploited, and there is promise for the future. The history of the Church, particularly in the later Middle Ages, has engaged the attention of scholars, and the picture of the currents and crosscurrents of the time is gradually becoming clearer.[32]

Any organization is subject to internal quarrels and tensions; but when one considers the medieval Church, with the large

variety of organizations with varying traditions and purposes
within it (and, by the fourteenth century, without serious external
enemies), it is no wonder that internal strains of considerable
magnitude would develop. In the case of the friars, a relatively
new type of religious order, aggressive and intellectually superior,
it is not surprising that they encountered considerable hostility.
The monks, as the foremost representatives of the contemplative
or virginal status in the Church, were especially aroused. The new
orders captured the universities and the intellectual life of the time.
By their activities in the world they attained popularity, wealth,
and influence and drove the monks, who up to then had gloried
in their superior role, into a defensive position.[33] And worst of all,
in the eyes of the monks, the friars could claim the highest status
of the militant Church, level with the position the monks had
long assumed for themselves alone. The monks were thus forced to
redefine and rethink their definition of perfection. The friars also,
by their interference with the parish priests and their sources of
income, deeply offended the secular clergy.

In thirteenth-century England we can see this monkish hostility
towards the friars, above all in Matthew Paris; and in the fourteenth century the situation became worse. One of the first steps
the monks took to strengthen their position was to create their
own colleges at Oxford. At the end of the thirteenth century
Durham and Gloucester Colleges were founded there, and in 1361
Canterbury College was established by the monks of Christ
Church, Canterbury. We have much evidence that the monks
turned towards theology and entered university disputation, and
we know that many monasteries made great efforts to send some
of their inmates on to Oxford.[34]

Even though there are no statistics easily available for the fourteenth century, one may contrast this situation with that revealed
by P. Glorieux's *Répertoire* of thirteenth-century masters of
theology.[35] Father Glorieux lists 425 masters of theology, of whom
only 19 are Cistercians or Benedictines. There is no doubt that
the friars and, to a lesser extent, the seculars dominated learning
in thirteenth-century Paris; and we may take this situation as
characteristic of learning everywhere. In England, at least, the
monks by the fourteenth century made an attempt to correct their
intellectual deficiencies; and although no statistics are at hand, with

three colleges at Oxford as opposed to none in the thirteenth, there must have been some lessening of the disparity. The names of the great theologians of the thirteenth and fourteenth centuries bear out this analysis. In England, the Franciscans had an especial pre-eminence in scholastic thinking, but it is not until the later century that any monk-theologians appear. Then one can find active Adam Easton, William Rymington, Uthred of Boldon, and Nicholas Radcliffe, all respectable if not notable thinkers—all of the last half of the fourteenth century.

Still another line of defense was the direct written word. Monks began to examine their origins and their rights, and composed defenses of their role. The argument from history was most popular, since the monks could at least claim antiquity on their side. In this attack on friars they frequently joined forces with the seculars, who were also attacking them for different reasons. The most notable secular attack on the mendicants since that of Guillaume de Saint-Amour in 1256 was that of Archbishop Richard Fitzralph, whose writings caused reverberations all over Europe and who is easily the dominant figure of the whole anti-friar movement of the period.[36] Later in the century, Wyclif took over the leadership in the attack. Fitzralph no doubt had the support of the monks, financial[37] and otherwise. But they were not silent on their own account.

Finally, the monks struck back by means of their chronicles. History was their province and had been so for centuries.[38] If they could not compete with the friars on the field of philosophy, they were more than their equals in historiography. By concentrating on their role in history and *Heilsgeschichte*, and on their antiquity, the monks felt that they could hold their ground and even re-taliate—especially as they were the main purveyors and recorders of medieval history. Their defense took various forms, all the way from claiming that monks founded the universities[39] to a bolstering of monkish self-confidence by listing their great men, and even to a re-urging of the claim of being under the special care of the Holy Ghost. Then, too, using an argument the Middle Ages could appreciate, they could claim the friars were newcomers and disrupters of the divinely ordered universe. All the figures of the Old Testament, including Adam, who could possibly be claimed as monks were employed to crush these mendicant upstarts.

Some of these documents and histories in the fourteenth century indicate the line monastic apologists took and the attacks they had to meet. They must be looked at, however briefly.

One of the most interesting and amusing parodies in the later Middle Ages is the so-called Devil's Letter, which appears in a variety of forms.[40] It is possible that Langland had this form and the related Devil's Charter in mind in the charter of False (II, 73–113), since a well-known example presumably written to the Papal Court at Avignon was widely circulated in the 1350's. It is always written in papal and imperial style, and grants or urges upon its recipients the rights and duties the devil would prefer. It thanks the recipients for their good services in the past. In general it is a brilliant parody and satire on ecclesiastical abuses. Paul Lehmann finds examples of the Devil's Letter as early as the eleventh century, and it turns up with suitable modifications throughout the later Middle Ages.

W. Wattenbach prints from Digby 98 in the Bodleian an English example written by Belial in which the English Franciscans attack the Benedictines. He dates it 1305, but Lehmann, in spite of the date of 1305. at the end of the letter, prefers a later date in the same century. It begins: "Belial apostatarum, prepositus et magister invidie, abbas claustri superbie, prior gule, custos et dominus Acherontis ..." and thanks the monks for their good services in preferring salmon to Solomon, in hunting, and in despising the cloisters. Belial links the monks with Sergius, the supposed Christian teacher of Mohammed, and Julian the Apostate. He recommends all of the seven deadly sins to them, as well as a host of others. In best parodic style it concludes, "Dat. in conventu nostro inferni de communi consilio generali sub sigilli nostri caractere in robore premissorum. Anno incarceracionis nostre millesimo trecentesimo quinto. . . ."

This kind of skillful satire is a good example of what the monks had to face from their lively and intellectual opponents. But even more serious was the direct attack against their possessions. In 1371, Friar Bankin and another Austin friar, possibly Thomas Ashburne, laid before Parliament a petition, preserved ironically enough in British Museum, Harley 638, fol. 222, from the Abbey of St. Edmund at Bury, asking for the disendowment of the monasteries for the common good—the financial stability of the realm.[41] This indeed was a serious blow and is revelatory of the depth of feeling the wealth of the monasteries provoked. It is perhaps to cases like this that Langland was referring (in XX, 271 ff.) when he says that Envy sent the friars to school to learn law and contemplation and to preach to men of Plato and Seneca[42] that all things under heaven ought to be in common.

Evidence of the reaction of the monks on a literary level is not lacking. The great collection, *Documents Illustrating the Activities of the General and Provincial Chapters of the English Black Monks, 1215-1540*, edited by W. A. Pantin, provides us with some clear-cut reactions, especially in the third volume (miscellaneous documents). Number 203 (pp. 28-29), for instance, is a letter *c*. 1357-1363 from the prior of Norwich to the prior of students at Oxford, stating that he cannot send Adam Easton back to the university because he is needed to help with the preaching and in silencing the Sadducees (the friars).[43] Number 232 (pp. 79-80), from the proctor of the English Black Monks at the Court of Rome (*c*. 1378), speaks of the attacks, chiefly by the friars, on the monks, the only remedy for which is a strict adherence to the rule.

Magdalen College, Oxford MS 147, fols. 228*b*-229*a*, contains a short historical chronicle which Henry Coxe, the cataloguer of the manuscript, appropriately calls a *Chronicon Infortuniorum*. It briefly lists the fires, floods, plagues, and earthquakes in England from 1132 to 1382. Inserted in this list for 1204 and 1214 are references to the founding of the Dominicans and Franciscans and for 1224 an allusion to the entry of the latter into England. I may be misreading the meaning of this catalogue, but it looks as if a monk were ridiculing the friars.[44] If so, it is a deft piece of satire.

A notable defense of monasticism is to be found in the various treatises on the origin of monasticism[45] which proliferated in the fourteenth and fifteenth centuries after the original had been written before the 1360's at Bury St. Edmunds. Mr. Pantin lists fifteen manuscripts besides echoes of the work which can be found in various writers, including Rymington and Thomas of Elmham. Langland, too, may be added to this list of those influenced by this notable monument of monastic apologetic.

Following the outline as given by Mr. Pantin, the original contained twelve chapters followed by two lists—of monastic saints

and of various orders (including the friars).[46] The work is fundamentally historical and bases its claim for the pre-eminence of the
monks on their antiquity. After the first chapter, which argues
that there were monks before St. Augustine, Chapter 2 discusses
the monks of the Old Testament—Samuel, Elijah, Elisha, and
others. Chapter 3 deals with the Essenes and Chapter 4 with
cenobites in the New Testament, especially John the Baptist. Peter
and the Apostles are also claimed as monks. Chapters 5 and 6
argue for a continuity of monasticism from the Apostles to the
rise of Egyptian monasticism, and Chapters 7 and 8 discuss the
symbolism of monkish habits and tonsures. Chapter 9, which is a
key chapter, deals with the Benedictine Rule and justifies the
monks by their role in the quest for perfection and their sponsor-
ship by the Holy Ghost—a clear-cut statement of monastic philosophy. Chapter 10 discusses anchorites and hermits as being at the
peak of monastic life. The last two chapters are devoted to the
evil *sarabaites* and *gyrovagi*.

The oldest preserved version in Vatican, Reg. Lat. 127, written
c. 1365, besides being followed by the two lists just mentioned,
concludes with *Questio utrum perfeccior sit ordo mendicancium
vel possessionatorum*, which is partly printed by Pantin.[47] The
issue to the author, probably the same monk of Bury St. Edmunds,
is which type of poverty is more perfect—*paupertas mendicans
valida* or *paupertas abiectis propriis contenta vite necessariis et sibi
sufficiens*. The author, who quotes Henry of Ghent, Maimonides,
Jerome and Augustine, and others, is a thorough-going scholastic
—probably a new product of the schools. He praises manual labor
and in his final answer of course finds for the monks. Monkish
poverty helps to extinguish cupidity, encourages the perfection of
humility and the tranquillity of the heart, and aids in the search
for heavenly wisdom. True, that is monkish, poverty recognizes
human needs and hence does not have to depend on begging. It
is better to live in common poverty than to seek out alms individually.

Chapter 9, containing a theoretical defense of the superiority of
monasticism, reveals the existence of an active sense of monastic
philosophy in England in the fourteenth century. One did not have
to go to the great writers of the past for a knowledge of its
principles. The fourteenth-century monk was quite prepared to

use these arguments again and answer his opponents by means of them.

This whole work is an excellent fourteenth-century English example of the *mystique* of monasticism and in general is like Joachim of Flora's *De vita sancti Benedicti et de officio divino secundum eius doctrinum*,[48] although there is probably no question of direct influence. The first part of this Joachite work describes the high mission of monasticism in history. Monasticism itself has a long history, and its geographical expansion is an index of its spiritual development. As Dom Cipriano Baraut puts it, Joachim conceives the history of the *ordo monasticus* as a spiritual pilgrimage to its final fulfillment in history and beyond in heaven. The laics are the concern of the Father, the clerics of the Son, but the monks of the Holy Ghost.[49] This is an idea that occurs elsewhere in Joachim's writings and in those of later figures like Bonaventure.

The English writer is not concerned with a third age, as was Joachim, but he is conscious of the high role of the monks and describes it in Joachite terms—with parallels to the Old Testament and with the use of generations as a chronological key to history and with a sense of expectancy. The monks are the crucial element in history. The monk of Bury St. Edmunds knows of the time of the Father and the time of the Son.[50] He sees a concordance in generations between St. Benedict and Elisha. St. Benedict clarifies what was dim and inchoate before him and reveals the secret which was always present in history—the supreme role of the monks. "Cenobite igitur ante legem Abraham. sub lege Moysen. Samuelem. Heliam. Heliseum et prophetas sub evangelio vero iohannem baptistam Christum et apostolos ... ad ultimum legis latorem eorum institutionis beatum Benedictum produces et aduocatos in extremo examine hinturi sunt."[51] There is no doubt that this argument is Joachistic, however modified; and it provides the best example of this aspect of Joachism in England, or as far as I know, on the Continent, in the later Middle Ages.

Although in general the high role of the monks in Joachim's system had been taken over by the Franciscans in the thirteenth century—the Spirituals especially—after all Joachim had actually made the coming age of the Holy Ghost the time of the flowering of the monks, when all mankind would become more or less monasticized. And there was no reason why the Benedictines or Cistercians should not appropriate this idea even if they were not prepared to go all the way with Joachim. Besides, it fitted into their own high view of themselves as envisaged in monastic philosophy.[52] This English work may be conceived of as a theoretical contribution to the fourteenth-century revival of monastic philosophy, and in many ways it is one of the most interesting of them all. Although, as Appendix I will show, there is much evidence for a knowledge of Joachim and pseudo-Joachita in England in this century, this particular manifestation is, for my purposes, the most important. It should be noted, however, that the writer of this treatise draws back from the full implications of Joachim's theory; for by this time such views, although not officially condemned, were at least looked on with suspicion.

An early fifteenth-century sermon delivered before a General Chapter of the Black Monks, significantly enough after the Mass of the Holy Ghost, is another piece of eloquent if verbose testimony to the prevalence of monastic philosophy as developed by the monk of Bury St. Edmunds, in later medieval England.[53] Here there is the same historical approach and the same emphasis on the high dignity of monasticism. Monks will endure to the end of time; and in spite of individual sinners there will always be good monks who will preserve the high ideals of the group. A remnant will save the monks, as a remnant saved Israel. "A patriarcha namque excellentissimo firmiter est fundata [ordo monachorum]; a prophetis et Esseis superedificata, et ab apostolis consummata, ac post apostolos per principes sanctissimos educata...." With such a history and such great men in its ranks, monasticism need not despair. The tone is defensive but firm, and its appeal reveals the kind of thinking serious monks in the later Middle Ages were indulging in.

Uthred of Boldon (d. 1397) was the foremost monastic defender of the century. Most of his works are still unprinted, but many of them have been commented on in our time by scholars of the period. His most vigorous opponent in 1366–1368 was the Dominican William Jordan on certain theological propositions that were adjudged erroneous by Archbishop Simon Langham in the latter year and that certainly embraced some of the general points of issue between friars and monks.[54] These articles of Uthred show some interesting points of contact with Langland, particularly on the salvation of the righteous heathen. Uthred seems, like Langland, to have believed that Saracens, Jews, and pagans can theoretically be saved by natural law, although there seems to be no clear trace in Langland of Uthred's peculiar theory of the clear vision of God whereby non-Christians can be saved immediately preceding death.[55]

The two main treatises written *c.* 1374–1376, wherein Uthred treats of his theory of the monastic life are as yet unedited, but they have been the subject of a long and satisfactory analysis by W. A. Pantin.[56] This analysis of *De substancialibus regule monachalis* and *De perfectione vivendi in religione* is the source of the following summary. Both treatises are reasoned discussions of the ideals of monastic life, and they raise and answer, in good scholastic fashion, the objections to Uthred's arguments.

The *De substantialibus* argues for the rational and divine sanctions for the Benedictine Rule, which, although formulated by Benedict, actually existed from the beginning of monasticism, which Uthred traces to the Garden of Eden. The rule is in some measure binding on all men, but in especial and to the highest degree on monks. Its essence is moderation and temperance in goods and passions and in obedience. Monasticism adds no perfection to the law of Christ but only helps its observance.

De perfectione deals with the nature of the perfect life and contrasts the claims of seculars and regulars as to its meaning. Uthred leans to a great extent on the Pseudo-Dionysius, who described the monastic life as the most perfect status here below. Evil members no more destroy its eminence than the rebel angels did that of the angels. The high calling of monasticism cannot be impugned.

Uthred is also the author of a meditation, a literary form that seems to have been a favorite with fourteenth-century monks.[57] William Rymington is the author of some notable ones, as is the anonymous monk of Farne, whose work has been recently published.[58] This type of composition goes back to Anselm and the eleventh century and is a relic of the last great flowering of monastic spirituality in that and the twelfth century. These meditations are a manifestation of that interiorization and psychologizing of life which begins then. But clearly, this aspect of monastic interest and literary activity does not seem to be reflected in Langland. Langland was not primarily interested in probing into the self and its relation to God. Whatever psychological interests he had, and he had many, were manifested in personification allegory and debate. The intense intimate spirituality of fourteenth-century monastic meditations is not to be found in *Piers Plowman.*

If, however, one turns to the chronicles and histories of the fourteenth century, most of them the product of monkish activity and coming from abbeys, one finds a different story. Here one is moving in Langland's intellectual milieu and under the urgency of *Heilsgeschichte.* These literary works offer an insight into monastic thinking about history which is reminiscent of Langland's historical and social orientation.

Although the monks did not dominate historical writing in England in the fourteenth century so much as in the two preceding centuries, it is still true to say with John Taylor, "To the end of the fourteenth century in fact, the Benedictine tradition is the core of historical writing."[59] The four major centers were Benedictine houses—St. Albans, Glastonbury, Malmesbury, and Bury St. Edmunds—and in all of them there was some activity in the historical field; in some cases, like that of St. Albans, great activity. To the monkish histories in the fourteenth century one must add some works by friars and laymen—the *Chronicon de Lanercost* or Thomas Gray's *Scalacronica,* for instance. Yet the overwhelming majority were of monastic origin and authorship. Their general attitude to history, their love of historical periodization from a Christian point of view, their predilection for prophecies, their hope or despair for the future, their sense of expectancy—although not all historians manifest all these features—reveal the accents of monastic philosophy and illuminate Langland's sense of history. Their histories are stuffed with prodigies, portents, and prophecies. The story of humanity has a deeper religious meaning, and God has placed his signs in history and nature for those who can read them. At the end of Galfridus le Baker of Swynebroke's *Chronicon,*[60] completed in 1347, someone has writen, quoting from the pseudo-Joachite *De semine Scripturarum,* that we are now in the last century "usque adventum Christi." This attitude is characteristic of the historians, although not many would go out on a limb, even a safe century away.[61]

In order to be a little more specific, and to avoid cataloguing various fourteenth-century historians,[62] a closer look at one chronicle, the *Eulogium historiarum sive temporis* by a monk of Malmesbury is necessary.[63] Here we find all the stuff of an apocalyptic view of history, especially when the monk is dealing with his own time, up to 1366. His continuators, who take the narrative down to the late fifteenth century, also shared this view. The monk speaks of a king who will destroy the evil men of his time and reduce the clergy to their pristine state and renew the privileges of the Church which formerly prevailed.[64] This is followed by another well-known prophecy, "Anglia transmittet leopardum...," and the monk's commentary thereon. Politics and weather seem to be his particular prophetic sphere. Under 1366, on October 8 and October 22, curious lunar phenomena are described; under the second date he speaks of the moon sending out arrows of fire towards the north. This may have something to do with Langland's "By syx sonnes and a schippe · and half a shef of arwes;/ and the myddel of a mone · shal make the Iewes to torne." (III, 324). The famous wind of 1362 is also referred to and many another celestial phenomena. This monk is concerned with defending the antiquity of his profession and seems to be familiar with the apology of the monk of Bury St. Edmunds.[65] In short, he is an excellent representative of the apocalyptic monastic view of history that Langland also reveals. History is moving towards a renewal, and the social and natural orders give all the evidence needed to the perceptive man. The whole world is agonizing towards a new birth.

An excellent example of Langland's point of view may be seen in a sermon by a Thomas Wimbledon of Merton, which strangely enough seems to have been ignored by *Piers Plowman* scholars. This homily was preached at Paul's Cross in 1388 and was extremely popular down to the eighteenth century, having been printed at least fifteen times. In fact, G. R. Owst says, "there can be no single sermon by an Englishman of our two centuries [the fourteenth and fifteenth] of which so many copies in contemporary manuscript, and later printed book can be found" than this on "Redde rationem villicationis tuae" (Luke 16:2).[66] Its post-Reformation popularity can no doubt be attributed to a misunderstanding of its attacks on the abuses of the time. Of the author, little is known, although he was probably a chaplain.

This sermon is very interesting from our point of view since it shows the kind of thinking at the basis of *Piers Plowman* without the violence of similar Lollard works but yet sharing many of their presuppositions. Langland has many similarities with the Lollard point of view but does not share its doctrinal concerns. Wimbledon's sermon, like the works of the chroniclers and historians discussed above, reveals that the same concern for the renewal of the world and Church, the same interest in Antichrist and the same belief in the imminence of a profound change in the Church, were by no means confined to heretics.

The theme of this sermon is dictated by the Lucian text—"Give an account of thy stewardship." The preacher points out that everyone must give account of his stewardship for his *status* role to God. Society consists of three groups—priests, knights, and people —the first two accountable for themselves and other people as well. The first part of the sermon develops the meaning of this tripartite division and discusses the sins of the world. In the last part the preacher is concerned with what kind of reckoning man must make and to whom. There are two judgments awaiting him— the particular and the general. The three summons to the particular judgment are sickness, old age, and death. The signs of the Last Judgment are the sickness, feebleness, and end of the world. Wimbledon moves on to the subject of Antichrist and when he may be expected. Quoting Joachim (actually the pseudo-Joachite *Commentary on Jeremiah*) and Hildegarde of Bingen, he argues that the world will stand under God's final judgment in the seven thousandth year from its creation, of which six thousand six hundred years have passed. But the point is not, of course, that the human race has four hundred years to go, but rather that the end of the world is near and little time really remains for reformation and a fundamental renewal. Elsewhere in the sermon the author argues that the great Antichrist will arrive in the year 1400.

This historical and apocalyptic sense of urgency and this ideal of each *status* performing its right duties and the parallel drawn between man and society are very close to Langland; and although there is no question of influence both because of the date and because of the wide acceptance of such thinking, the kind of political and historical thinking that lies in Langland's mind can be approached through Wimbledon.

Although there is no new evidence at hand, we must now look at the accepted dates for the three versions of *Piers*; for the political prophecies of the later Middle Ages can give, I am convinced, some clues as to when Langland was moved to write down his poem, especially the A-Text or first version of the poem.

The attempts to date the three versions of the poem have generally relied on presumed allusions to contemporary events within each version. This method, owing to the proclivities of the human animal at all times for getting into trouble and the dreary repetitiveness of human existence, has its pitfalls. The ins and outs of these attempts at fitting contemporary history into the various, for the most part vague, allusions in the poem need not be traced here.[67] The details are complex. It is easy enough to be cynical about them and to think that one cancels out the other; but in the absence of other information, and this is almost the case here, such speculations, unsatisfactory as they may be, must be used.

The only firm evidence for dating the A-Text is the allusion to the famous wind storm of January 15, 1362, which provides the *terminus post quem* of the work. In his attempt to find allusions to Alice Perrers and certain other events in the history of the royal family and of the Hundred Years' War, B. F. Huppé wishes to date this version late, *c.* 1373. J. A. W. Bennett chooses 1370 because of A, IV, 111, where the expression "Rome-renners" occurs, for the Papal Court was in Rome only from October 1367 to 1370. This is probably a case of excessive literalism, for Rome could very well be used symbolically.

My own feeling is that the A-Text was written 1362–1365. Besides the argument from contemporary prophecy, there is one further piece of evidence for an early date, to which M. E. Richardson has called attention and which has been ignored.[68] In A, V, 140–141, there is an allusion to Rose the regrator (the retailer), the wife of Avarice, who has been in business for eleven years. There is a record of Rose la Hokestere, who was tried and convicted for forestalling in 1350. Rose would have been in business for twelve years at least, and a reference to eleven years in retailing would not be amiss. Finally the term "this" applied to the southwestern wind would argue for an early date after the catastrophe.[69] Langland also uses the term "thise pestilences" (V, 13) in the same passage, which could refer to the resurgence of the pestilence in 1361–1362. The other allusions found by Huppé and Bennett to current history are not entirely convincing.

The B-Text must be after 1370, for there is an allusion to John Chichester as mayor of London (XIII, 271), an event which can be dated in that year. Bennet and Huppé seem to be agreed on 1377–1379 for it. The fable of the Belling of the Cat probably alludes to political events in 1376–1377. A. Gwynn, however, wishes to move the composition of part of B back to 1370–1372, since he assumes Friar William Jordan, who is attacked in B XIII, must still be alive at the time of its composition. The date of Jordan's death is unknown except that it is after 1368, and Father Gwynn feels that by 1377 he would probably be dead. Gwynn's other arguments are based on presumed allusions to earlier events, but he does admit that the fable must allude to the "Good Parliament." All in all, there is really no good reason for questioning the generally accepted date of B—about 1377.

The date of the C-Text has been given by W. W. Skeat, in his great edition of this poem, as 1393, on the basis of some supposedly contemporary allusions. Skeat believed (as we no longer do) that Langland wrote *Richard the Redeless* (now known as *Mum and the Sothsegger*), clearly dated 1399; and inasmuch as he had to be kept alive to that date, there was no objection to giving him something to do in the 1390's. N. Coghill argues for a similar date because he wishes to account for the omission in C, VI, 177, of the reference to the Abbot of Abingdon in the corresponding line in B, X, 326.[70] There was trouble with the Abingdon's tenants in 1394, and Coghill conjectures that Langland, aware of these events, wished to remove any possible contemporary allusion. He had apparently taken this abbot's name by chance in 1377–1378 when he wrote the B-Text, because Abingdon was a well-known wealthy monastery and because the name alliterated nicely.[71]

However, John But, who probably died in 1387, alludes to Langland's death, and it is probable that Thomas Usk, who was executed in 1388, quoted from the C-Text.[72] It is more likely, then, that this version was written *c.* 1385.

My concern with the dates of *Piers Plowman*, especially that of the A-Text, is motivated largely by my desire to suggest that the prophetic forebodings of the 1360's were behind Langland's attempt to write what was to prove to be the first version of his poem. It is merely as a hypothesis that I make this suggestion, since proof is obviously impossible; but the year 1365 was accounted by all mid-century prophets as a crucial one, and the pressure of fear may very well have made Langland compose his poem.

Let us, however, first turn to a brief discussion of fourteenth-century prophecy. Prophecy is a favorite form of discourse at all times, and he would indeed be foolhardy who would attempt to speak of any period as favoring vaticination over any other—too many documents of the past are lost and oral examples are ephemeral. Yet we know that political and eschatological prophecy was extremely widespread and popular in the later Middle Ages, and I have the feeling that this period was a high mark in the history of prophecy.[73] Perhaps the strongest argument for this conclusion besides the subjective impression is to be found in the numerous attempts in the fourteenth and fifteenth centuries to date the coming of Antichrist. No longer are general predictions sufficient, but actual dates are desired. And, on the other hand, many scholastics argued, in the face of this interest, that the date of the coming of Antichrist could not be determined by the human mind.[74] Their protests do not seem to have been of much avail.

The great English libraries all contain a large number of prophetic manuscripts or parts of manuscripts. The mere enumeration of these would take up much space and would not advance the argument. Well-known names like Merlin, Hildegarde, and Joachim, not to speak of a host of lesser-known ones, occur again and again. Some of these prophecies are suitably cryptic; others are relatively open. Many are interested in political or ecclesiastical events, and others concentrate on Antichrist. Many make use of astrology and astronomy. Animals are favorite masking symbols. Numbers and letters follow in bewildering profusion.

The author of perhaps the most popular prophecy of the later Middle Ages in England, the pseudepigraphical *Prophecy of John of Bridlington*, is the Austin friar, John Erghome. He is an interesting figure in the prophetical stream of the fourteenth century, a man about whom one would like to know more. His library was given to his own house of Augustinian friars at York. We are fortunate in possessing a catalogue of this library with the names of the donors of books; and hence it is possible to reconstruct from this catalogue Erghome's personal library.[75] Erghome probably died in 1390.

The interesting fact revealed by a perusal of Erghome's titles is that he had gathered a large group of books on prophecy and related subjects. Here was an educated man of the fourteenth century who could collect a notable library on prophecy and was sufficiently interested to hand his books over to an important religious house. His own *Prophecy of John of Bridlington* contains Bridlington's supposititious prophecy and a commentary.[76] The whole work is dedicated to Humphrey de Bohun, Earl of Hereford (as Earl, 1361–1372), a reference that enables us to date the work roughly. Like all respectable prophecies, it begins with *vaticinia post eventum* posing as *ante eventum* in order to win that suspension of disbelief which is vital in works of this sort. These safe prophecies go to about 1363, a chronological fact that establishes a more exact date for the work. The political purpose of the prophecy, according to Sister Helen Margaret Peck, was to encourage Edward III in his struggle with France by giving it an apocalyptic meaning. Edward is carrying out the will of God. It is strongly opposed to Bishop William of Wykeham, whose period of great influence with the king embraced the 1360's. Father Gwynn, apparently unaware of the Sister's researches, sees it as written primarily to praise the Black Prince and to satirize rather nastily contemporary events and personages. This prophecy gives an excellent picture of the prophetic and apocalyptic thinking of the decade in which Langland began to write, although there is no evidence of any influence on him.

In the preceding decade Jean de Roquetaillade in France reveals a similar, if more deranged, attitude. His works are filled with political prophecy and are just as pro-French as Erghome's are pro-English. He is even more concerned with Antichrists than Erghome and, regardless of inconsistencies, throws out date after date. To Jean, a Franciscan Spiritual, his is the time of the Antichrists, and he declaims his anathemas to a receptive audience found all over Europe including England.

Interestingly enough, the dates Roquetaillade favors for the coming of Antichrist—and he is not alone in this—are 1365, 1378, and 1388, dates which approximate the composition of the three versions of *Piers Plowman*. In his best-known work, well represented in English libraries, the *Vade mecum in tribulatione* written in 1356, Jean de Roquetaillade thinks that things will reach their nadir in the 1360's and that renovation will begin before 1370. From 1360 to 1365 the world will be a prey to terrible catastrophes. A Western Antichrist will appear between 1362 and 1370. An angelic Pope will appear in 1367 to start to roll back the tide, and a new King of France will work with him hand in hand.[77] Less widely known, the *Liber ostensor*, written in the same year—1356—uses more or less the same dates; 1360–1365 is to be a crucial period of troubles. In an earlier work, *Liber secretorum eventuum*, stimulated perhaps by the Black Death, the Franciscan favors 1366 for the arrival of Antichrist. Here, he argues for the necessity and utility of Antichrist; for the worst must be expected before the best can come. He will, moreover, purify the Church by separating the sheep from the goats. He is indeed a *flagellum Dei*. In this work, revival cannot be expected before 1415.[78]

Jean de Roquetaillade was no doubt partly influenced in his choice of dates by his own interpretations of contemporary events, but in general he was relying on predictions made earlier in the century by Arnold of Villanova and John of Paris, who had, respectively, chosen 1378 (or 1388) and 1366 for the appearance of Antichrist.[79] John, however, is less sure than Arnold and much more sober in his approach.

Current in England also in the 1350's was a prophecy, attributed to Joachim, usually entitled "Prophecie Ioachim in maiori libro de concordanciis" (*sic*), found in various manuscripts.[80] These different versions show a variety of dates, for nothing is so useless as a false prediction after the date has passed. Like all well-known prophecies, this one turns up again and again with changed dates.[81] The original version probably was written before 1250, but it was quickly adapted to the dreaded 1360's. In this prophecy, Abbot Joachim is supposed to have predicted two Popes—one at Lyons and one at Rome—in 1357. In 1360 the Church will reach a low point in public esteem; and in 1365, when Jupiter and Saturn are in conjunction, the Greek Church will return to the fold to strengthen the Church of Christ for the attacks of Antichrist.

One of the main reasons 1365 was particularly feared (or hoped for, depending on the point of view) can be seen from this prophecy. In that year a conjunction of Saturn and Jupiter and other unusual conjunctions were expected; and these astronomical events presaged misfortunes. The conjunction of Mars, Jupiter, and Saturn in 1345 was widely held to have been the cause of the Black Death.[82]

In general the astronomers of the period confirm what we have already seen in these prophecies. John of Bassigny, a French astronomer of the period, predicts a bad time for the world for the whole period 1352–1376. John of Murs, his contemporary and colleague, in a letter to Pope Clement VI, is concerned with the conjunction of Saturn and Mars in Cancer in 1357, and Jupiter and Saturn in the eighth degree of Scorpion on October 30, 1365; for both of them will be serious for the Church, and 1365 will be crucial.

A similar line is taken by an English contemporary astronomer, John of Eshenden, who emphasizes the horrors of these well-known dates, and especially the importance of the conjunction of 1365.[83] Yet at the same time he is dubious of the attempts of Joachim and others to foretell the end of the world.

The prophecies of the period agree remarkably that the fifties, sixties, and seventies of the fourteenth century are dangerous times and that 1365 in particular is a year to be watched.[84] These are written by the major prophetical figures of the whole century— Arnold of Villanova, John of Paris, Jean de Roquetaillade, and the most notable astronomers.

It seems likely that Langland, whose apocalyptic sense of history was acute, was stimulated to write down his poem as a warning to the world before matters reached an even more crucial stage. It is out of this heated atmosphere of expectancy, which both the chronicles and the prophecies reveal, that the immediate motive for writing it at a particular time probably came. Even if that is not the case, this prophetical surcharged atmosphere explains the similar strain in *Piers*, a strain to be discussed in some detail in Chapter IV. It explains Langland's prophetical and apocalyptic view of things, in the sense that it is not unique; and in the 1360's such a poem would very well have been possible. And when looking at the poem with this fact in mind, we shall see at how many points it makes contact with some of the strong currents of its age.

Although the monks, both as defenders of monasticism and as

historians, had a strong interest in the apocalyptic view of history (and especially in their own eschatological role), they were by no means the only group in the Church who did. This attitude can be found among laymen, seculars, and friars. The radical friars, especially those known today as the Spiritual Franciscans, maintained a fundamentally apocalyptic point of view. At the very end of the century this attitude is evident among various heretics, in England among the Lollards especially. But this element is rather late and cannot be a factor in assessing Langland's background. The Spirituals themselves were frequently adjudged heretical, and some were burnt.

Among the Spiritual Franciscans, who openly espoused Joachim's and Peter John Olivi's teachings, the issue frequently turned on the problem of poverty and the literal following of St. Francis' Rule. The story of the Spiritual movement is too vast to be discussed here; and besides, for Langland, it is for the most part irrelevant. I did not always think so, for when I first began the investigations that led to this book, I was convinced of its importance in understanding Langland's poem. Now I am no longer so convinced, though perhaps it is a minor factor to be taken into account in assessing the poem. Joachism, which may well be an important factor in Langland's intellectual milieu, was not primarily associated, in England, with the Spirituals, but rather with biblical exegesis, especially on the Apocalypse, with monastic philosophy, and with the apocalyptic and prophetic view of history in general.

The chief objection to finding Spiritual echoes in Langland, however, is that the English Franciscans were not deeply affected by this movement. It was basically a Continental movement.

Although the English Franciscans were rather conservative about poverty, at least in theory, and although some were involved in the famous Chapter-General at Perugia in 1322, which led to John XXII's bull *Cum inter nonnullos* in 1323 and the defection of Michael of Cesena and Occam, they were not involved, with a few exceptions, with this radical activity. There was also the affair of 1329 at Cambridge when four Franciscans, among them Henry de Costesy (or Cossey), were arrested, presumably for defying the Pope and taking a strong stand on poverty.[85] There are only a few Spiritual writings connected with England, and they all circulated on the Continent. The Spiritual works of Occam were all written after his permanent departure from England and were primarily attacks against papal power rather than arguments for a Franciscan Joachism. The manuscripts of Olivi in England were almost all his non-Spiritual writings, and Ubertino da Casale was admired only for his intense spirituality.

Hugh of Newcastle's *Tractatus de victoria Christo contra Antichristum*,[86] written in 1319, is the only real Spiritual work written by an Englishman, and even this last point has been questioned. In any case he seems to have lived most of his life in France.[87] Two manuscripts of the work were apparently in England, one of which (formerly at Queen's College, Oxford) is now lost. It is a sober treatise on Antichrist consisting of a prologue and two books, the first of which is devoted to the temporary victory of Antichrist and the second to Christ's final victory. Hugh is concerned in Book II, over whether the time of Antichrist's coming can be predicted, and of course he answers affirmatively. In the same book, he uses the pseudo-Joachite *De semine Scripturarum* and says that according to this book there are only twenty-nine years left from now (1319) to the Final Judgment.[88] This would give us 1348, but the *De semine* seems to have been read in various ways. Like a good Spiritual, he takes as the surest sign of the coming of Antichrist the persecution of those who follow the poverty of Christ. Many prophecies are drawn on, and here is a real apocalyptic work. Yet one can see no sign of any particular influence from it on Langland and on England generally, and it is best taken as merely another evidence of the fourteenth-century apocalyptic frame of mind.

There is no evidence in *Piers* of any special Spiritual doctrines. Langland's apocalypticism, praise of poverty and of "poor fools," need not be interpreted as evidence of Spiritual Franciscanism.[89] In any case, *Piers Plowman* is not fundamentally a work of a Spiritual, except perhaps for one fact—that a solution to the problem of the world turned to a great extent on the reform of the friars. This may be held as evidence for Spiritual influence, but it can also be explained on the basis of Langland's concern for the regulars, which included friars and monks. In any case it is the only evidence for such a view; and, considering the rarity of radical Franciscan thinking in England in this century, it is unlikely that Spiritualism was his source. Ideal monastic thinking and ideal Franciscan thinking intersected at many points. One cannot force Langland's concern with perfection into a Spiritual point of view, nor his emphasis on temperance and order. These last points will be developed further.

Thus Langland may be regarded as a clerk in minor orders who was born in the West country near the Malvern Hills, who, as his knowledge of scholasticism and interest in ideas suggest,[90] probably studied at a *studium generale* of a cathedral or order, or at Oxford, who had some contact with monks, who moved to London, where he lived out his life at the minor ecclesiastical tasks he could perform, and who sometime in the sixties, probably before 1365, convinced of the great travail of his time, began to write what was to prove an endless task for him, a great poem embodying his craving for Christian perfection and evincing a sense of apocalyptic urgency.

CHAPTER IV

History, Social Theory, and Apocalyptic in
Piers Plowman

ALTHOUGH in the Judeo-Christian tradition the notion of perfection was always more than a metaphysical idea and embraced society as well as the individual, in the later Middle Ages the political and social aspects of perfection were heavily stressed, perhaps as a response to the rising age of individualism. The great sense of expectancy that is characteristic of the last part of the Middle Ages, whether Joachist or not, was molded and stimulated by the concept of perfection, the perfect man and the perfect society.[1] As Hanno Helbling has pointed out, we have the paradox in the later Middle Ages of a strong belief in both the imminent end of the world and a great coming future, a *renovatio*. The pull between this world and the next is part of the crisis of later medieval thought, which found a solution in the Renaissance with its tendency to separate the two realms.

It was, however, Joachim of Flora who provided unconsciously one possible solution to this tension by his theory of the three ages; for the imminence of a new age under the Holy Ghost could satisfy both optimists and pessimists. As one age passes into another there are persecutions of the righteous and the advent of Antichrists; a time of troubles comes upon the world. But only for the ultimate purpose of renewal. "When Almighty God wishes to consume the old, in order to set up the new, he permits some persecution in the Church, deserting what He wishes to be finished and protecting what He wishes to last so that the new, . . . the good hidden in the shadows, when the occasion presents itself, may be led forth to the light."[2] Thus Joachim consoles the persecuted, explains the terror and holds out hope to the suffering. In the troubled times of the fourteenth century, these views were especially important. Joachim brought perfection into history in a new way. The very sufferings of the age and of the Church were proofs of a coming new age or profound reformation. The idea of fulfillment as applied to the Old Testament could be applied to the modern period. Within the present time of troubles with its corruption and sin affecting laity and clergy alike, a new pattern of fulfillment was working itself out and another *plenitudo temporis* could be expected.

Not all or even most medieval thinkers could accept Joachim's coming age of the Holy Ghost, but his thinking and that of his followers did infuse hope into many who despaired, and he reemphasized the truths of the Kingdom of God. Society must be made perfect before individuals could be perfected in this world. God was, however, on the side of perfection. Joachim made the apocalyptic a political and social phenomenon. He and his followers historicized eschatological concepts like Antichrist. As Charles Péguy has said, "Tout commence en mystique, tout finit en politique."

On the other hand, the mystics of the fourteenth century stressed, in contradistinction to the monastic and older tradition of the Kingdom of God in history, individual perfection and union with the divine. The great figures of German and Flemish mysticism as well as those in England, Dame Julian of Norwich, Richard Rolle, Walter Hilton, and the author of the *Cloud of Unknowing*, were not fundamentally social thinkers. They were primarily concerned with the perfection of self and the union with God.

In this period it is always unrealistic to make too clear-cut a distinction between those who stressed social perfection as a prelude to individual perfection and those who stressed personal salvation. It is certain that neither prophet nor mystic would deny the importance of the other in the total world scheme.[3] But for convenience the two may be separated. Strictly speaking, only those who stressed individual perfection are true mystics. Peter John Olivi, Angelo Clareno, Langland, Wyclif, and Hus are not mystics but apocalyptic thinkers—men who stressed social perfection and the attainment of the Kingdom of God on earth. The world must become a paradise fit for unfallen Adams. But man must create his own paradise, with God's help; and to Langland this would be impossible without a reformation of the world, and in particular of the friars as the apex of the Church Militant.

through the finding again of Piers Plowman by Conscience. Such a reformation would be a return to apostolic and Adamic purity.

Langland understands the *imitatio Dei* in a very different fashion from that of Thomas à Kempis or the general devotional school of the later Middle Ages, which dwelt on the human aspect of Christ and His living example and which concentrated on His passion and death. Conrad Pepler is the only student of *Piers Plowman*, as far as I am aware, who has made this point. He writes, "The realistic and emotional devotion to the humanity of Christ, so typical of fourteenth-century piety, finds little expression in the Vision of Piers Plowman."[5] The Bernardine and Cistercian revolution in this aspect seems to have passed Langland by. The poet concentrates on the kingship of Jesus, the Pantocrator, and on the transformation of society into the Kingdom of God. In this he goes back to an older monastic and Christian tradition, a tradition less psychologically oriented and more closely rooted in the liturgy and Bible than the later monasticism.

Medieval thinking, then, applied the notion of perfection not only to the realms of being, of society, and of self, but also to some extent to the realm of history. In some ways the problem of the perfection of history is the most interesting of all. The concept of perfection is closely connected with a rationalistic view of the universe, that is, the conviction that the universe is for the most part capable of explanation by reason. It assumes that the multiplicity of singulars in the universe can be reduced to or subsumed under certain principles. But history is the realm of singulars or the unique, if it is recognized as a separate realm at all. If the concept of perfection is to be applied to history, one must consider the unique, the particular and the singular, at least somewhat rational and meaningful. To put it another way, if history is meaningful, as the Judeo-Christian tradition teaches, it is related to some extent, at least, to perfection. History is not merely the arbitrary and the capricious.

One can, as the ancient Greeks and Romans did, make history significant by reducing it to nature and giving it a cyclic form. The concept of the eternal return made history into a more unruly, but nevertheless rational, nature. In effect, however, all this is making history meaningful by eliminating it as history, by crushing its essential quality—the unique. To many Greek thinkers and others, the historic was a mere accident of things, an unessential detail in assessing the meaning of an event; or it was a storehouse of examples, a branch of rhetoric.[6]

In the Christian tradition, following the Hebraic emphasis, history must be distinctive. God is a God of history, and his providence extends over all. To the Israelite, in both flesh and spirit, history has a meaning because salvation has come and will come through it. It is not just a repetitive cycle, nor an accident of things; it reveals the will of God. God may interfere and has interfered with the process of history. History is partially redemptive and moves towards a final end. No one in the Judeo-Christian tradition can ignore history, and the claims of Christianity and Judaism as religions rest upon the historicity of certain happenings in the past.

Then, too, there is the eschatological side. The Day of Judgment sets a termination of the world, and the end explains the beginning. The Kingdom of God, however that elusive concept may be defined, is clearly a part of the Judeo-Christian tradition.

The meaning of history could not be purchased, however, as with the Greeks, at the cost of its uniqueness. This was the Judeo-Christian historical problem—how can uniqueness of event be wedded to a conviction that the world had been created by God and was meaningful in time as well as in space? If this problem could not be solved, then one had to rest content with history as a series of meaningless events, an eternal repetitiveness, or, at the most, a number of admonishing or encouraging *exempla*. To solve this dilemma, the answer generally provided was the concept of world ages, which, as opposed to the Greek cycles, combined the unique and the pattern. Paul speaks of or implies the ages before the law, under the law, and under grace. Augustine adds a sevenfold periodization. And one can list many other systems that divide history.[7] There are repetition and progress in history; and in terms of itself each age is justified and unique, and in terms of later ages it is a preparation and a type of it. Joachim of Flora was to carry through to the bitter end all the implications of this thinking and by tying in his ideas with the Trinity, produced the goal of a new third age of the Holy Ghost, which he expected in 1260. In the eyes of some, such as Hugh of St. Victor, within each age there is progress too. To him the history of man since the

Fall is a long *restauratio* to the paradisaical condition, in which the central but not the exclusive event is the Incarnation. John of Salisbury and Thomas Aquinas also held theories of modified progress; and indeed, recognizing an increase in knowledge in time and believing in reason, they could hardly avoid the conclusion that progress in history was possible. Not all medieval thinkers were to take such optimistic views, but such opinions were not uncommon.

History, then, in spite of its intellectual intractability, could be brought under the aegis of perfection. It was rational in some sense and could be understood and justified, at least in general, both because of the soteriological events that had happened and continued to happen within it and because of its end and transcendence in a bodily resurrection, a Final Judgment, and a Kingdom of God to embrace all the saved. To some, this historical perfectibility has been a heady brew; and when secularized, it has led to much Utopian thinking, not all of it bad.[8] But with the Kingdom of God as the goal, both social and individual, history does have a rationale and is in some sense perfecting and perfectible.

Before turning to the apocalyptic elements in *Piers Plowman*, it is necessary to say something of Langland's political theory, a subject most closely related to his apocalyptic view of history, although not always its inevitable concomitant. Later medieval political discussion was largely centered around the problem of the conflicting claims of Church and State, the *sacerdotium* and *regnum*. This complex and elaborate subject I omit as being irrelevant to my purpose.[9] But behind all this discussion was a view of society, originating with Plato and Aristotle, which was remarkably stable. For it is this picture that Langland has continually in mind, and he specifically describes its features. What was Langland's ideal society, and how was it organized?

Langland viewed society as a precisely articulated institution with each part performing its proper function and thereby realizing its perfection. In essence, this was the standard view of society in classical and medieval times, and beyond. It may be taken as the classic political and social theoretical framework of Western thinking and owes its origin to Plato.[10] The Christian notion of the Mystical Body of Christ, to which all Christians belong, added a new dimension to, without fundamentally changing, the concept.

How far this society was corrupted by original sin was a debatable question. With many different emphases, this picture of society was the normal one for the period, and it fitted in perfectly with the dominant hierarchical view of the universe. Secular society, like nature and the Church, was organized in hierarchical levels, which were called *status* or states.

Langland, like most medieval men, was *status*-minded. Each human being was part of various *status*, and his true liberty consisted in performing the demands that his *status* called on him to live up to. There were certain norms established by reason or grace which his participation in social living made the standards of his actions.[11] These *status* and norms have an objective existence; and in the case of social ones they impose by natural law an obligation to be lived up to.

Every large unit has parts, and parts imply a limit. God had ordered the universe according to weight, measure, and number (Wisdom 11:21), and society too has its divisions and limits. The basic division in the fourteenth century varied somewhat. but in general it comprised clergy, knights, and workers. This tripartite division could be defined and subdivided in different ways. The Middle Ages loved threes, even at the cost of comprehensiveness or confusion. The merchants and professional men were badly served by most of these schemes, for they were put together with peasants. Even worse were Thomas Brinton's *status*—prelates, religious, and workers—for here (Sermon 30) the temporal lords were lumped together with all nonreligious occupations. The *De triplici ecclesia*, a work of the period, has clerics, temporal lords, and "vulgares qui in operarios, mercantes et yconomos sunt multipliciter divisi" as the basic social *status*.[12] The clerics should teach others in deed as well as word. The lords temporal should dominate society "seculariter" and be opulent. The "vulgares" should live by bodily labor and be moderately concerned with temporal goods. Even revolutionaries like John Ball wished no more than the proper relation of each class to the other, which was the only foundation for social justice.

What Ian Watt says of Fielding's vigorous satire on the upper classes—that it "should not be interpreted as the expression of any egalitarian tendency: it is really a tribute to the firmness of his belief in the class premise"[13]—may certainly with justice be applied to Langland. "Such was the limit of peasant aspirations [in the later Middle Ages]; the people longed for justice, even social justice; but that did not mean that they aspired to social equality. Each man should be content with his lot, and the poor man shall be allowed to live in peace and enjoy the fruit of his toil, without hindrance from the rich."[14]

One may assume from what Langland says that his tripartite over-all scheme was divided into the religious, the lords temporal, and workers, with subdivisions within each broad classification, and that his ideal implied that the religious would spiritually sustain, the knights would defend, and the workers would materially support society. Justice consists in the right relationship between classes. Measure and temperance are the social virtues par excellence. Restitution, *redde quod debes*, is of the essence of justice; for by its means, balance is restored after temperance has become intemperance and measure, immeasure.[15] In the last chapter I shall analyze Do-best in some detail; for it is the crowning portion of the poem, and in it these virtues are stressed again and again. Against all tradition, Langland exalts temperance over the other cardinal virtues there, and if my argument has been followed, it should now be clear as to why this virtue, along with restitution and measure, occupies such an exalted position. But these virtues grow out of Langland's monastic philosophy as well as his political philosophy—for temperance is the virtue of chastity, moderation, and control and brings together the two worlds of the cloister and of general society, uniting realms in the way medieval man loved to do.

It is clear that there are apocalyptic elements in *Piers* and that the whole poem implies the hope of a better world which is predestined to solve the crisis of Langland's own time.[16] It will perhaps be useful to look again at the poem to see how extensive this belief is and how it is woven into its fabric.

First of all, the very subject of the poem, Christian perfection, in its social form, bespeaks apocalypticism. Social thinking on the subject of perfection, above all in the fourteenth century, had to be apocalyptic. The transcendence of society to a new level was thought by many to be the only way out of the crushing dilemmas. The sad state of the contemporary Church could be explained only on these grounds. God was planning, if not a new age, at least a renewal of the good and the just. The evil was the result of the birth throes of the good. What was hidden "in the womb of time" would be revealed at the proper moment; and as Antichrists[17] assailed the true Church, Unitas, a new life and renewal was being prepared, soon to manifest itself. The true Church would reassert itself, and the false Church would be overcome.

In recent years there has been a tendency to find in *Piers* the odyssey of a mystic towards God, and perhaps in one sense this is true. But *Piers* is first of all socially oriented—that is, apocalyptic in its view of perfection. History and society must come first, and the last parts of the poem show this very clearly.[18] The journey of the individual soul to God is perhaps also implied, but it is not central. It is Piers, not Will, who, starting as a simple peasant, becomes the human aspect of Christ and in effect passes through the three grades of perfection to become Christ as man. Piers, not Will, is deified, or gradually revealed as deified.[19] This distinction is interesting and significant. Man can be raised to God only through outside aid. It is not revealed how Piers becomes elevated to his high dignity, since the reader sees the events of the poem from Will's point of view. Will's quest is for the three "Do's"— that is, Christian perfection—and he grows old in it; but he knows that Piers Plowman must be found by Conscience and returned to Holy Church before he can find the answer. He must be prepared to cooperate with the grace Piers represents and the Christ he stands for. But Piers is sought to save Holy Church, not primarily to save Will. And this is what makes *Piers* first of all an apocalyptic, not a mystical, poem. Both Will and Piers in some senses are Everyman, but Will is basically diachronic, whereas Piers is synchronic, man. Will is incomplete, whereas Piers is complete man. *Piers* is not fundamentally the story of the *itinerarium mentis in Deum*, and the three "Do's" of the Vita section are not fundamentally the purgative, illuminative, and unitive ways of the mystic; rather they belong to an older tradition, a monastic one originally, of the states of Christian perfection that entail the Kingdom of God.[20]

Second, the basic symbol of the poem, Piers, and its attendant agricultural imagery, together with other important classes of images in the poem, such as food and clothing, reinforce the apocalyptic point.[21] Any poem thus organized must at the very least in a Christian society have eschatological aims.

The history of agricultural imagery in the Judeo-Christian tradition is too long and complicated to discuss here. The Hebrews ever since their transformation from a nomadic and pastoral people into a farming and agricultural community were prone to express their spiritual experiences in imagery borrowed from their predominant economic activity. From the story of Cain and Abel,[22] the latter, often to Christians, the symbol of the true Church or the founder of the Church, through Mosaic law ("Man shall not live by bread alone," to take one example), through the prophets, and down to the New Testament, the very language of religion is impregnated with the images of agricultural and pastoral life. The same is true of the New Testament, especially of the parables of Jesus. The seed and sowing, the plow and the harvest,[23] the tares and the crops, the farmer and peasant, the mill and the field— all these are to be found in the greatest religious passages of the Bible and in the works of the Fathers. Above all, eschatological imagery is highly agricultural. Jesus, interpreting his own parable of the tares, says, "He that soweth the good seed is the Son of man; The field is the world; the good seed are the children of the kingdom; but the tares are the children of the wicked one; The enemy that sowed them is the devil; the harvest is the end of the world; and the reapers are the angels" (Matthew 13: 37–39).[24]

The harvest is paradise or salvation, and those who tend it lead man to his proper end. Christ is the supreme harvester or plowman, and all plowmen to some extent are symbols of his true followers—priests, religious, or even laymen who are creating or bringing in the harvest. Jesus was historically a carpenter and could be associated with the making of plows. The plow is the tool whereby He prepares the field of the world for His harvest of souls. Just as Pentecost is the feast of the Church, of the mission, of the Holy Ghost, and also the feast of the end of time, of the Church Triumphant, so the Plowman is both the ecclesiastical and eschatological image par excellence.[25]

It is fundamentally this tradition that Langland is following in his ideal figure, although the plowman is also, and especially in the fourteenth century, the figure of the poor and the exploited. The true peasant is the symbol of Christ and all that He implies—the salvation and the perfection of man.

Thus, it is not surprising that the field and the vineyard and the plowman and husbandman were widely used in the thirteenth and fourteenth centuries to express the Christian truths of the meaning of existence. Owst has shown how common they were in sermons of the period.[26] Pope John XXII, in his bull (1329) condemning Eckhart's errors, clothes his exposition in terms of the field of the Lord, of which he is the custodian who must eliminate the chaff. To the writer of the *Distinctiones monasticae et morales* (I, 10), an Englishman of the thirteenth century, the field is a symbol of the soul, the Militant Church, the Bible, and finally the Triumphant Church, all at once. Langland could not have been unaware of these associations connected with his agricultural imagery.

Piers Plowman is an eschatological figure—both the way and the goal of Christian perfection. He is both the model and the norm of human existence for Christians, and he can lead them into the transformed society—the Kingdom of God, which may also be an age of the Holy Ghost.[27] He will lead them back so that they may go forward to their proper destiny.

Robertson and Huppé have drawn attention to the predominance of imagery of food and clothing in *Piers* and its unifying role. Its purpose in *Piers* is, I think, to further the aims of the poem; and in general these images in the tradition have been interpreted as grace and perfection symbols. Food as spiritual sustenance and as Christian (or Jewish) truth is widely used in the Bible and later religious writings. Its meanings are fairly clear from the context. Food also had eschatological meanings in the Bible, particularly in the New Testament; and the Last Supper is in one aspect a Messianic banquet, as some of Jesus' comments show. We shall eat and drink in the Kingdom of God. Food, in the fatal apple, and food, in the Eucharist, have been the means of both man's downfall and his salvation. Besides these eschatological associations, which can also clearly be seen in lines like "Thou preparest a table before me in the presence of mine enemies" (Psalm 23:5), satire directed at monks, often by monks, had for a long time concentrated on the sin of gluttony. The gluttonous doctor of divinity in Passus XIII (who is probably William Jordan, O.P.) might almost be a figure from the satires of Peter Damian or

Bernard of Clairvaux.[28] If this satirical image is not a *topos*, it is certainly a conventional point of attack. In spite of these other purposes, food and drink generally in *Piers* have apocalyptic associations.

Clothing is also an important symbol, although its meanings are perhaps less obvious. Much of the traditional interpretation of clothing has centered upon the story of God's clothing Adam and Eve, and this tale was frequently tied in with the story of the good Samaritan.[29] Clothing is often the symbol of grace, of the new man. New or different clothes make a new and different man. Yet old clothes can be sin and corruption, the old man. Our flesh is clothing, and this garment will be put off. Like many profound symbols, clothing is an ambiguous image. In this poem, it may be found in the arms that Piers as Christ puts on, and in the new clothes that Will dons to search for the answers to his questions, as well as in the spotted clothes of Hawkin the Active Man. Clothes are man's hope and his despair. With monks, too, they have a deep and spiritual significance. When he enters his order, a monk puts on new clothing, as a child being baptized. It is a symbol of his new life, like that of the angels and Christ, and the perfection of his *status*.[30] Clothing as imagery, therefore, has deep moral, metaphysical, and theological implications.

An examination of certain parts of the poem where the apocalyptic element is strong will disclose what role these parts play in the total structure of *Piers*.

The field full of folk of the Prologue is a picture of society divided into its various grades as medieval religion conceived them, with the overhanging suggestion of the Kingdom of God. It is a *heilsgeschichtliche* vision—man in his social relations struggling through the field of existence between hell ("a depe dale" and "dongeon") and heaven (a "toure on a toft"),[31] trying to live and flourish. Most men are merely concerned with the field itself and only a few with their proper end. The majority are evil. The Prologue then points particularly (vv. 58 ff.) to the sins of the friars who preach for their own profit, glossing the Bible to justify themselves in their evil ways, and who dress in fine clothes, for charity has become a merchant. Unless Holy Church and these friars hold together better, however, great mischief is to be foreseen. This point is made again more strongly at the end of the poem.

The B and C versions of the poem following the above scene, give a famous picture of the ideal king and the fable of the rats, which may have a contemporary significance. This emperor-saviour or ideal king is one of the important eschatological figures, along with the angelic Pope, of the later Middle Ages. The famous passage in the Prologue beginning, "Thanne come there a kyng ·
kny3thod hym ladde" (v. 112), has been much commented on but usually with the contemporary political scene in view. This approach, while partly true perhaps, is not the only approach, and it obscures the passage's essential apocalyptic nature. This king whom "mi3t of the comunes" (v. 113) made to reign is not merely Edward III and the situation is not merely the tangled political events of 1376 or 1377, but rather the *rex justus* and the new or reformed age to which history was tending. As Donaldson has shown, the "comunes" is not the House of Commons but the community in general or commonweal.[32] Langland is here uttering a commonplace of medieval political philosophy and canon law that the *communitas*, the whole society, provides the basis and sanction for the king's rule. The good king, the *rex justus*, supported by the nobility and the clergy, and counseled by practical reason, sets up the ideal commonwealth in which each class will have its proper role to play. A lunatic speaks up to praise him, probably a fool in Christ, someone like Will, and an angel speaks from heaven in Latin. Only fools and angels can speak the truth. The angel in the air (possibly in this case Bishop Brinton) was probably suggested by Revelation 18 or John 12:28–29 and is a traditional device for making portentous announcements.

The short Latin poem in the text stresses the double traditional role of the true king, a representative of God on earth who is also both just and merciful.[33] The "goliardeys, a glotoun of words," then grieves the king and answers the angel, by referring to the presumed etymology of the word *rex*, a mode of argument that had much validity in the Middle Ages. "For *rex* is said to have its name from *regere*; he has the name without the thing unless he strives to maintain the laws." This is an ancient definition going back at least to Isidore of Seville's *Etymologies* and can be widely found in the Middle Ages.[34] It is significant that the goliardeys stresses justice only. Justice is the crying need of the times even more than mercy. The proverb was used to prove that the king had no power to do anything except command what is right.

One then learns of the unhappy land whose king is a boy.[35] Thereupon follows the fable of the rats, which is presented not as a speech of any character but as an action. The rats agree that someone must do something about the cat who is tormenting them and decide that he must be belled; unfortunately, no single rat has the courage to attempt this feat. A good solution must be practical or it is worthless, the fable teaches us. This fable may well primarily refer to local political problems and fears[36] attendant upon the last days of Edward III; yet it serves to bring contemporary history into an apocalyptic range, even at the cost of destroying the simple effectiveness of the Prologue as it is found in the A-Text. The problem of belling the cat has something universal about it, and suggests the difficulties, because of human weakness, in establishing the just society.

The king is an important figure in the poem and appears more than once. He is an apocalyptic figure in *Piers* but also an ideal king about whom the Middle Ages loved to speculate. The king as the key to the political problem is a favorite subject of medieval admonition; to this the numerous *specula principis* of the later Middle Ages provide abundant testimony. To some extent, Langland's criticisms of the king also partake of this tradition. His kings are at once good kings and divine envoys—at once ideal and apocalyptic. I am stressing the apocalyptic in this chapter because I think the contexts demand it, but I am not denying a less eschatological side to these figures.[37]

The Prologue then presents the scene of *Piers* in an apocalyptic setting of a social decay that has promise of renewal, a setting which points up the issues of the poem. Langland is concerned not merely with local problems or with contemporary issues but with the world and society in a Christian perspective; and he correspondingly presents us with images and pictures to convey his eschatological vision. This is a world *sub specie aeternitatis* and under the eye and judgment of God. Its evil has corrupted Christian society and the Church Militant; yet out of evil good may come, for God allows evil to flourish and the Church to suffer while He plans for its rebirth and regeneration.

The next scene, the dialogue in the first passus between Will and Holy Church, poses the problem that the fair field full of folk has implied—the problem of salvation and perfection. Holy Church explains the meaning of the previous scene and discusses some of the general issues involved in perfection. Here is the Church Triumphant, the true Church, which enables Will to see clearly his duty and man's destiny. In the early part of her speech, Holy Church stresses temperance and moderation—a point which is again made at the end of the poem. All that is superfluous should be given to the poor, and need should regulate our social dealings.[38] By right, a man must possess only what he needs. The active basis of justice in society is the doctrine of superfluity and, as Robertson and Huppé say,[39] its necessary measuring rod, need. This is why both need and temperance occupy such important places in the apocalyptic vision of Do-best. But here at the very beginning of her speech, Lady Holy Church (I, 17 ff.) makes this very same point. "Mesure is medcyne · thou3 thou moche 3erne. / It is nau3t al gode to the goste · that the gutte axeth" (I, 35–36). The ideal society, the just society, must be reared on the virtue of temperance.

Holy Church, after introducing herself, goes on to praise truth, which probably here means truth or loyalty or sincerity obligatory on all men by natural law. Only on loyalty to one's duties can a just society be based—and men all have within themselves (by "kynde knowing") powers to enable them to follow truth. Truth teaches that love is the most valuable virtue of all. "Loue is leche of lyf · and nexte owre lorde selue" (I, 202).

Then follows the Meed episode. Lady Meed is that which destroys truth and love and makes right relationships between classes impossible. Meed (the desire for reward) is the great enemy of measure and temperance. Only the King, guided by Reason and Conscience, can put her down.[40] Meed seduces all classes, especially the friars, and misleads mankind. The King is, of course, the ideal king, God and the individual soul. Following W. Erzgräber,[41] I think Conscience is a combination of the two scholastic terms, *conscientia* and *synderesis*; and in the psychological sense what is here is the Scotistic picture of the practical intellect (the King) under the influence of practical reason (Reason) and synderesis and conscience (Conscience), stimulated by the will and in turn stimulating it to act justly. But the King is also the ideal king and the supreme King of kings.

Conscience in her great speech before the King breaks out into an apocalyptic vision (III, 282 ff.). "Shal na more Mede · be maistre, as she is nouthe, / Ac loue and lowenesse and lewte togederes, / Thise shul be maistres on molde · treuthe to saue." Love and conscience shall come together in the earth and create such peace and perfect truth that the Jews will at last be convinced and be converted, and all weapons will be destroyed. As she reaches her climax, Conscience breaks out into a mysterious prophecy.

> "And er this fortune falle · fynde men shal the worste,
> By syx sonnes and a schippe · and half a shef of arwes;
> And the myddel of a mone · shal make the Iewes to torne,
> And saracenes for that si3te · shulle synge *gloria in excelsis &c.,*
> For Makomet and Mede · myshappe shal that tyme"
>
> (III, 323–327)[42]

Langland's predilection for prophecies, usually of the most difficult kind for us, is further evidence of his apocalyptic frame of mind. Obscure prophecies are the stock-in-trade of all those who are convinced that history is soon about to undergo a profound change. They satisfy those who love the obscure and are a delight to those who look for self-justification and social reform. To men convinced of their truth, they make sense out of the current miseries of history. This type of prophecy was also difficult to disprove and the same prophecy may be applied again and again *ad libitum,* not to say *ad nauseam.* Above all they prove the superiority of *Heilsgeschichte* to secular history. In a time of crisis, such as the later Middle Ages, they were very popular, especially with those concerned with the writing of history.[43] These enigmatic prophecies are, however, of the essence of the apocalyptic view of life.[44]

In the fourth passus during the dispute between Peace and Wrong, Reason also lays down negatively the conditions necessary for his intervention (vv. 113–142). I shall not intervene, Reason says, in this quarrel (in which Lady Meed is also by now involved) until lords and ladies all love truth and hate wickedness, until Pernel's finery be put away and children properly chastised and the holiness of ribalds be seen for what it really is, and so forth. This

ironical picture is also an ideal one and emphasizes the distance
between Langland's own time and his deepest social dreams.

Finally, at the end of this section (and passus), the King promises
to submit to Reason and Conscience and punish Meed. The gift
of counsel has in effect been given to the King so that he may
exercise *discretio* and really become the just ruler and saviour-
emperor.[45]

This whole section (II–IV) is fraught with an apocalyptic sense
of urgency, and Langland's allegory is centered around the problem of the king, who is a multidimensional symbol but whose
majesty can unite the religious, social, and psychological realms,
with the social (and political) bearing the main emphasis. The
plea is for the transformation of society and the right use of *bona
temporalia*. Lady Meed is exposed, and Conscience and Reason
are invited to take their proper places.[46] Conscience and Reason
create the necessary circumstances for the awareness of sin, and
hence the confession scene in the next section follows logically.

The last three passus of the Visio are concerned with repentance
and absolution, as in the scene of the Confession of the Deadly
Sins, in the scene of the planned Pilgrimage to Truth, which is
permanently interrupted by the plowing of the half-acre (in the
telling of which Langland is enabled to sketch out his ideal
society), and finally in the scene of the Tearing of the Pardon, with
its repudiation of the pardon by the priest, apparently without
Piers' being convinced of its complete worthlessness. The major
concern here is with the apocalyptic elements in these wonderful
passus with their richness of detail, humor, and *élan*.

Closely related to the prophetic frame of mind is the tendency
to find eschatological signs in natural phenomena, especially those
of weather and the sky. Nor are these wanting in Langland,
although they are not perhaps very common. To Langland, contemporary social phenomena were his main signs; and one of the
main themes of his poem, both explicit and implicit, is that
current social evils provide the main evidence that a new or reformed age is about to dawn. The evils of his time afford the best
proof to him that if God and His Church are realities—and to
Langland there could be no doubt on these matters—good was
to come out of evil. The persecution of the just and of the true
Church was a fundamental proof of their coming rehabilitation,[47]

if not rebirth. Deep down, Langland, like all millenarians, was an optimist.

But nature, too, enters into the scheme. The prophecies just discussed all predict or explain eschatologically dire events in nature. This attitude towards nature was widespread in the Middle Ages (and before and since), and is abundantly illustrated in the chroniclers of the period, who not only recorded the death of kings but faithfully reported unusual natural disorders.

In V, 13 ff., Reason begins his sermons by referring to the recent pestilences (which had devastated England in 1349, 1361–1362, 1369, 1375–1376) and above all to "the southwest wynde on Saterday at euene," all of which were, Reason assures us, due to the sin of pride. This allusion also occurs in the A-Text, and it is the most important piece of evidence for the *terminus post quem* of the first version of *Piers*; for both this disastrous Saturday wind storm and its exact date January 15, 1362, (1361 old style), are recorded in many contemporary sources.[48] This typifies the reasoning of the seeker for signs and is so closely related to the prophetic mood that we cannot be surprised at finding it. A more general statement about the matter occurs in Anima's speech in XV, 348 ff. Things are so bad now that the weather and sky have all the "experts" at their wits' end.

> "Astrymyanes also · aren at her wittes ende;
> Of that was calculed of the element [air] · the contrarie thei
> fynde.

> (XV, 363–364)

The harmony of nature is upset, for this is really Antichrist's time.

It is in the second part of the Visio that Piers first makes his appearance as the guide to Truth. The true journey, after the false journey by Meed to London in the first part of the Visio, is now being made after the mass confession and absolution of all classes. Langland indicates the social nature of these confessions by using, in some cases, various figures of the seven deadly sins, which shift as he speaks. The sin as he confesses becomes a representative of various classes and groups—he is both one man and Everyman. The acknowledgment of sin, leading to penance, is a preliminary step—and of course a most important one—on the road to salvation and perfection. But as the sequence (in Passus VI) shows, this is a perpetual struggle; for man falls back into sin again and again, as the folk helping Piers did after all their splendid resolutions. The journey to Truth is only described by Piers (V, 568 ff.); it is never undertaken.

Through the various pilgrims attempting to help Piers, Langland presents a picture of the ideal society, with the knights defending the peasants and the state, and the clergy serving all their needs. But again to work hard at one's appointed task is too much for the ordinary run of humanity, and some do not wish to work at all. Hunger restores order and after appeasing his appetite departs. But again only the worst is to be expected. The scene ends with Langland's direct exhortation to all to do their duty and a warning that Hunger and pestilence and flood will return even within five years.

There is no need to enter here into the many problems connected with the last passus of the Visio, the famous and puzzling Pardon Scene; but I do wish to point to its apocalyptic element, part of which does not seem to have been hitherto noticed.[49] The crux of the problem is whether Truth and the Pope, who issued the pardon in the first place, are to be preferred to the priest who impugned it. Either horn is sharp and unpleasant, but the least discomfort comes from the assumption that it is the priest whom Langland is criticizing, however one may interpret the incident. The end of the poem also justifies this interpretation, for Christ's pardon there is practically the same in sense (XIX, 177 ff.) as Truth's. The words of the pardon in the Visio, "Et qui bona egerunt, ibunt in vitam eternam; Qui vero mala, in ignem eternum," come, as has been pointed out by N. Coghill, from the Athanasian Creed, and were clearly present in contemporary versions of that Creed.[50]

Now the interesting thing from my point of view is that these words in the Creed do not refer, as is generally thought, to the personal but to the general judgment. In other words, to those who knew their Creed, the pardon does not indicate the immediate fate of the soul at death but at the Second Advent and Last Judgment. What this means altogether is not entirely clear, but the priest impugns the pardon perhaps because it alludes to the final judgment of souls when all pardons will be too late, and not because of the inadequacy of natural reason and law.[51] Lang-

land may be criticizing the priest because he does not fully understand God's judgment which is hanging over society. This is the
constant theme of the poem—remember the final social reckoning
—and is evidence of Langland's apocalyptic frame of mind. It fits
in too with the final portion of this passus when Will admonishes
his audience and warns them sternly of the Day of Judgment,
when all shall "comen . . . bifor Cryst · acountis to ȝelde." The
words may be considered a pardon in the sense that we must
remember that God's final judgment always looms over society
and man, a situation that makes divine pardon necessary. On this
eschatological note, the Visio, as the Vita will too, comes to a conclusion.[52]

The long last part of the poem, the Vita, is divided by apparently
authentic rubrics into three sections—those of Do-wel, Do-bet,
and Do-best—and the problem of what these divisions mean has
always exercised scholars. The crux of the difficulty is the first
of these sections, Do-wel, which is not only difficult but badly
organized. Passus XI, which in B takes up where A apparently
had been finally bogged down, is the worst of all. In recent years
valuable analyses of the Vita and Do-wel have been written, and
Wells, Coghill, Chambers, Meroney, Gerould, Donaldson, Robertson, Huppé, Frank, Kane, Erzgräber, to name some major names
in *Piers Plowman* research in the past thirty years, have made
contributions to the unlocking of its secrets.

The chief difficulty is not in line by line analysis, although that
method can still be fruitfully used, but in the over-all significance
of the divisions, a difficulty compounded by the inordinate length
of the Vita, especially Do-wel. The Wells-Coghill interpretation
of these three divisions as the active, contemplative, and mixed
lives has recently been subjected to strong criticism.[53] The weakness
of this analysis is that with one exception (XIX, 104–183) in the
life of Christ in Do-best, references to the triad, if manuscript
rubrics are omitted, occur only in Do-wel, and nowhere else, and
that there the three Do's are defined in six or seven different ways.
Even though G. Kane and J. A. W. Bennett[54] believe that these
definitions are cumulative, it is not easy to see how one definition
builds on the other. Some seem different from the others, and
some reinforce the others. In some cases Will is dissatisfied with
the answers. This may be more of a reflection on Will than on

the answer, but we know from Will's further searching that more can be said on the subject and that one cannot take any one answer as definitive.

Do-bet is built around the Tree of Perfection or Charity and is concerned with the theological virtues, culminating in the Harrowing of Hell. It concentrates on the theological virtues of faith, hope, and especially charity and full trust in God. Jesus is the dominating figure, and the section comes to a conclusion at Eastertime. Do-best is an apocalyptic vision of the age with emphasis on the Holy Ghost, the Church, and the four cardinal virtues. But about Do-wel one cannot be so categorical. After Will's wanderings (in B) to the friars, Thought, Wit (intelligence), Study, Clergy (learning), Scripture, Lewte (integrity and justice perhaps), Reason, Imaginatif,[55] Conscience, and Patience, Do-wel ends with a plea for patient poverty and humility and presents a vivid picture of Hawkin the Active Man. No simple summary can do justice to the wealth of topics here—marriage, predestination, learning, social justice, the necessity of speaking out at evil, the meaning of nature, minstrels, the sins, faith, the salvation of the non-Christian, and so forth. In some ways the impression created by Do-wel would satisfy the criteria for the active life, but then Do-bet and Do-best cannot be made to fit, as far as I can see, the complementary two stages of the triad—the contemplative and mixed lives. And as S. S. Hussey has said, the evidence for the knowledge of this particular triad in England before Hilton is very slight.

Threefold divisions of the life of perfection are common, however, even if this particular one is not. Nor are characterizations of some of them as good, better, and best, unknown,[56] even if they are not common. The idea of increasing qualitative improvement, of grades of perfection, is and has been widespread in Christendom, especially in monastic theology and philosophy. A further example may be given here. Abbot Abbo of Fleury divides Christian male society into three orders—laymen ("agricolae," "agonistae," and "principes"), clerics, and monks—which are characterized as good, better, best. The female orders consist of married, widowed, and virgins. All these divisions are, as we know, traditional, but Abbo makes some special twists that seem to be his alone. There is no question here of direct influence on Langland; in any case it is hard to see how Do-wel corresponds to laymen, Do-bet to clergy, and Do-best to monks, although in a few ways the parallels fit. The Joachite triad of Father, Son, and Holy Ghost provides a better solution; but again to equate the Father with Do-wel is not entirely satisfactory, although the last two fit very well. Even in the first there are "haunting though obscure harmonies"[57] with Joachim. This possible parallel has been noted and cannot be dismissed. We may also say the same of Donaldson's parallel with Bernard—that the three Do's represent humility, charity, and unity.[58] We may yet find the source.

Possibly Langland himself was confused, especially in Do-wel, which it seems likely he had much trouble in composing.[59] This solution is perhaps an easy way out, but at present there seems to be no other. And it may be that Langland had several schemes of grades of perfection in mind and that he could not successfully bring them all together, especially in Do-wel, where he was overwhelmed by the difficulties of his problems. Then one must remember that the quest for truth is actually basic to his whole scheme. He could not perfect his poem on perfection because of the magnitude of the problems facing him. He does give an answer, but it is an answer which involves a struggle through history and time. Will's quest is basic to the structure of the poem, and a quest is a record of difficulties. In a poem on the search for perfection, they must involve the author.

Do-best clearly seems to be devoted to the work of the Holy Ghost, and Do-bet most probably related to the Son; hence Do-wel may have been intended for the Father. The triad of marriage, continence, and virginity—or lay, priests, and religious—is also relevant,[60] and possibly Donaldson's Bernardine triplet. But Langland could never resist wandering, and in all three sections the triads appear—more or less. Perhaps all one can say is that the grades are grades of increasing perfection, and that the whole section of the Vita is eschatologically oriented, finally culminating in a social transformation, to arise in Do-best out of the ashes of contemporary impiety and sin. Will learns that patient poverty and charity, the fundamental answers to his quest given in Do-wel and Do-bet, must lead to a social transformation that is basically an ecclesiastical transformation; for the Church under the aegis of the Holy Ghost is the ideal society, as hoped for but not attained in

Do-best. It is proper that this reformation be under the Holy Ghost, who is charity in action and whose special care is the Church itself, as manifested at Pentecost (with which Do-best itself begins) and in the later history of the Church.

The use of the grammatical concept of comparison to indicate these three grades is characteristic of scholastic thought, with its love of grammatical analogies. From the twelfth century on, scholastic writings are full of grammatical categories; in fact for a while, grammar competed with logic as the formal framework of scholasticism. Throughout all this period there are also treatises of *de modo significandi* type, which dealt with philosophical grammar. As the long passage in C, IV, 335–410, for which no source as yet has been found, shows, a passage in which Langland makes an elaborate distinction between *mede* and *mercede* based on the notions of direct and indirect relations, as between noun and adjective, Langland no doubt was attracted to grammatical reasoning and naturally fell into a good, better, best pattern to clarify the degrees of perfection. In this he was encouraged most likely by Jesus' use of "better" to characterize Mary's part in the Bible.

To become more specific about apocalyptic elements in the Vita, let us turn to some sections that deserve special attention. In VIII, 78–106, Thought gives Will one of the many definitions of the three Do's he is to receive. It need not be taken as definitive, but it certainly contains some truth. It is one possible answer to the complex question of what the three grades of perfection, as traditionally conceived, are. Do-wel follows, Thought says, whoever is an honest and sober workman; Do-bet includes this and more— humility and active charity, which correct the injustices of avarice and preach to the people. Do-best is a bishop who saves men from hell and protects Do-wel. Do-wel, Do-bet, and Do-best have chosen a king to guard all three and to rule according to their advice.[61] This king is the ideal ruler, the saviour-emperor, who is a recurrent feature of the poem, and the bishop is probably an ideal Pope, an angelic Pope. But as in Dante, for the maintenance of justice and love within the state, the king is above the Pope. However in *Piers*, the king is also Christ in His majesty.

Wit (the *spiritus intelligentiae* or wisdom) in IX in the course of a long speech defines Do-well as "trewe wedded libbing folk"

(v. 107) or the well-known *status conjugatorum*, the lowest rung in the ladder of perfection. This part of Wit's speech, which continues to the end of the passus, is a long section on marriage, full of practical advice, as well as superstition, which holds up Noah as the ideal type of married man. Langland blames at least part of the troubles of his time on the violation of the spirit of true marriage, that is, true lay spirituality. He concludes that Do-wel is to do as the law teaches; Do-bet to love friend and foe; Do-best to give to and protect young and old and to heal and help. Then for good measure another phrasing—Do-wel is to dread God, Do-bet is to suffer, and Do-best, which arises from both, is to bring down the obstinate and wicked.

Langland does not here equate Do-bet with the clergy or widowhood, or Do-best with monks and virginity; but given such a well-known parallelism, it is hard to avoid the conclusion that it is clearly implied. These three grades also presuppose the Father, the Son (the supreme exemplar of love), and the Holy Ghost (the supreme exemplar of all spiritual activity). One must admit that Langland leaves a good deal to implication and that one must be cautious in drawing conclusions. Yet this passage is probably to be reckoned among the apocalyptic ones.[62]

Of the next, however, there can be no doubt, for Langland (X, 230 ff.) is as outspoken in his apocalyptic vision as Conscience was in Passus III. In the midst of the discussion of the three Do's by Clergy (spiritual learning and perhaps too the ideal clergy) occurs the most Joachite of the various definitions of these enigmatic grades of endeavor. For Langland strongly implies that Do-well—which "bilongeth to bileue"—is to be equated with the Father, Do-bet—"to suffre for thi soules helth"—with the Son, and Do-best—"to be bolde to blame the gylty"—with the Holy Ghost. Again Langland is not absolutely clear. The whole context, however, demands this interpretation.

Will tells Clergy that he was sent thither to learn what the three Do's are. Clergy begins by saying that although it is common enough to believe in the Trinity, its mysteries cannot really be explained by human reason. Then he proceeds to define the three Do's by relating the first to belief (faith by which the Old Testament saints were saved), the second to suffering (of which Christ is the greatest exemplar), and the third to boldness in attacking sin and evil (God in action).[63] These characterizing nouns are best explained by the individual members of the Trinity to which Clergy has just referred.

The discussion of Do-best (blaming the guilty) then broadens out into a discussion of the sins, especially the ecclesiastical sins, of the time. Clergy alludes to Hophni and Phinehas (I Samuel 4), the classic example of faithless and evil priests, and tells the correctors to correct themselves, quoting the well-known saw about the guardian dogs who will not bark—an interpretation of Isaiah 56:10 going back ultimately to Gregory the Great.[64] Clergy lashes out at sins of the religious, culminating in an attack on monks for neglecting their cloister, which is "hevene on this erthe." Finally the saviour king is brought in.

> Ac there shall come a kyng · and confesse ȝow religiouses,
> And bete ȝow, as the bible telleth · for brekynge of ȝowre reule,
> And amend monyales · monkes and chanouns
> And putten hem to her penaunce · *ad pristinum statum ire,*
> And barounes with erles bete hem · thorugh *beatus-virres* techynge,
> That here barnes claymen · and blame ȝow foule. . . .
>
> (X, 317–322)[65]

After the King effects a reformation of the monastic orders, Langland predicts that the friars will find a key to Constantine's coffers, whence they will have their "finding" (the basic necessities of life). It is with this hope, which is related intimately to his theory of poverty, that Langland will end the poem.[66] The Abbot of Abingdon will "have a knokke of a kynge · and incurable the wound," but before that king comes, Cain (Antichrist) will awake, but Do-wel will "dyngen hym adoune."

Here is the apocalyptic vision in all its glory. It represents essentially the implied outcome of the vision of Do-best at the end of the poem. The evil of the present, especially the sins of the clergy, is in fact proof of God's mysterious ways, for the contemporary crimes of the Church are only a sign of the coming great renewal and return to the pristine status of apostolic purity.

Anima's long speech on charity in Passus XV is also an apocalyptic picture of the times. She begins by rebuking poor Will for his boundless curiosity. It is a form of pride and is best illustrated in the learning of the friars who "moeuen materes inmesurables to tellen of the trinite" (v. 69) and only create doubt. Their energy could be better expended in good works. These preliminaries lead Anima into a long disquisition on the sins of the clergy and religious from whom charity has fled. The health of society under God depends on the spiritual health of the clergy, but alas they are sick, and poison from them spreads everywhere. Then finally she reaches the heart of her speech, which is a long discussion of charity and love (the section in C actually called by the scholastic phrase "distinctio caritatis"). But no one can know charity without Piers, for charity is spiritual recklessness which throws itself on God for its needs beyond the essentials.

Charity has been seen with kings occasionally and with saints but never with beggars (an aspersion on the friars). Long ago in St. Francis' time, he was once found in a friar's frock, but not very often since. He can come to the king's court if "the conseille is trewe / Ac if coueityse be of the conseille · he will nou3t come ther-inne" (vv. 230–231). This is obviously a reference to the earlier Lady Meed episode of the Visio. Then Anima goes on to praise the early monks who exemplified charity and faith in God, and did not care about their bodily wants. Riches are the cause of much trouble, and the heavenly and meteorological signs of the day show that all is not well and that the order of the cosmos is disturbed. Clerks, Anima continues, are ignorant, and even Mohammedans and Jews understand charity more than Christians do.

Only by emulating the Apostles, and acting as Anthony, Dominic, Francis, Benedict, and Bernard did, can we hope for salvation. Finally Anima returns to the sins of the Church and concludes with a long peroration on its evils. The Church has been corrupted by money and wealth, and Constantine's donation has been a curse. However, love and patience will win out.

There are elaborate parallels and metaphors underlying the Tree of Perfection in Passus XVI.[67] Briefly, this Tree of the three grades of perfection is a symbol of *Heilsgeschichte* and looks to the future, possibly even to an age of the Holy Ghost, but certainly to a profound reformation inspired by the Holy Ghost. This is the Tree of Perfection, growing on land owned by *Liberum Arbitrium*, free will,[68] which, flowering and fruiting through history, produces charity. The Joachite overtones in this image and the parallels between the grades of perfection and the Persons of the Trinity all suggest the apocalyptic vision.

Abraham, a herald, and Moses, a spy, symbolizing faith and hope, become the center of the action after the Tree scene—both forerunners of the knight (the Samaritan and Piers) who is to appear shortly and who is Christ and charity.[69] These figures prepare the way for the most famous passus in the Vita, the Harrowing of Hell (Passus XVIII), the culmination of Do-bet.

In the *heilsgeschichtliche* vision of the world there are various turning points or highlights—the Creation; the Fall; the first covenant; the Incarnation; the Passion of Christ; the Harrowing of Hell; Pentecost and the establishing of the new covenant with its instrument of realization, the new Church and New Law; the missionary period to save as many souls as possible; the period of Antichrist (or periods of Antichrists in some versions); the Millennium (optional), and the Resurrection and Final Judgment. Of these, Langland chooses to concentrate on only two, although of course the others (or most of them) are not ignored—the Harrowing and the Antichrist period,[70] and they are treated towards the end of the poem. It is proper to raise the question of why these two were especially stressed. The attacks of Antichrist as seen in Do-best deserve a separate development, for this section is the key to the poem and brings together most of the themes already discussed.[71] But it is clear that inasmuch as Langland felt that since it was this phase of *Heilsgeschichte* through which he and his contemporaries were passing, it would be only natural to concentrate on it. The period of Antichrist was timely and up to date; it was Langland's own period, and it is to be expected that his apocalyptic mind would treat it extensively and as a climax.

But the question remains: Why did Langland concentrate on the Harrowing of Hell rather than, say, the Incarnation or Passion in the culmination of the Do-bet section? This question cannot be definitively answered, but good reasons can be shown for this choice, reasons that make a possible and indeed likely answer.

First of all, the Harrowing of Hell is much more dramatic and fits Langland's over-all scheme better. His artistic progress by debate and conflict, a major formal element in the poem, can best be served by the tremendous dramatic power of setting Christ against Satan. This inherently dramatic clash is heightened by the introduction of the debate between the Four Daughters of God into the scene. The Harrowing is the resolution of their conflict and is presented through their eyes and partially by their reports. This conflict surrounding a conflict, unique in all of the literature on this theme as far as I know, is a brilliant literary tour de force and enables the Harrowing to be perfectly assimilated to Langland's artistic scheme. I cannot see how the Passion itself could have been presented in similar fashion. The victory of Christ comes later.

Second, the concentration on this scene enables Langland to solve a problem of meaning that has been haunting him throughout—how to reconcile love and charity (of which the Incarnation is the supreme example) with justice and reason. In the Harrowing of Hell, reason and love become one,[72] and life triumphs over death. The just who lived by faith are saved by the divine love; and the balance of forces is re-established. Christ's death is both an act of love and an act of justice; but until the just are freed in hell and Satan bound and Hell confined, His sacrifice is not complete. The liberation from hell is the final and necessary step in establishing divine justice. Without it, the scales could not be balanced; but when at last they are, cosmic and moral order are re-established.

Finally, the Harrowing is the only display of Christ in His majesty before the final scene of His return; it foreshadows the Last Judgment. But Langland cannot, rooted as he is in history and especially the history of his own time, portray that Last Judgment. The Harrowing of Hell is the next best thing and a reminder to his contemporaries of the last solemn event in *Heilsgeschichte*. And Do-best, which follows immediately on this culminating scene, begins with a long discussion of Christ the King.[73] The majesty of Christ, the ruler of the universe, and the royal, prophetic, and priestly power centering in him,[74] were first displayed to the Magi (XIX, 81 ff.); but in general He did not often exercise the rights of His divine and temporal kingship until His death. But then in the liberation of the Old Testament saints for the first time we see Him in human form ("in alle my3tes of man," XVIII, 253) exercising His royal power and prerogatives as He will exercise them at the end of time.[75]

Langland, who in Do-best takes up the question of Christ the King and whose emphasis on the Kingdom of God demanded it, gives us at the end of Do-bet the best example of Jesus' kingship that he possibly can—a vivid picture of His majesty destroying the power of Satan and releasing the souls of the just. All this is a foretaste of what is to come in history, and as Satan and his minions were overcome, so finally will Antichrist and all his hosts be subdued—when Conscience finds Piers Plowman, and when the religious orders will be able to take over their fundamental task of transforming the world. The Antichrist scene, which ends the poem on a realistic note, is the anti-vision to the vision of the Harrowing of Hell—the present reality as opposed to God's reality, but the vision of Do-bet foretells the true end to the Antichrist vision of Do-best. It is not necessary to tell the final outcome, and the poem can end in apparent but realistic gloom.[76] However, to thinkers like Langland, the very presence of Antichrist is actually evidence for the imminence of renewal and fundamentally a hopeful sign.

The ideal king who has appeared several times earlier in the poem, in the apocalyptic passages mentioned above, now disappears, and in his place appears Christ the King. The Harrowing of Hell scene is the culmination of these ideal king scenes earlier in the poem. Christ at the end is the ruler of the *regnum* and *sacerdotium*. In the last analysis he is king and spiritual shepherd, and deputies are no longer needed. Not the suffering Christ but the victorious Christ is Langland's theme, and his theology is a theology of glory.

In a profound sense, the powerful scene of the Harrowing of Hell is the true end of the poem, of the quest for Christian perfection which this poem exemplifies. The end of the quest cannot yet be, but it is coming—the end when the Church Militant finally becomes the Church Triumphant, when the true Church, which has been in the shadows, will emerge, when the persecutions of the just will be over, when love and complete faith in Christ will flourish. Langland, still in history, could not put the renewal of the Church, the supreme manifestation of Christ's power in history, at the end of his poem; but towards the end in Passus XVIII he could give the reader a reasonably good foretaste of what was to come because of what he believed had already come.

Piers Plowman is thus deeply immersed in the apocalyptic vision of the world and its history. The ideal Pope or spiritual leader is seen in Piers, who is a multidimensional symbol, and the saviour-emperor or ideal king appears in *propria persona* in several of the more notable apocalyptic passages. These two figures of late medieval apocalypticism—the angelic Pope and ideal king—are united in the figure of Christ in His majesty Who harrows hell and Whose power and dignity are carefully described in Do-best. Although Do-best as a section of the poem is under the aegis of the Holy Ghost, at the same time it concentrates on Jesus as Conqueror, King, and Judge. Individual perfection becomes in the last analysis a problem of social perfection, and social perfection to a convinced Christian means the Kingdom of God.

Piers Plowman begins with a vision of society, a fair field full of folk, and ends with a similar vision but with the forces of Antichrist unleashed against the true Church and the society of the elect, Unitas. In between comes first the problem of society and of the proper distribution of *bona temporalia*, then the desire for salvation, which is frustrated, and finally the journey of the self towards enlightenment in perfection, which leads inevitably back to society.

But the only answer is the help of God and His inscrutable will, which ordains in this time of *Heilsgeschichte* that sufferings be undergone so that the just and the merciful may finally come into their own and a great social renewal may take place on the road to the Kingdom of God. The final victory of the King of the Kingdom of God is foreshadowed in His victory over Satan as He harrows hell. This knowledge can comfort and strengthen man in the days of tribulation that have come upon him.

CHAPTER V

Piers Plowman and the Quest for Perfection

ALTHOUGH the Harrowing of Hell scene is in some ways the culmination of the poem—especially in the picture of Christ the King and Judge—yet in other ways the true climax comes where we might expect it: in the last two passus of the poem, the Vita of Do-best. As the title indicates, Langland portrays the search for the highest grade of perfection in the conclusion; it is concerned, not, as the two earlier sections of the Vita are, with the search for authority and the self or with the search for faith, hope, and charity in the events of Christ's life and death, but with the establishment of the Christian society in his own time and in the future. Here is not only the usual dialogue and interplay between Will and the world, although Will has become again more passive, but a kind of parallelism between the two: The decline of the world before its transformation is similar to the decline of Will as a person when old age approaches.

Just as Will is both historical and normative—he is both William Langland of London and every questing sinful man—so the settings and events of this final section—the attack of Antichrist on Unitas, the Church—are both particular and typical. The age of Antichrist is with us now, Langland is saying, but it is also a recurrent feature of *Heilsgeschichte*. The struggle with Antichrist is a perpetual element in eschatological history, but there are acute phases when he actually appears and causes an apocalyptic crisis. It is with such a crisis, because Langland thinks it is historically relevant to his age, that the author is primarily concerned. However, above and beyond the acute crisis of his time, the general notion is not forgotten. Until the Millennium, Antichrist—seductive and vicious social evil—will be the continuing problem for the true Church. This sense of time and of timelessness helps to explain some of the puzzling chronological leaps in this last section, a recurrent movement between past and present.

The last part of the poem is socially oriented in accordance with Langland's thought as it is here being interpreted. Here is no unitive stage of the mystic, no beatific vision, no absorption into the divine, but rather the fate of the social order, and above all of the Church, which is the ideal society of Christians, the mystical body of Christ. Divine judgment in the form of persecution descends upon the Church, as old age and impotence, which are God's judgment too, descend upon Will. The failure of Will in these passus is equated with the failure of society. Social forces, especially the sins of the religious and above all of the friars, make possible the assault and imminent success of Antichrist, just as natural forces within Will make possible the assault and imminent success of death.[1] Although Langland is not specific in either case, both death and Antichrist may be defeated; for God's justice and love are at work in time.

This portion of the poem, just after the Harrowing of Hell has been portrayed, opens with Will at home, awake from his last vision, dressing and going to Mass. In the midst of the service our somnivolent hero falls into his usual state and dreams his second-to-last vision. It is significant, and ironical too, that the body of Will should be in a real church while he dreams of the quest for the highest grade of perfection and of the preparations to defend the Church, which are the subjects of this vision. While the Church is blissfully unaware of the problem, preparations for its defense are being undertaken. Piers is working to reform the Church and redeem the remnant while the character who is visualizing him is sleeping through Mass.

Conscience, who has been a prominent character throughout, reappears and explains to Will that Piers, whom he has just seen "paynted al blody," is the human aspect of Christ.[2] It is now necessary that there be no further ambiguity about the highest, but not the only, meaning of Langland's key figure. Only the return of Piers, that is, the supreme model for human beings and the only possibility for their divinization, can make social revivification possible; for then the friars, as the type of all religious, can have their "fynding" and be reformed and pride will be destroyed.

Christ is the Christian conqueror, Conscience, using the imagery of the Christ-knight that has been basic to the preceding passus, tells Will. Christ is the king and warrior par excellence. Will immediately wishes to know why he is called Christ rather than Jesus, His right name.[3] This question enables Conscience to give a sermon, as Frank calls it,[4] on Jesus' name and life and their meaning (vv. 26–193). Christ is the King of Kings, and his whole life exemplifies the three Do's, that is, perfection.

The first part of her sermon (vv. 26–64) deals with the name Christ and its significance. Conscience begins by saying that one and the same person may be knight, king, and conqueror, and that these titles are desirable in increasing degree. The Jews who despised Jesus lost their status as free men, whereas every Christian becomes by virtue of his baptism a free man.[5] Yet the Jews called Him King; and when He ravished Hell, He became conqueror and awarded all his loyal lieges places in paradise. He protects mortals from the foul fiend and all evils; and He died on the Cross to teach man to love poverty and penance and to suffer woe willingly.[6] The name Christ means Conqueror.[7]

Christ the King is the theme of the last three passus of the poem; for both the Harrowing of Hell and the anticipated victory over Antichrist are supreme manifestations of His regality, and in terms of social judgment and rejuvenation in the apocalyptic vision of the world, this is the aspect of Christ that is most important.[8]

The second part of Conscience' sermon deals with Jesus' life from two points of view: as the exemplification of perfection, and as creating the means for all men to attain this perfection. To do this, Conscience divides Jesus' life into the three grades of perfection, the three Do's. But His role as King is never forgotten. The story of His birth, as Conscience tells it, emphasizes, not its humble surroundings nor the maid Mary, but the reverence paid to Him by angels and kings. Jesus, however, was at birth only a knight and not yet a king or conqueror. The Magi recognized what He was to be; and, in the three gifts, offered Him reason, justice, and mercy, the three attributes of a good ruler.[9]

Jesus then grew through the three stages of perfection. He assured his mother through the miracle of turning the water into the wine that His was truly a virgin birth, a very puzzling remark (vv. 116–117). This was his first step in Do-wel. Next he healed the sick and comforted the sorrowful and moved into Do-bet. Now He was King and was called the son of David. Then followed His death and resurrection.[10] He revealed Himself first to

Mary Magdalene, because what women know may not be kept secret, and then to the Apostles, even to doubting Thomas. Jesus now by these acts entered upon Do-best.

On departing, He left Piers the power of pardon, through which His mercy and forgiveness could reach all men provided they recognize the principle of *redde quod debes* (Matthew 18:28).[11] Whoever does not give satisfaction and make restitution will be punished on the Day of Judgment, when the good will go to the godhead and great joy, and the wicked will dwell in woe without end. According to Langland, the last words of Jesus to his Disciples ("And what persone payeth it nou3t · punysshen he thinketh, / and demen hem at domes daye · both quikke and ded; / The gode to the godhede · and to grete Ioye, / and wikke to wonye · in wo with-outen end" [XIX, 190–193]) are approximately the words of the Pardon of Piers, which he tore when it was impugned by the priest in Passus VII. Jesus is here guaranteeing the value of the torn pardon. In theology the priest may have been right, but I cannot see how, with these last words of Jesus in mind, Langland intended him to be so. These are the words of the Athanasian Creed dealing with the Last Judgment, and Langland interpreted them in terms of justice and *redde quod debes*.

It has often been said that the main point of *Piers* is love, and no one can deny the importance of this theme throughout the poem. It is less frequently, if ever, said that justice is Langland's theme, but it is certainly true that Langland values justice as much as love and, because of the crisis of his own time, probably rated it higher. Justice without love is deficient, but love without justice is equally deficient; and indeed without justice, there can be no society in which man can be perfected.[12]

Redde quod debes is a recurrent theme of the Do-best section, is the essence of Truth's pardon in Passus VII, and is a central point in the confession of Avarice in Passus V.[13] It needs, therefore, a further investigation, even beyond the excellent analysis of R. W. Frank, Jr.[14] I believe it is a basic feature of Langland's political and social thought and a key to one of the meanings of the poem.

The primary significance of the phrase "to return what one owes" is to be sought in the Sacrament of Penance. Restitution is a basic part of contrition, for to make restitution for sins committed against one's neighbors is evidence of contrition. To receive absolution one must be contrite, must confess to a priest, and must pay for one's sin; by punishment and by special obligations imposed, one "satisfies" God.[15] The complicated problems connected with restitution figured in much theological and legal thinking in the later Middle Ages, especially as it was frequently impossible to pay back the injured party.[16] Although restitution is, strictly speaking, evidence of contrition, it also presupposes satisfaction; and treatments of this part of penance, especially in the high Middle Ages, sometimes involve the problem of restitution. The details of these matters serve to show the practical importance of the matter in the later Middle Ages.

Duns Scotus, like practically all the scholastic thinkers, is very firm on this point. He writes, "Restitutio igitur semper est necessaria faciendo in facto, si possibile sit, vel in voto...."[17] Archbishop Fitzralph and Bishop Brinton come back to this subject again and again in their sermons.[18] And some made this point the gravamen of their attacks on confession to the friars. That friars who did not know the confessant were not strict in their demands for restitution is a recurrent complaint in the fourteenth century,[19] so much so that those scholastics like Bradwardine who stressed God's grace in salvation were offended. Restitution is part of natural law, and these men felt God's power was limited and the mystery of God's grace debased by those who emphasized this element in their writings and preachings on confession. Bradwardine in *De causa Dei*, for example, calls those who say restitution is necessary for absolution "Cainistae."[20]

But as Frank says, "To think of *redde quod debes* as nothing more than part of the sacrament of penance is to miss part of the poet's purpose in choosing the phrase."[21] This phrase would immediately suggest more to any literate medieval man, for it is frequently used in the definition of justice. Thomas Aquinas, for instance, defines justice formally as *reddere debitum unicuique*.[22] This of course is an old definition, although sometimes expressed in other words, going back to Plato, Aristotle, and the Bible, and universally repeated. With this definition of Thomas Aquinas and of others, however, the Platonic-Aristotelian notion of each receiving his due is assimilated to Christian morality. Christian perfection must in part, if not fundamentally, be social, and hence must involve action. Justice, as summed up in *redde quod debes*, is Christianity in action. As the German contemporary of Langland, Jordan of Saxony (or Quedlinburg), who died *c.* 1380, wrote, "*Redde quod debes*, because the completing (*complementum*) of Christianity consists in rendering each his due as the apostle in Romans XIII [:7] says: *Reddite omnibus debita*."[23]

By using this phrase, *redde quod debes*, in his parting speech (XIX, 182), Jesus is guaranteeing the torn pardon of Piers, and Langland is making his apocalyptic point about the Kingdom of God. Justice, while it may not be man's final need, is the crying need of his time. Until man's relations with man and to God are set on a just foundation and each *status* performs its proper functions, no true reformation of society is possible. Until we get such a reformation, love or grace cannot fully manifest itself. Justice involves the proper ordering of society so that the self may be properly ordered. A true spiritual and social balance has to be re-established—and God's grace must be at the beginning as at the end.

Now Pentecost arrives, for Easter has come and gone (Passus XVIII); and the poet describes how the Paraclete comes to Piers and his fellows (XIX, 196 ff.). The feast of the birth of the Church and unity is upon them.[24] The Church is Christian society and under the special protection of the Holy Ghost; and Pentecost celebrates its creation (and that of New Law), just as in Judaism it celebrated the giving of the Old Law. The Holy Ghost descends in lightning and fire,[25] and Will is afraid. Conscience tells Will that what he has seen is Grace, who comes from God. Greet and worship him, he orders Will. Then Grace goes with Piers and asks him and Conscience to summon society.

The Vita of Do-best is under the special protection of the Holy Ghost, just as the Vita of Do-bet is under the special protection of Christ and the Vita of Do-wel is more obliquely under the special protection of the Father. The emphasis here on Pentecost, the feast of the Holy Ghost and of the Church, His instrument for saving the world and leading it to perfection, makes this quite clear. The Holy Ghost is perhaps being used as the symbol, not of the Joachite age of the future, but merely of the perfecting of humanity. Nevertheless Langland conceived of this perfection in social terms and in terms of the defeat of Antichrist, which involved the future. The Holy Ghost then is the special patron of reform and reformation, and it is eminently fitting that He be the essential motivating force in this last section of the poem. Above and beyond all this, monastic philosophy puts a strong emphasis on the Holy Ghost as the protector of the monks and on their particular society as the ideal pattern and apex of the Church. In what follows it must be remembered that in spite of their differences and different contexts of meaning, grace, love, and the Holy Ghost are closely related concepts.[26]

The poem now turns to Grace's efforts to strengthen Piers and the society of which he is the head—the Church—before he departs; for bad days are coming (XIX, 210–330). Grace first says he will give his gifts, treasure to live by and weapons to fight with, to every sensible creature; for Antichrist is coming to grieve the whole world and trouble Conscience. Evil days (which Langland obviously means to be his own time) shall come with false prophets, flatterers, and deceivers who shall "be curatoures · ouer kynges and erlis, / And Pryde shal be pope · prynce of holycherche, / Coueytyse and Vnkyndenesse · cardinales hym to lede" (vv. 217–219). Here again, we find the emphasis on the corruption of Holy Church by its leaders. This is the great sin, the betrayal of God's trust by violating the great principle of justice—*redde quod debes.*

Grace goes on to give his gifts of different kinds, in different proportions, to different groups and men in society—gifts designed to make society work and to bring men to salvation—to priests, lawyers, merchants, laborers, artisans, astronomers, philosophers, righters of injustices, monks, and hermits.[27] He bids them work with each other and coordinate their efforts. They must love one another. Piers is to be Grace's agent and registrar "to receyue · *redde quod debes.*"

Piers is set up with a team of oxen and the imagery becomes agricultural. This whole scene parallels the earlier plowing of the half-acre in Passus VI. The allegory deepens. Piers as the terrestrial representative of God (Grace) is the plowman of the earth.[28] His plow is drawn by four oxen, the four Evangelists, with John the gentlest of all.[29] Behind, four bullocks, the four chief Western Fathers, Jerome, Augustine, Ambrose, and Gregory, were to harrow what the oxen plowed, with two harrows, the Old and New Testaments. Piers was given four kinds of seeds, the four cardinal virtues, to sow in man's soul. Then Grace instructs Piers to build a barn to store the crops, but at Piers' request builds it himself with the Cross and the blood that Christ shed thereon. The building is to be called Unitas, or Holy Church. On his departure, Grace gives Piers a cart called Christendom with two horses, Contrition and Confession, and a hayward, Priesthood. Piers himself presumably at this point stands for Satisfaction, the final part of the Sacrament of Penance, for he is to receive *redde quod debes*, as related above (v. 254).

Most puzzling in this episode is the emphasis on the cardinal virtues, which are normally part of natural law and hence not particularly or uniquely Christian. It is true that Langland (vv. 307–308) speaks of love growing from the four virtues to destroy the weeds of vice; but grace, which is of the supernatural order, would not ordinarily be granting these natural virtues. But the cardinal virtues are essentially the social virtues. After all, it is with society—the ideal society of all Christians—that Langland is concerned in this final apocalyptic section; and these virtues are the ones that need to be cultivated in the reformation of society. Besides, the cardinal virtues are not necessarily completely natural. They can be acquired naturally through human effort, but they may also be infused by God. There is no doubt that Langland is here thinking of the infused cardinal virtues,[30] but even so one would expect the theological virtues or the Gifts to be the special donation of the Holy Ghost. Yet this would be to misunderstand Langland's apocalyptic orientation. The theological virtues have already been stressed in Do-bet, wherein man's relation to Christ the King has been dealt with. Now at the end, the poem returns to society again and to the kingdom of the just.

The remainder of Passus XIX, 331–479, deals with the preparations for an attack by Pride (or Antichrist) and his minions on the barn, Unitas, which Piers and Grace have established. Piers has gone off to plow while Conscience and Kind Wit attempt to order the defense, but brewers, vicars, lords, and kings, representatives of the three basic social classes or *status*, are all unwilling to enter Unity and submit to Conscience or Kind Wit; or if they are willing to do so, they misunderstand what is required of them and abuse and violate the cardinal virtues. All social classes are corrupt, but many Christians do penance and more or less join the beleaguered Unitas. A good deal of this last part of the passus is again devoted to the sins of the clergy, especially the cardinals and the Pope, who "sendeth hem that sleeth suche as he shulde save" (v. 427)[31] and who "pileth holykirke" (v. 439). The King is an anti-king, the antithesis of the *rex justus*, and sets himself up as above the law or as the law itself. Will awakes.

The same vision is continued in the last passus (XX) of the poem, but there is first, before Will falls asleep again, an interlude of extraordinary interest. The betrayal of trust, on the part of all groups in society, but above all by the leaders of the Church, has been the cardinal sin of society; and the only way to remedy it is to do just the opposite—throw oneself on God completely. Live without solicitude as Adam and Eve did and return to paradise.[32] To live thus, however, one must give up all superfluity. But need is the determinant of superfluity, the crucial issue in man's humanity to man. Need at this point, then, appropriately appears to Will and reproaches him for having doubts about poverty and for not completely trusting in God, and praises the virtue of temperance over all the other cardinal virtues. One must recognize legitimate need so as to be free for spiritual activity. True temperance and moderation create the conditions for true perfection.

Langland is here carrying out the parallel between Will and society that has previously been suggested. Just as contemporary society has violated order and natural limit, so Will himself has neglected temperance, of which need is the regulating principle. Need attempts to bring to the stumbling hero of the poem a sense of order which can be determined only by need.

To our eyes Langland here seems to be trying to reconcile the irreconcilable—to justify poverty in terms of temperance.[33] Man throws himself on God and becomes needy without solicitude for worldly cares, and at the same time he is manifesting the virtues of temperance. In line 35, Need is actually equated with temperance, as the whole structure of the argument shows. Need argues that temperance or the "spirit of temperance" is superior to the other virtues. Beginning at line 25, he takes up each of the other cardinal virtues and evaluates them, showing their weak aspects. Fortitude violates measure, justice is subject to popular pressures, and prudence fails because of miscalculation. But need (which must mean temperance, as the context shows) is always humble and avoids riches, as Jesus Himself did when he took on human flesh.

However, to medieval thinking neither poverty nor virginity violated the principle of the mean or of temperance. Thomas Aquinas specifically discusses this matter in connection with poverty where he says that "the mean of virtue is taken according to right reason, not according to the quantity of a thing. . . . It would, however, be against right reason to throw away all one's possessions through intemperance, or without any useful purpose; whereas it is in accordance with right reason to renounce wealth in order to devote oneself to the contemplation of wisdom. . . . Much more therefore is it according to right reason for a man to renounce all he has, in order perfectly to follow Christ."[34]

Need argues that a man in true need is justified in getting food and clothing in any way. This too is a scholastic commonplace. Thomas argues that it is lawful to steal in extreme need; and Fitzralph in a sermon summarized by Aubrey Gwynn tells us that in his days in Paris, a beggar, if caught in the act of stealing, would be hanged if he had money in his pockets, but if penniless, would be allowed to go free.[35] One then can throw one's self on God by giving up all care; and even by natural law, let alone God's grace, be assured of existence. Need concludes his address by saying to Will

> For-thi be nouȝte abasshed · to bydde and to be nedy;
> Syth he that wrouȝte all the worlde · was wilfullich nedy,
> Ne neuer none so nedy · ne pouerere deyde"
>
> (XX, 47–49)

Will then falls asleep and dreams his last dream.

In this section the role given to temperance is most curious and, as far as I know, unique. Perhaps Need is merely boosting himself in saying temperance is the highest of all the cardinal virtues. I think not, however, for temperance and its related concept of superfluity is one of the basic themes of the poem. The fact that it is Need who appears at this critical juncture is also significant. Order and balance, moderation and measure, the elimination of superfluity, and humility, poverty, and spiritual chastity—these are the virtues on which monastic philosophy and Langland put stress.

In view of all this, I cannot think Need is ironically (from Langland's point of view) merely praising himself.

Traditionally, either prudence or justice takes pre-eminence among the cardinal virtues. Thomas specifically denies that temperance is the greatest of the cardinal virtues; and in fact he makes it the lowest, especially since, unlike justice and fortitude, it concerns the good merely of the individual rather than of the many. Prudence is highest, for it is partly an intellectual virtue. Thomas admits without going into details that in some respects, because of its greater generality, temperance may be greater than fortitude and justice; but even in this concession he does not place temperance above prudence. In this tendency to rate temperance as a lesser cardinal virtue, Thomas is following tradition, yet it is significant that he felt that this was a proposition to refute.[36] Among some thinkers at least, although who they are I have not been able to discover precisely, temperance must have been given absolute pre-eminence among the cardinal virtues.

The popular *Moralium dogma philosophorum* of the twelfth century rates the virtues in the following descending order of merit: prudence (because it pertains to *cognitio*), temperance (because it pertains to self and others, the family, and the state), justice, and fortitude.[37] Possibly Thomas Aquinas had in mind writers such as the author of the *Moralium*, for he is principally concerned with vindicating fortitude and justice over temperance, rather than prudence over temperance. Note, too, the much broader definition of temperance that the composer of the *Moralium* makes, as compared to the narrower one in which Thomas limits temperance to the self. It is not a social virtue to the latter.

The *Moralium dogma philosophorum* is echoing an older tradition going back to classical times which, if it does not put temperance over justice, at least stresses this virtue highly. In Cicero's *De officiis*, temperance embraces the other three virtues and is highly praised.[38]

As Arnold Stein points out, temperance and justice are closely linked, and temperance was often assumed to comprehend justice. Temperance appealed to Cicero, for it enabled him to bring together both individual virtues, such as modesty and gravity and self-restraint, and social virtues, such as justice and harmony—and perhaps also a universe with limits and boundaries.[39]

Although I cannot trace the steps from Cicero to Langland, we do have the evidence of the *Moralium* as a signpost by the road; it is this pre-scholastic and monastic concept of temperance that seems to be in Langland's mind as he praises temperance so highly. Thomas and other scholastics demoted temperance largely because they did not include its social aspects in its definition, thus separating it strictly from justice.

There are, however, several other approaches to this problem. Thomas and all the scholastics following Aristotle emphasized that virtue is a mean between two extremes. Yet many of them, including Thomas, did not seem to associate temperance, which of all the virtues comes closest to the quality displayed in choosing the mean, with the measure used in exercising all virtues.[40]

Yet in practice Thomas does seem to conceive of temperance as measure and moderation in all things. In his discussion of temperance in the *Summa* at one point at least, he recognizes two meanings for temperance: a general sense affecting all virtues and a particular sense controlling the appetite to pleasure.[41] In general Thomas takes it in the latter sense, but the older tradition, which persisted into the Renaissance, emphasized its broader and more noble sense.

The last part of the Middle English *Book of Vices and Virtues,* a fourteenth-century translation of Friar Lorens d'Orléans' *Somme le Roi* of 1279, is, for instance, devoted to the "vertue of attemperaunce and sobernesse," which the highest gift of the Holy Ghost, Wisdom, sets in the hearts of his devotees. Here temperance is the fruit of the highest gift of God, and its various degrees are carefully presented. Finally the author tells us that "alle vertues ben braunches of this" and that its practice gives us unity with and rest in God, "wherefore sche [the heart] fyndes al here comfort and her ioye and hire delit þat passeþ all oþer delit."[42] Such is Langland's view, though he places temperance among the cardinal virtues, for it is of them and yet beyond them—the principle underlying all virtue. In I, 158, Langland puts into the mouth of Lady Holy Church the remark that love itself is a mean between heaven and earth. The term "mean" probably signifies both a bridge or channel and a middle point.

This subject must be looked upon from still another position which will bring us closer to monastic philosophy. One of the basic notions of metaphysical perfection was based upon the verse in Wisdom 11:21 [20], which stated that God created the world according to measure, number, and weight. In the Middle Ages these terms were widely used, though variously interpreted, to justify the conception of an ordered and perfect universe. They could easily be translated into Greek, especially Aristotelian, philosophical categories. The limited is the knowable and the perfect.[43] A perfect universe demands measure and limits—in the natural, social, and personal spheres. This particular concept, especially the idea of perfection involved, created difficulties, since an infinite God without any limits, except for a few commonsense ones, had to be fitted into the scheme.

Various attempts are made to equate these three principles with the Persons of the Trinity, an undertaking that led to difficulties. Albertus Magnus wrestles with these problems manfully in his *De bono* and tries to solve the problem by showing all three principles are the same.[44] In Article 3 of the same *questio*, Albertus points out that each of these qualities, *numerus*, *pondus*, and *mensura*, from different aspects refers to each of the three Persons or at least to two of them. *Mensura*, for instance, insofar as it means limitability and continence, refers to the Holy Ghost and, insofar as it means the end of things by species, refers to the Son.[45] It is significant that Albertus connects *mensura* with the Holy Ghost, who is the guiding Person of Do-best.

Thus temperance is a complex term embracing ideas belonging to various orders of thought and has both a narrow and a broad meaning. In its broad sense it comes close to being the generic term for the basic quality of all virtue and indeed of the whole order of the universe.

Even in its narrow sense, it embraces many virtues. From Philo[46] on, it especially referred to the control of the concupiscent part of the soul. As Scotus says, "proprius habitus concupiscibilis est temperantia," and it pertains especially to the control of appetite[47] in the scholastic sense of the term. *Cupiditas*, which is perverted love, is then controlled and suppressed by the virtue (or *habitus*) of temperance. When temperance is lacking, self-control is lacking, and the world and its pleasures dominate the soul of man.

A glance over the *questiones* devoted to temperance in Thomas' *Summa* discloses the following virtues treated as parts of this virtue: honesty, abstinence, fasting, sobriety, chastity, virginity, sexual continence, clemency and meekness, modesty, humility, and studiousness. To his master Albertus Magnus, as *De bono* shows, continence, chastity, clemency, and modesty are the main sub-divisions of temperance. Duns Scotus follows the same general pattern, although he stresses, more than most scholastics, humility as a part of temperance.[48]

These are the virtues of *ascesis*, of self-control, which is the first stage of the journey to perfection and which creates the possibility for the return to paradise or deification. They are the supreme monastic virtues that enable man to be in but not of the world. These are the virtues stressed in the Benedictine Rule and by all commentators on it. The great monastic writers, such as Bede, Peter Damian, and Bernard, concentrate their efforts on elucidating and propagating these virtues, for they will lead to charity and love, the crown of all—when we love only God and ourselves because of Him.

In Do-wel patient poverty is the most desirable virtue, and in Do-bet, in the passion and Harrowing of Hell part, patience[49] was united with majesty and power in Christ, and now in Do-best temperance in the broadest sense of the word, is offered as the root of all virtue, of an ordered society, and of an ordered universe. Patience or humility is the first step towards perfection. "De patientia perfectio nascitur. . . . Patientia est radix & custos omnium virtutum."[50] Humility bears the tribulations of the world and enables one to throw oneself on God completely. "Because thou hast kept the word of my patience, I also will keep thee from the hour of temptation, which shall come upon all the world, to try them that dwell upon the earth."[51]

Humility is one of the few virtues to get a chapter to itself (VII) in the Benedictine Rule, and here Benedict distinguishes twelve grades of this virtue. When the monk has climbed the twelve steps of the ladder of humility, he finally comes to the love of God which drives out all fear. Joachim, like all good monks, stresses humility "qui vincit omnia."[52] In fact "humble" is the equivalent of "spiritual" for him.

Bernard, too, wrote one of his most famous works taking his departure from this chapter, the *De gradibus humilitatis et superbiae*. In humbling himself, man raises himself towards God.

Humility leads to true knowledge of oneself, which in turn enables human beings to discover God in themselves.[53] Humility is in the last analysis love, for it means submission to the will of God. Finally Christ in His human life from His birth to His death taught us above all, humility; and the Incarnation itself is the supreme manifestation of humility.[54]

Since Old Testament times, humility has also always been linked with poverty. One can be truly humble only if one is not involved in the riches and honors of the world. This point too is stressed by Benedict and Bernard.

Benedict and commentators on Western cenobitical life always emphasized the virtue of moderation inherent in the Western rules,[55] moderation in terms of the extremes of asceticism and worldly joy. To an outsider this moderation could also appear as sheer extremism. From the point of view of one dedicated to Christ and God, throwing oneself on God, giving up the world, and entering a round of prayer, meditation, and work were indeed moderation itself. Thus, monastic vows are comprised in temperance and humility.

The opposite of humility (or patience or temperance, in Langland's usage) is pride, as the title of Bernard's work indicates. Thus it is only natural that Antichrist in *Piers* be known by his name of Pride. Humility—or Langland's temperance—is the only way to defeat this most mighty of all foes. Temperance in its manifold meanings is the only answer to Antichrist, for it is the soil of all virtues and above all of humility, which is the specific antidote to pride, the first of the sins. As Thomas puts it, humility is the "spiritualis aedificis fundamentum."[56]

Temperance is thus the capital social virtue, the key to the just society and the ordered universe. It leads the individual to charity; in all its forms it guides society to a right functioning of its parts; and it imposes on the universe its proper limits. In relation to temporal goods, which it is the function of secular society to produce, the guide to action is temperance which regulates superfluity; for all that is superfluous should be given to the poor. The doctrine of superfluity is thus also connected with temperance and need. "It must needs be that man's good in respect to them [earthly goods] consists in a certain measure";[57] and beyond this measure of need all superfluous things must be given to the poor.

Measure and temperance are necessary to the determination of superfluity, which establishes in practice what charity in action must be. The problem of what is superfluous in each case, and for each status, occupied and still occupies Roman Catholic thinkers.[58] But there is no question as to the principle. Following Jesus' direct commandment in the matter is a clear obligation.

At the beginning of the poem, Holy Church stresses temperance and moderation in worldly goods, and here at the end Need is making the same point to the same man, Will, but with more personal force. The highest form of temperance is to throw oneself utterly on God. Here all except mere sustenance and clothing would be superfluous, and one would indeed be following Christ.

This point has not been made so clearly before in B, although there are references to absolute trust in God.[59] In C, however, probably after Langland had written the Do-best portion of B, Reckless in all his ambiguity becomes a chief character in Do-wel, which primarily has to do with the self—as represented by Will, who is both Langland and Everyman. Donaldson has called attention to this change in C.[60] In particular he analyzes Reckless' long speech to Clergy (XIII, 88—XIV, 128) which extols patience and poverty. "Indeed," Donaldson writes, "the passage would serve as a guide book for any one who is looking for authority to cast his burdens upon the Lord and to renounce all anxiety for the affairs of this world." Note too, for this is one of Langland's main points, that it is Clergy (spiritual learning and the clergy) who is the recipient of this harangue. The clergy, above all the friars, must rethink their conception of superfluity and re-establish their trust in God. They must obtain their "finding," their minimum for livelihood, and be satisfied.

Langland is not arguing that all should throw themselves utterly on God, but only those who would obtain perfection in their *status*. For the clergy, the guardians of Unitas, this task is absolutely necessary, beginning with Will himself as Langland, for the shepherds must set the example. Then all *status* can revaluate their own need, with an attendant awareness of superfluity. Conscience must be man's guide in this task for social regeneration. Conscience will tell man what his need really is, and then he may be able to reorder his life under the new economy, the signs of the coming of which may be seen in the attacks of Antichrist.

Nor was Langland alone in this attitude in his century. In the pseudo-Occamite *Dialogus inter militem et clericum,* translated by John Trevisa towards the end of the century, the very same point is made about the clergy.[61] "And all the ouerplus besyde clothe and foode, ye [clergy] ought to spende in dedes of mercye & pitie, as on poore people, that haue nede and on suche as be sycke and diseased, and opressed with misery." Fitzralph makes approximately the same point about the friars, who, he insists, must make restitution for their surplus of goods and privileges gained unjustly from various Popes. Wyclif makes this point again and again. Bishops should give their superfluity to the poor.[62] Neglect of the concept of superfluity, especially among the clergy, has resulted in the present state of injustice.

To return to the text, the last passus reveals that after Need's speech, Will falls asleep again and dreams his last apocalyptic vision. Antichrist comes and overturns the crop Piers planted and makes False grow and increases man's needs (v. 54). Guile grows in place of truth. Antichrist is welcomed by friars and religious who ring bells and come forth to him. Only fools do not join the merry throng. They would rather die than live any longer since justice ("leute") is so flouted. These saintly fools (of whom Will is in part one) defy Antichrist and his followers and curse the kings who comforted them. Pride (who is now Antichrist's chief lieutenant, not Antichrist himself), ordered by a sensual lord,[63] raises Antichrist's standard, and Antichrist's army moves against Conscience. The latter calls upon his fools[64] to withdraw into Unity, Holy Church, and resist until Nature ("kynde") comes and defends them all for the love of Piers the Plowman.

Nature hears Conscience and comes from the planets, sending down diseases upon the people and frightening especially the sensual lord. Age and Death move in, and Nature herself appears. All classes fall before Death (vv. 99–104).[65]

Nature and his aide-de-camp, Death, leave off at Conscience' bidding. But Fortune flatters the few who are alive and sends Lechery among them. They gather together again and make preparation for battle against Unity. Avarice leaps into the fray and sends Simony to corrupt the courts and destroy justice and true matrimony.[66] Conscience admires Avarice's assiduity and zeal and wishes he were a Christian. Life[67] sets himself up as an ally of

Pride and takes a leman Fortune and begets Sloth, who grows fast and marries Despair. Life and Age fight, and Life flees to Physic, who gives him a glass hood (that is, protection of no use). He returns to fight and soon sees it is useless. He flees to Revel, while Age suddenly pursues Will. Age passes over Will's head, making him bald. When Will rebukes him, he hits him over the ear, making him deaf, and knocks out his teeth. Then he assails him with gout and sexual impotence, the latter to the intense dislike of Will's wife.

In despair, Will sees Death approach and appeals to Nature for help. She advises him to enter Unity. Will then asks what "craft is best to lerne" (v. 206) and is told to "lerne to love." How can I feed and clothe myself, he asks. Nature tells him that if he truly loves he will lack nothing. So Will goes through Contrition and Confession and comes to Unity[68] to witness the attack of the seven giants (seven cardinal sins) on the building guarded by Conscience. The interchange between Nature and Will is highly reminiscent of part of the dialogue between Holy Church and Will in Passus I; and Nature's answer to Will's question is approximately the same as Lady Holy Church's.

The role of Nature in this scene needs further elucidation. The drive towards perfection is aided by Nature herself, for she punishes those who are attacking Unitas. The stars, in a very literal sense, are fighting for the triumph of the true Church and the elect who gather under Conscience's banner. Medieval man believed that there were compelling forces making for perfection and righteousness, not only within the individual and society but also in nature. Nature also produces signs as a warning to sinners and as encouragement to the just. Whether these signs and afflictions are special effects by God through nature, or are of internal origin as secondary causes, is not told. Langland could have believed both or either. In any case the hierarchical organization of nature is in harmony with itself, and the various levels of being reinforce each other. Nature has its norms which should not be violated.

The story of the battle between the soldiers of Christ and of Antichrist continues as the poem moves towards its end. There is now a heightened sense of urgency and of desperation, which is conveyed by the rapidity of the action and the tenseness of the alliterative meter. Contemporary allusions may be interspersed here, as in the reference to the "mansed preste of the marche of Yrlonde" (v. 220),[69] since Langland is strongly concerned with his own time. The scene narrows to the beleaguered community, assailed both from without and from within. The cardinal social sin of his own time—the betrayal of their trust by the clergy—becomes the central point of weakness. Proud priests join with Avarice in the attack. Conscience, in despair, calls on the clergy for help. Only the friars, whom Conscience distrusts, answer his call. Need appears again and warns him against them, ironically telling him to let them beg. They have no patrimony and will do anything for money, for begging corrupts the spirit.

Conscience, laughing at Need's speech, calls the mendicants in but warns them not to be envious but to live according to their rule. He guarantees them a sufficiency to live by, provided they leave logic and learn to love. If you wish to have the cure of souls, Conscience says, you must not violate the basic principles of nature —that God made all things in measure and set limits to everything in creation. Your great sin is that you violate the order of the universe by your tendency to multiply. Except for the friars, all other institutions, both secular and religious, set a limit to themselves—courts, soldiers, monks, and nuns. God numbered the stars and gave them names; but the friars "wexeth out of noumbre" (v. 268). Heaven has an exact number; only hell is numberless.[70]

The friars, by their insatiable greed, preach communism[71] and, by giving easy penance and ignoring restitution, destroy the Sacrament of Penance. They corrupt society. Their overweening cupidity and intemperance destroy all that is good and holy, and annihilate moderation and balance both in the world and in society. They violate the virtue of temperance as Langland conceives that quality.

The friars, who should be setting an example on the highest level of perfection, as their status as religious demands, are the worst sinners of all, violating both the natural and the social order. That the perfect has limits and is understandable, that is, rational, is a commonplace of Greek philosophy, as seen in Aristotle and Plotinus and probably in Plato.[72] Like so many classical concepts, this principle of limit, as one may call it, was a Christianized or at least made a presupposition of Christian thinking from earliest time, in spite of some of the logical difficulties it created in dealing with God. Origen, for instance, writes "quia ubi finis non est, nec comprehensio illa nec circumscriptio esse potest."[73]

We find the same principle in the Pseudo-Dionysius and Augustine.[74] John of Salisbury in the twelfth century writes, "All things other than God are finite. Every substance is subject to number because it has just so many, and no more accidents. Every accident and every form is likewise subject to number, although in this case because of the singular nature of its subject, rather than a participation of accidents or forms. Everything also has its own weight. . . ."[75] The same idea occurs again and again in the writings of the great scholastics.

In the fourteenth century in England, at least, this metaphysical principle was taken out of its proper context and unfairly applied to the phenomenal growth of the friars. Archbishop Fitzralph may have been the originator of this application, for he is the first apparently to use it against them. The Trevisa translation of his sermon *Defensio curatorum* says, "þe philosofer in his secunde book *de anima* seiþ þat þe worst þat is in kynde is passyng resoun of gretenesse & of encresinge, þanne it folewiþ þat þei holdiþ nouȝt þe lawe of kynde but forsakiþ hit, for þei [the friars] wexiþ grete & encresiþ wiþ-oute eny ende. Also Holy Writ techiþ vs, Sapiencie XI C⁰, þat God made & ordeyned al in mesure, noumbre, & wiȝt."[76] We also find this complaint in Wyclif, who in *De apostasia*, says the friars are "sine numero limitato."[77] This argument was apparently a common weapon in the arsenal of those opposed to the friars. Yet in Fitzralph and Wyclif it is one of many points to be scored and does not seem to be central to their case.

In Langland it is a different matter. The violation of nature's order on the part of the friars is a serious charge. It is prominently developed in his picture of his times—the age of Antichrist—and it is part of his whole argument on the virtue of temperance. Metaphysical limitation is another facet of this virtue, which to Langland is central in the reform of the world. Temperance is violated by men and especially clerics and religious, not only in the moral realm but also in the cosmological realm. The excesses of mankind, especially those of the friars, who should be in the vanguard along with the monks in the quest for perfection, tend to destroy the very basis of intellectual and ontological existence.

They are turning the world into an undifferentiated hell which is the model for nothingness and infinite confusion.

The friars apparently give up their attempt to enter Unitas, except for one Flatterer who worms his way in, past Peace the porter, on the pretense of shriving the sick. Even Contrition has become sick. Conscience welcomes Flatterer and asks him to salve his cousin Contrition. Friar Flatterer's confession is as corrupt as can be and so beguiles Contrition that he forgets to cry and weep. The friar goes among the besieged and hands out absolution right and left.

The attack is renewed, led by Sloth and Pride. Conscience cries again for help from Clergy and Contrition. Peace tells him that Contrition and many others "lith and dremeth" (v. 376) all bemused by the friar. In despair, Conscience says that he will become a pilgrim to seek Piers, who can destroy pride and enable the friars to have "a fyndyng that for nede flateren" (v. 381). May Nature avenge me, he cries, and send me good luck until I have Piers Plowman. He calls aloud after grace until Will awakes.

Conscience, like Will at the beginning of the poem or the repentant sinners in Passus V (vv. 517–519), now sets out on a pilgrimage. He is superior to the hero, as he was then, only insofar as he knows whom he must seek—Piers—and what the world needs—the reform of the friars. The repentant sinners then gave up their desire to go on a pilgrimage at Truth's urging, probably because they were not really ready, an unreadiness the sequel (Passus VII) fully confirms.[78] The end of the poem comes around to the beginning, and the quest must go on.

Throughout these last two passus, grace and the Holy Ghost have been considered identical, a somewhat unusual but not unknown conjunction theologically speaking. Langland, however, equates grace with the Holy Ghost, just as he had earlier equated freewill with the third Person of the Trinity.[79] Conscience at the end is crying aloud for Grace, presumably the Holy Ghost who built Unitas for him, to defeat Antichrist.

Normally, too, it is Christ in His second coming who will defeat the final Antichrist; but for lesser Antichrists, as Pride here seems to be, there appears to be no regular pattern. The fact that Conscience cries after the Holy Ghost, or seems to, suggests again a Joachite point—that the new age will be that of the Holy Ghost.

But as always with Langland, the matter is not clear-cut, and one can argue that he is using grace in its ordinary sense here, as may well be.[80]

The meaning of the quest for Piers, the ideal or angelic Pope or, by extension, the ideal clergyman or religious, the plower of souls and Christ himself, seems clear enough;[81] for throughout, the corruption of the best, or those in the highest *status*, through pride, the sin of excess self-love and intemperance, has been Langland's chief complaint. Piers is to be the model for the reconstitution of society; and a quest for him seems natural. But the introduction of the friars may seem anticlimactic, especially as all Conscience asks for is that they may have "a fyndyng" (sufficient provisions for life).

By exploring the meaning of this request a little further—at the cost of some repetition—I shall show the importance of this matter to Langland; and in so doing I shall bring together the main points of my argument.

Langland, in his prayer for a "finding" for the friars, is adopting the same point that the monk of Bury St. Edmunds makes in his question on mendicancy and endowment. If a man seeking perfection does not take care of his minimum needs, he will be forced, out of solicitude, to use other methods, such as mendicancy, which lead to all kinds of abuses. Poverty properly defined entails a man's having sufficient to live on obtained by labor with the hands. "Poverty which has the necessaries of life, not desiring any other things, it seems, is more perfect."[82] This is one reason why Need is such an important figure in the last passus. The recognition of legitimate need on the part of the friars is the first step in the reform of the friars. If they abandon their erroneous concept of poverty and realize that the quest for perfection requires a minimum of food and clothing, which can be obtained by legitimate labor, they can then give up their concern for wealth, with the inevitable corruption that attends upon it, and truly become, as their status on the highest level as religious demands, genuine seekers for perfection. They would then presumably set an example for all other *status* and lead the way to a regeneration of society. By going further and suggesting a Joachite age of the monks in Langland's mind, one may say that the future belongs to them and to all religious orders dedicated to the quest for perfection, and that the age of the Holy Ghost will be ushered in. This last point goes beyond the clear evidence, but it is a possibility.

Need, however, is to be taken not only in the sense of a recognition of the necessity for elementary sustenance but in the sense of the regulating principle of justice and harmony in society. Under Christ, temperance is the virtue the world needs most of all.

In the last analysis, the quest of Conscience for Piers and Grace, who are of course closely connected, is the quest for paradise and deification, which is the ultimate purpose of the human quest for perfection. Just as Piers begins as a plowman and ends as the Christ-man, man may become through imitation of him like God; and it is by pilgrimage that all mankind, as a holy society, the Church, must take its way to paradise. In a sense all must become monks, even if formally a distinction must be made between the various *status* in society. Langland was not ready to think primarily in individualistic terms, as Thomas à Kempis was. Perfection involves the lifting of society into a new phase or economy.

Piers Plowman is a dialogic and dialectical poem, and the quest for perfection gives the work its unity and movement. Since the quest for perfection is a perpetual struggle with opposites in order to transcend them, the form of a *conflictus* best expresses the significant content of that search. The dialogue of Will with his interlocutors, and the conflicts he sees, reflect the spiritual and material aspects of the journey of the soul and society to Christian perfection.

This form, which is one of the several genres Langland is trying to combine in *Piers*, was not of course invented by the author, but it is admirable for his purposes. The fundamental dualisms of life in all periods make the idea of dramatic clash appealing. In medieval times this conflict, which was conceived in terms of the opposition of certain basic ideas dear to the medieval Christian heart, appears in the formal dress of the *conflictus* or debate, in which two abstractions meet headlong, usually verbally rather than physically. The clash between reason and will, between God and the devil, between good and evil, could be dramatized in this literary form without sacrificing the intellectual clarity that medieval man desired. Rationality could be honored even in the fundamental tensions of medieval life. This too is a kind of temperance and moderation.

Langland in choosing this form was paying tribute to the facts of life as he saw them. But to him the conflict exists only in order to progress to perfection, as a dialectical movement towards deification; hence the *conflictus* as used by Langland is not static but dynamic. The passage, the pilgrimage, the quest, moves by means of the conflict. Often the hero is instructed and helped by authority. Will, the hero, is a pilgrim; the evil and weak characters in the action are at various times pilgrims, and Conscience becomes at the end a pilgrim with a goal that sets him apart from the others. Hence the debate is combined with the pilgrimage, which is normally part of allegorical vision narrative.

The need for the allegorical romance genre grows naturally out of the idea of clash and debate conceived as steps in a quest or pilgrimage. A poem with a central theme of the quest for Christian perfection would need to be cast in narrative form unless it were to be a mere treatise on the subject. John Lawlor puts it very well when he writes, "Langland's poem thus succeeds in communicating, not a cumulative effect of discursive thinking, but the very pressure of experience itself."[83] Life is a pilgrimage and should be a quest for perfection, and Langland wishes his reader to sense deeply just what all that means in terms of a historical and suprahistorical figure, Will, who is both William Langland of Malvern Hills and London and every Christian man.

But no quest for perfection can mean anything unless it centers on the hindrances to perfection in this world, and hence the large and important element of satire in the poem. The hero is seeking for perfection and does not know how it may be found. He is in very essence a child of God who is hoping for enlightenment—an *ingénu*. Hence this is the reason why Langland also thought of his poem as partly an encyclopedic satire. In this genre the innocence of the hero provides the motive force for the action and satire. It is an ideal medium both for presenting the dilemma of Will and for criticizing the cupidity and sins of his age.

Thus in order to dramatize his complex theme, with its mixture of quest, debate, and satire, Langland found himself, so to speak, in the midst of three literary genres that were well established before his time; and from its conventions he attempted to weave together a unified work of art, a work that would reveal his basic perplexities, dramatize and objectify them. He was perhaps attempting too much, and this alliance was not always successful. And beyond all this hovers the apocalyptic urgency that must have been the driving force in his character. If what he was trying to do can be seen, one can come closer to both the glories and the weaknesses of *Piers*.

The religious genres in the background of *Piers* are due, I think, to Langland's own experiences and life. Satire was associated with the sermon and the complaint, and in writing satirical poetry Langland, as a clerk in minor orders, could hardly fail to put his strictures in such a way as to suggest them. The commentary arises out of his intense concern with the Bible. To medieval man the Bible had to be seen through its exegesis, and in "speaking Bible," Langland had to speak as a commentator or exegete. Scripture is the guide to perfection, and it can be understood only in the light of the Catholic interpretation of it. This attitude forced his poem partly into the literary form of the commentary, the normal mode of understanding Scripture. In the later Middle Ages, in Langland's own time, the tendency was to incorporate biblical quotations harmoniously into the work, but Langland in following the commentary method only partly keeps to this principle.[84]

Langland, in a temperate middle style, argues for a temperate throwing of oneself on God, as a monk may do it, not as a friar who is guilty of excess. True "care-lessness," which must allow for man's normal needs and which can be obtained by manual labor, will make possible the new society and the finding of Piers again. Temperance is the keynote of the poem.

Although this virtue is stressed from the beginning, Langland, as he worked on his endless poem, became clearer and clearer about the implications of his doctrine. This increasing clarity is shown in the C-version; and in Langland's treatment of minstrels especially, it is very instructive.[85]

Donaldson has made a perceptive study of the use of the term minstrel in *Piers* and has shown how the C-version makes precise the rather widespread confusion in A and B concerning good and bad minstrels.[86] Langland comes to see that the profession of minstrel is ideally the prototype for the man who sensibly throws himself on God. God's minstrels are those who are *sorglos*, who trust in Him and who have implicit faith. They are the monks of the spirit. The bad minstrels are the friars who pander to the gross needs of the lords and ladies on whom they rely for support. On the highest level, "He þat most loueþ god, syngeþ hiȝest."[87] But the corruption of the highest is also the worst. The corruption of the religious ideal by the friars is equivalent to the corruption of the "minstrel of God" ideal by ordinary minstrels. This division of minstrels is not clear in A and B, but by the time C was being written, Langland knew what he wanted to say. Hawkin the Active Man is both a confectioner and a minstrel, and Will too has some of the characteristics of a minstrel. The minstrel at his highest is the ideal man of God.

The speech of Holy Church in Passus I really sets out the "message" that Langland is bringing to his age and perhaps ours. Because the disordered nature of the poem has been stressed so much, it would perhaps be useful to look at her speech again. She begins by stressing the importance of moderation and need. A proper recognition of need—the right to have clothing and shelter, food and drink, "in mesurable manere" (v. 19)—is the first prerequisite for Christian perfection. "Mesure is medcyne · thouȝ thow moche ȝerne (v. 35)." How, Will then asks, can possessions be properly divided in this world? The answer, Lady Holy Church says, is to be found in the Bible in Jesus' command to render unto Caesar that which is Caesar's and to God that which is God's. "Riȝtful reson shulde rewle ȝow alle (v. 54)." One should take possessions only as rightful reason and kind wit dictate for one's need. She also tells Will the meaning of the tower and the dungeon he has seen in the vision of the fair field full of folk. They are heaven and hell, the final destinations of man and the eschatological goal of all redemptive history.

Will then asks how he may save his soul, and Lady Holy Church responds with a long speech on "Trewthe" (loyalty to the social and spiritual norms of existence). One must preserve in one's social relations the proper moderation, which consists in fulfilling the duties of one's station and status. The prototype of all rebellion against "trewthe" is Lucifer, who broke the original pattern of the universe.

What force within me, Will asks, can help to keep this principle? This question provokes Lady Holy Church to call him a "doted daffe (v. 138)." He is told he has a natural knowledge of what to do and how to love if he would but perceive it. He is told to teach others the truth and to look to Jesus, who provides an example for us all. Share your wealth with others, Lady Holy Church continues. Chastity without charity is worthless, and the greatest sinners are the clergy. Faith without works is dead, and "give and it shall be given unto you."

The theme of the whole poem is explicit in this scene, and the rest of the poem is a working out in detail, sometimes endless detail, of the speech of Lady Holy Church. The end of the poem makes again, in an apocalyptic setting that Langland saw in his own time, these very points. In spite, then, of his propensity to ramble, to develop, to divagate, Langland is firm and single-minded in his essential point—in A, B, and C, and from beginning to end. The expansions and changes in the different versions do no more than add more material to build up the essence of what he has to say; they all reveal the hard struggle for Christian perfection. The basic answer, though, the answer Langland never doubted, is set out in Passus I of the A-Text—moderation in self and society, victory over the betrayal of ideals, especially by the clergy, the need for love and justice. In these essentials Langland never wavers.

Will is both actor and spectator and sums up in himself both the practical and speculative aspects of *Piers*. Will is also historical and normative and presents in himself the problem of Langland's time and the Christian problem for all time. He is involved and detached; he is of time and eternity. In his final failure is the failure of mankind and society, and yet in this very failure is hope. The miseries of the world are the strongest evidence of a coming renewal.

It has been the main purpose of this book to argue that it is in the older monastic view of man that we can best find the intellectual framework of *Piers Plowman*. The concern for perfection, the concept of grades of perfection, and the social orientation of the notion of perfection all bespeak an older tradition that we have called monastic philosophy. Monasticism helps to explain the crucial role of the virtue of temperance in the poem as well as its apocalyptic view of life. Life as a pilgrimage, the goal of deification, the return to paradise—all these are monastic commonplaces.

The literary genres in *Piers* also show this influence—the debate, allegorical romance, and encyclopedic satire are especially appropriate to the monastic way of life. The religious genres were those cultivated in the monasteries. If we do not use the term too strictly, we may say that *Piers Plowman* is a fourteenth-century English apocalypse.

The lines of the connection in the fourteenth century between Langland and monasticism have been laid out here, but much more remains to be done as our knowledge of fourteenth-century English culture deepens, especially of the culture favored by the monasteries, although by that time it had long spread beyond the confines of the convent. A desperate monasticism, fighting back in the fourteenth century at the superior and newer movements, revived sufficiently to affect the life of the period. Somehow and at some time Langland must have been influenced by that aroused movement, for it has left its strong traces in *Piers Plowman*. How this influence came about we cannot say, but making this assumption seems to me to be the only hypothesis that brings together the apparently discordant elements in the poem's structure and meaning. It does not explain everything. Much is still unknown both about the movement and about various parts of the poem. But if I have been able to direct the investigation of *Piers* towards the right questions, even if I have not provided all the answers, I feel that this work has not been in vain.

APPENDICES

APPENDIX I

Joachim of Flora in Fourteenth-Century England

ALTHOUGH in this book I have refrained from associating my argument closely or fundamentally with the thought of the twelfth-century Calabrian Abbot Joachim of Flora, I have on more than one occasion pointed out in *Piers Plowman* certain similarities to Joachism that make some kind of relationship theoretically possible. It is not my purpose to connect the case argued here with Joachism, but I by no means wish to rule out the possibility of some kind of influence that has been more or less vaguely suggested by *Piers Plowman* scholars since the time of J. J. Jusserand.[1] The time is not yet ripe to argue the case positively, for much more needs to be known about the intellectual life of fourteenth-century England than is possible at present. Too much important material lies buried in Latin manuscripts not well known or not easily available for study.

One link in the chain connecting Joachim and Langland can, however, be forged at present: that Joachim's writings were known in England in the fourteenth century is beyond question. Yet this very fact has been questioned, even recently, by scholars,[2] and I think the matter should be made clear here. The following evidence is by no means complete, but there is enough of it to leave no reasonable doubt that Joachim's works were known directly in fourteenth-century England.

In dealing with Joachim we are face to face with the problem of pseudo-Joachita, for under his name numerous works were circulated which are not genuine. A great many of these pseudo-Joachite works, mostly prophecies, can be found in manuscripts of English provenance, and some were heavily pillaged by English writers;[3] but only two well-known and substantial pseudo-Joachita, the famous *Commentary on Jeremiah* and *Commentary on Isaiah*,[4] will be used as evidence. In some of the references to Joachim below, in the last list, it is not absolutely clear that the works were directly known; but included are only those cases where the knowledge is detailed or unusual enough to imply direct acquaintanceship. Since the name of Joachim was often loosely bandied about, it alone, without taking into consideration the context, is of little value to my purpose. Even if I have erred in one or two cases, it is unlikely that I have done so in most instances.

As a preliminary statement, it should be pointed out that the Florensian Order, which Joachim founded, seems to have owned much property and many benefices in England in the thirteenth century. Although by the fourteenth century it had lost a good deal of its vigor, in the first half of the thirteenth century its drive and zeal seemed to many to make it one of the most important orders in the Church. Gregory IX, for instance, in his bull canonizing St. Dominic referred to the Dominicans, Franciscans, Cistercians, and Florensians as the four pillars of the Church. There is also some evidence that after the condemnation of Joachim's Trinitarian theories by the Lateran Council in 1215, the order was less zealous about the sanctity and glory of its founder than previously. Nevertheless, the connections between England and Italy created by the Florensian Order's property could have provided an easy channel for the passage of Joachite manuscripts to England.[5] Although the history of the manuscript is not known, it is possible that it was through this channel that the very precious manuscript of the Joachite *Liber figurarum*, now known as Corpus Christi, Oxford 225A, came to England.

Surviving Manuscripts[6]

1. Corpus Christi, Oxford 225A—*Liber figurarum*.
2. British Museum, Harley 3049, fols. 135^a–218^b (new foliation) (from Durham Cathedral Priory)—*Expositio in Apocalypsim*; and fols. 245 ff. (new foliation)—extracts from the *Commentary on Isaiah*.
3. British Museum, Harley 3969, fols. 216^a–224^a—excerpts from the *Expositio in Apocalypsim* (according to index in the MS, fol. 235^a).
4. British Museum, Royal 8.F. XVI A (owned by Richard Kylmington [or Kylvington], Dean of St. Paul's, d. 1361)— extensive excerpts from Joachim's works (*Evangelium aeternum*) and Protocol of Anagni report of 1255 condemning that

work. Printed by Denifle in *ALKG*, I (1885), 99 ff. (but not from this MS).

5. British Museum, Sloane 156, fols. 34*a*–41*b*—excerpts from *Commentary on Isaiah*.
6. British Museum, Cotton, Tiberius B.V, Part II,[7] fols. 4*a* ff.—part of *Commentary on Isaiah*.

Library Inventory and Catalogue References

1. Boston of Bury's famous, but as yet unpublished union catalogue of MSS in English monasteries, indicates, as Professor R. A. B. Mynors of Oxford, the editor, has kindly informed me, that both the *Expositio in Apocalypsim* and *De concordia* were in the Library of the Oxford Franciscans *c.* 1400. It is also quite clear that under the title "Super libros prophetarum commenta" the *Commentaries* on Jeremiah and Isaiah are referred to, although it is not clear where they were.
2. Professor R. M. Wilson of Sheffield, who in recent years has thoroughly explored extant medieval library inventories, informs me that a copy of the *Expositio in Apocalypsim* was at Exeter in the Middle Ages.
3. The Library of the Augustinian Friars at York, whose fourteenth-century catalogue with additions is extant (ed. M. R. James in *Fasciculus Ioanni Willis Clark dicatus* [Cambridge, England, 1909], pp. 2–96), and to which we have already referred, possessed a copy of *De oneribus prophetarum*, among other pseudo-Joachita, an interesting "tabula Joachim de concordantia testamentorum" (part of the *Liber figurarum?*), a simple "de concordancia [for *concordia*] testamentorum" and "Joachim super apocalypsim."
4. Syon Monastery Isleworth had in the early sixteenth century (see *Catalogue of the Library of Syon Monastery Isleworth*, ed. Mary Bateson [Cambridge, England, 1898], p. 75 ([I 26])), a copy of Joachim's *Expositio in Apocalypsim*.

References to Joachim in Fourteenth-Century Writings Showing More Than a Routine Acquaintance with Him[8]

1. The influence of Joachim's Commentary on the Apocalypse in late thirteenth- and fourteenth-century England, especially on the Franciscan biblical exegetes of the period, has been

adequately dealt with by Dr. B. Smalley, and I need do no more than refer to this article.[9]

2. Henry of Harclay, Chancellor of the University of Oxford (*c.* 1270–1317), was much concerned to prove that the date of the second coming could not be predicted, and in refuting Joachim's views shows that he had read him, or at least part of his work, carefully.[10]

3. Archbishop Stratford in the 1340's quoted the pseudo-Joachite *De oneribus prophetarum* in a knowledgeable way in a sermon at a point when he is discussing the decline of the world.[11]

4. Bishop Bradwardine in his *De causa Dei,* I, 46–47, attacks Joachim's Pelagianism but speaks of him with respect, or at least in such a way as to indicate that some of his contemporaries held him in respect.

5. The Monk of Bury St. Edmunds' "Treatise on Monastic Origins" shows a deep knowledge of Joachim as discussed in Chapters III and V above.

6. Thomas Wimbledon's sermon "Redde" shows a knowledge of the *Commentary on Jeremiah.*[12]

I have taken only the most clear-cut examples, but I think that one can without difficulty conclude that Joachim, although not the most widely known of ecclesiastical writers, was certainly known in England in the fourteenth century. He was widely mentioned, but I have not included in my list the numerous references to his name or the many prophecies attributed to him. His name frequently served both as a sign of a misguided thinker and as a model of prophetic perspicuity. There is no reason to doubt that it would have been possible for Langland in fourteenth-century England to know him and his works.[13]

APPENDIX II

Langland and Scholasticism

ALTHOUGH it has been my purpose in this book to stress the older monastic or Christian philosophy of perfection with its social orientation as the basic matrix of Langland's point of view, I do not wish to give the impression that he was uninfluenced by other intellectual currents in his century and especially by that of scholasticism, which was the dominant mode of thought in his time.

England in the fourteenth century, especially up to the time of the Black Death and even as late as Wyclif, was a notable center of scholastic thinking, especially at Oxford and among the Franciscans. It is unthinkable that anyone who was intellectually alive and seriously interested in theological and philosophical problems in that time could have avoided contact with scholastic thinking, and indeed there is much evidence in *Piers Plowman* that its author was affected by this powerful theorizing and thinking that we call scholasticism.[1]

The two great names of the English Franciscan school of this century, Duns Scotus and William Occam, are of course well known. They are among the great figures in the history of Western philosophy. But it is not common knowledge that there were a host of other English philosophers who were important if not world-shaking figures and who left their mark in the development of philosophy. Men like Harclay, Bradwardine, Adam Woodham, Holcot, Rodington, Buckingham, Fitzralph, William of Alnwick, Thomas Walleys, Hugh of Newcastle, and John Wyclif were all notable philosophers, though most of their works are not easily obtainable today. Except for Wyclif, most of their writings are either unprinted or, if printed, are in rare incunabula and sixteenth-century books. Even some of Wyclif's philosophical works are as yet unprinted, for it was not this aspect of his writings which appealed to modern editors. The English Reformation destroyed the interest in preserving the works of these men, which were also written in outmoded forms, and it is only recently that a revival of interest in their productions has arisen.

The work of these men, along with that of Scotus and Occam, provided the kind of scholasticism with which Langland came in contact. No doubt the great names of the thirteenth century, especially Thomas Aquinas and Bonaventure, were known to him, as they were to these English philosophers. But these men did not hold the position of pre-eminence that we assign them today, and it was not until the nineteenth century that Thomism, although certainly honored from early times, received the accolade as the Catholic philosophy par excellence.

In order to approach properly Langland's relation to his scholastic milieu, we would have to know more about it than is at present possible. Probably in the coming years, as more of this work and the related work in fourteenth-century biblical exegesis becomes available, many of the puzzles in *Piers* can be cleared up.[2]

It is quite clear that Langland in general belongs to the English Franciscan school in his emphasis on freedom of the will, natural virtue, and voluntarism and in his view of the nature of the soul.[3] In detail, however, the influences cannot at present be enumerated. My purpose in this appendix is to show the technical scholastic elements, sometimes merely the external signs, in *Piers* when these stand out clearly. In many cases no doubt I have overlooked such elements.

The question may arise about where Langland got his knowledge of scholasticism. Faced as we are by an almost blank biography, it is obvious that this question cannot be answered with any certitude, but one may reasonably speculate. The kind of knowledge of scholasticism that Langland displays could only have been obtained at some institution of higher education.

It has generally been assumed that Langland was not a very learned man. Certain mistakes, mainly in his Latin, are probably one of the reasons for this belief; another is the fact that the Vita, wherein he really displays his learning, is much less frequently read than the easier Visio. The opinion was probably thoughtlessly repeated by scholars, as I myself did twenty years ago.[4] Today, however, I prefer to agree with the older opinion of J. J. Jusserand and B. Ten Brink,[5] that he had a university education or its equivalent and would therefore have at least been introduced to the real learning of his time—and I think the poem bears out this assumption.

To account for his knowledge of monastic philosophy and scholasticism, an assumption that he attended a Benedictine college at Oxford would be perfect. This hypothesis, however, is difficultt to support. Had Langland been regarded so highly by his Benedictine house, assuming he at one time belonged to one, as to be sent to Oxford for further study, it seems unlikely that he would have ended up as a secular in minor orders. We have, besides, no sure evidence that he was ever connected with a Benedictine abbey, and certainly there is nothing in the poem save his monastic philosophy to show he ever had any Benedictine connections. It was entirely possible in the fourteenth century (or even earlier) to know monastic philosophy without being a monk at all.

Mother Catherine Elizabeth Maguire, recognizing Langland's "Benedictine bias," tries to account for Langland's dual knowledge by assuming he went both to a Benedictine or cathedral school and to a Franciscan *studium generale*.[6] This is a possibility. The *studia generalia* provided an advanced theological training almost on a university level, and attendance at any one would certainly be sufficient to account for the scholastic knowledge Langland displays. On the other hand, he may have attended Oxford (or less likely Cambridge) at an ordinary college and picked up his monastic philosophy from reading or from a friend. Possibly he was connected for a while with a monastic establishment but decided it was not for him. Whatever the answer to this question may be, Langland definitely shows signs of a scholastic training of a specialized sort that could have been obtained only at a university or an advanced school set up by an order or cathedral, the only places where such training was available.[7]

Langland is disturbed by the proper relation of learning to religion and its role in the quest for perfection. There is much satire on barren learning which does not lead to God. Conscience at the end of the poem, for instance, tells the friars (XX, 249) to leave logic and learn to love. In Passus X and XI, Will is wrestling with the same problem, and elsewhere we can see criticisms of the abuse of learning and philosophy. His final opinion, however, is probably that put into the mouth of Imaginatif (in Passus XII), who defends the right employment of learning—"And riȝt as syȝte, serueth a man · to se the heighe strete, / Riȝt so ledeth letterure · lewed men to resoun" (vv. 105–106). Severe criticism of the abuses of learning and logic does not, of course, preclude his indebtedness to them. The right use of learning is one of the major themes of the poem, and it is only natural that its misuse be strongly criticized and its evil excesses be exposed.

What then is the evidence that leads to the conclusion that Langland was acquainted with scholastic philosophy and theology in more than a superficial sense? One general point should be made: Scholars are by no means agreed on what Latin technical terms Langland was translating when using English equivalents. That he was attempting to translate scholastic terms at certain points in the poem there can be no doubt, but there is some uncertainty about what they were. In fact one could make up quite a list of modern contradictory interpretations that could amuse or bewilder the reader, but there is nothing to be gained from doing this. There was no intellectual vocabulary in English in the fourteenth century—it was only beginning to emerge—and the lack of agreement on English terms is characteristic of the period. This is especially the case when true English equivalents, such as "kind wit," were used. The principle that these terms should be merely anglicized Latin words was not yet generally accepted. Some words, like "conscience," were anglicized Latin vocables, and they of course cause no difficulty. Words like "inwit," however, present a more difficult problem.

The following is some of the evidence for the assumption that Langland knew scholasticism in more than a superficial sense.

1. Langland seems to be well acquainted with some of the technical terms of scholasticism. In refuting opponents or teachers in the Vita he uses *contra* three times and puts the words into the mouth of Imaginatif.[8] In the first instance, in the conversation with the two Franciscans, Will says, "*Contra*, quod I as a clerke · and comsed to disputen." It is clear that there the word "dispute" is being used in a technical sense: Will is beginning a disputation and proceeds in good scholastic wise to quote a biblical text to support his argument that all men are sinners.

Imaginatif also uses the abbreviation "Sortes" for Socrates. This shortened form of the name of the philosopher, a stock figure in schoolroom syllogisms, is the standard form of his name in medieval treatises on logic. Fourteenth-century English philosophy was especially devoted to logic; and these works and their authors were anathema to the Italian humanists of this century and the next,[9] to whom this logic was the chief enemy. Langland, too, seems particularly irritated at the logical side of contemporary scholasticism, and in C, XVII, 231, he refers to the predilection of the friars for "insolibles and fallaces," thinking no doubt of the *De insolubilibus* and *De fallaciis* types of logical treatise very much favored in his century. He need not have read such works to have been aware of these titles, but his mention of them does argue for some acquaintanceship with the logical works of the period.

In XV, 375, Langland refers to the scholastic form known as the *quodlibet*, a report of the *ex tempore* answers of a master in theology to whatever theological or philosophical question his students wished to raise. One also finds the use of "where" or "whether" (XIV, 101, and XV, 191) as the equivalent of the *utrum* found at the beginning of a scholastic *questio*. Patience in XIV, 275 ff., shows a knowledge of the scholastic *distinctio* in her analysis of the various meanings of the word poverty, although her starting point is a quotation from a non-scholastic source. In the corresponding passage in C this section is called in a rubric "Distinctio paupertatis."[10] The great scholastic textbook, Peter Lombard's *Sentences*, is divided into *distinctiones*.

2. Langland in IX, 52 ff., and XV, 23 ff., shows an awareness of the great dispute in the fourteenth century over whether the distinction between the soul and its faculties was a real or conventional distinction. This issue was particularly debated at Oxford in the 1330's and 1340's, when Langland could have been a student there.[11] There is no doubt that Langland subscribed to the general Franciscan theory that the distinction was a conventional one. *Piers Plowman* is not a philosophical treatise, and the case is not argued, but the mere fact of the point being made with a supporting quotation (Passus XV after v. 39) argues for an acquaintance with this philosophical problem of the period.

3. The C-Text (IV, 335 ff.) discusses the difference between "mede" and "mercede," which is made to accommodate the good and bad meanings of the Middle English word "mede" in that version only. This text includes a long philosophical discussion of

direct ("rect") and indirect relations, which are compared to the grammatical categories of adjective and substantive and their relation to each other. Neither I, nor anyone else as far as I know, has been able to find the source of this discussion, which in all probability lies buried in the scholastic writings of the period, but of its nature there can be no doubt. This passage is a real bit of scholastic argument based on grammatical analogy which was popular in the Middle Ages.

4. Langland also shows a knowledge of the scholastic theory of trade in III, 87 ff., and 255–256, and in the latter even uses the technical term "permutation" to describe the exchange of goods and services. This idea of equal exchange as the basis in justice for trade is older than Duns Scotus, but I believe it was he who first actually used the term "permutacio" to describe it.[12] This word is a clue then to Langland's knowledge of scholasticism.[13]

5. Randolph Quirk has carefully studied Langland's use of the terms "kind wit" and "inwit" in a recent article,[14] though he by no means claims completeness for his work. It is clear from this article, if not from the text itself, that Langland is well aware of the technical meanings of these terms, even though there may be some dispute as to what Latin words he is translating. Dr. Quirk's conclusion very well supports my own argument: "It is important however to note in conclusion that while, as we have seen, his [Langland's] usage differed considerably from that of most writers, the difference lay in his need to find terms with which he could express in a consistent allegorical framework complex concepts of scholastic philosophy, yet be intelligible to an English public" (p. 188).

6. The whole organization of Do-wel, whether it be autobiographical or not, argues for a knowledge of scholasticism on Langland's part. This part of the poem moves among psychological, religious, and ethical personifications and abstractions which indicate a quest among ideas and into one's own mind in a scholastic frame of reference. The major characters here, omitting the somewhat irregular figures of the Franciscan friars, are Thought, Wit, Study, Clergy, Scripture, "Lewte" (which is a polysemous figure but which primarily means justice and trustfulness), Reason, Recklessness, Imaginatif, Conscience, Patience, and Anima. This kind of personification, often as well as what is said, reveals an awareness

of scholastic speculation on the sources of knowledge and doctrine, especially in the late thirteenth and fourteenth centuries.[15] The basic sources of Christian knowledge and their relative validity are questions of primary importance to the thinkers of the period. The existence of the problem indicates an increasing self-consciousness and a questioning of the basis of objective historical and doctrinal knowledge. Scripture, reason, tradition, the Church ("clergy"), all jostle one another in *questiones* of the period on this subject.

Furthermore, the very nature of these abstractions indicates their birth in a scholastic milieu, and reveals their author as a product of the schools and as one accustomed to the scholastic frame of mind.

7. Finally, in the figure of Conscience, who occupies such an important role in the poem and who is the primary guide of Will throughout, we find combined both a scholastic and pre-scholastic (primarily monastic) conception of this important faculty of the soul. In the light of the theory argued in this book as to the sources of Langland's thought, these scholastic and pre-scholastic elements are put together in almost the same proportions that my argument would favor.

Conscience in the Visio plays essentially the scholastic role of judge. In combination with Reason, he decides on the moral value of human action. In his debates with Lady Meed and later as chief adviser with Reason to the King, his natural law aspect is emphasized.

The ruler, whether the king or the self, in order to act justly and put down human cupidity (Meed), must subject himself to both reason and conscience, which are his proper moral guides. This is the typical scholastic concept of conscience—a moral guide and judge of human actions. In Bonaventure, Aquinas, and Duns Scotus, for instance, the act of conscience (in the broad sense of the word) is conceived as a syllogism in which synderesis provides the first major premise—a moral generalization—superior or inferior reason the second major premise, and conscience (in the narrow sense of the word) the conclusion. In Thomas, synderesis is a permanent tendency (an *habitus*) of the intellect and conscience. Conscience testifies, binds, instigates, accuses, causes remorse, and censures.[16]

There are variations on this scheme and disputes as to whether synderesis was in the intellect or in the will or whether it was a power or *habitus* of the soul, but this schema fits the general scholastic picture. As is common in the later Middle Ages, Langland makes no distinction between conscience and synderesis and uses the former term to include both the faculties.[17] It is true that to some of these thinkers, and to the mystics in the later Middle Ages, synderesis in some regards is given a higher role. Thomas of Vercelli, for instance, in his commentary on the Pseudo-Dionysian *Mystica theologia* says synderesis is a cognitive faculty that surpasses reason. Meister Eckhart connects it with the *scintilla animae*, which is closely connected to God in the soul.[18] Even in Aquinas there are traces of this older view.[19] However, in general, among the scholastics, conscience is, as in the Visio, a rather matter-of-fact faculty that is essential to right action and morality. As the *Compendium theologiae*, a late scholastic compendium attributed to Jean Gerson, puts it, synderesis (which is taken as a synonym of conscience) "est vis motiva seu potentia *naturalis animae rationalis*" (my italics).[20]

The Visio contains no trace of the mystical older meaning of conscience, going back ultimately to Paul and Philo, wherein conscience is the link with God in the soul. In the later part of the poem Conscience, on the other hand, is no longer the scholastic quality of the natural reasonable soul, but much more. If it is not exactly a mystical faculty in the Vita when it introduces Will to Patience, when it comforts him and defends Unitas against Antichrist and goes at the end to find Piers Plowman and Grace, this is because *Piers* is not fundamentally a mystical poem concerned with the journey of the self to God, but an apocalyptic one. Nevertheless, Conscience' role has been considerably widened and in terms of monastic philosophy; for the term conscience before the time of the scholastics had other than mystical meanings.[21]

Conscience in Do-best is the power which can make us divine, not as individuals, but as a society of Christians. The Pseudo-Bernard *Tractatus de interiori domo seu de conscientia aedificanda* takes conscience as an interior temple of God—the site of God's dwelling in us rather than the voice of God himself. This tractate was probably written by a Benedictine. It takes conscience as equivalent to the house of wisdom built with seven columns

(Proverbs 9:1). "A good conscience . . . is the Temple of Solomon, a field of blessing, a garden of delights . . . joy of the angels . . . treasury of the King, the hall of God and the dwelling place of the Holy Ghost."[22] In an unprinted sermon by the monk Hugh of Pontigny (d. 1151)[23] three mansions of the just are alluded to—one exterior, one interior, and one superior, corresponding to the Church, conscience, and heaven. The house of conscience has the four cardinal virtues as its walls.

The Middle English *Abbey of the Holy Ghost*, a work roughly contemporary with *Piers*, contains a spiritual abbey of the soul built on the site of conscience. Conscience is the monastery of the heart, so to speak. In these examples we come close to Langland's view of the matter in Do-best. Conscience is the Church within us and heaven is, as in Hugh, the Church above us. I cannot here explore the full history of conscience as a monastic concept, but it is in monastic philosophy that we can find, I am sure, the explanation for Langland's unusual use of conscience as a social and apocalyptic virtue.

My point here, however, is merely to show how both scholasticism and monastic philosophy combine to explain Conscience in *Piers Plowman*. Scholastic philosophy explains part of its meaning, but to reach the final and richest part of the concept we must turn to monastic philosophy.

APPENDIX III

The Problem of Imaginatif

WHY does this relatively unimportant faculty of the soul in scholastic philosophy occupy so important a place in the poem as to be a chief instructor of Will in his quest for perfection? A whole passus (XII) is devoted to his discussion with the hero. Will has reached an intellectual impasse at the end of Passus XI on the problem of the value of learning, on the problem of salvation, especially whether man can be saved under natural law ("the righteous heathen"), and on the problem of the meaning of nature. Imaginatif in a long speech clears up these matters, a clarification that enables Will to go on to the heart of Do-wel, for to learn the value of patient poverty is its main point.[1] One would expect a higher psychical faculty—reason at least—to occupy this key role, but instead Imaginatif becomes Will's instructor. Why?

The history of the imagination is extremely complex, and although it has been studied by many scholars, no one has yet been able to synthesize it into a whole. And there are good reasons for this incompleteness, since both the concept and its terminology lack clearly defined limits or stability. This is true not only among various writers on the psychology of the soul but also, in the case of many, within the corpus of any one writer. There are good studies of individual psychologies, however; and even if intellectual order cannot be obtained, one can still arrive at some kind of consensus as to what many writers thought about the subject. It is merely on these general statements that I base my case; to do otherwise would require another book and possibly several on the subject alone.[2]

The two studies that have been devoted to Imaginatif in our poem bring forth valuable supporting material; H. S. V. Jones takes the concept in a very narrow sense, and Randolph Quirk concentrates on the lexicographical aspect of the word and though brief in his treatment of the history of the idea, is well aware of the complexity of the concept.[3]

Without going into great detail, I think I can make some clarifications not yet made. Briefly, imagination is the picture—or idea-making faculty of the human mind (as John Locke might put it). It has two essential functions in ancient and medieval psychology. The first is to create from the *sensibilia*, the data the external senses present to the mind, clear pictures or phantasms from which the active or agent intellect abstracts universals that are alone the subject of knowledge.[4] The human mind cannot, in most medieval psychologies, know singulars, which are the raw material of knowledge. Even in those schools such as the Scotistic which allow for some knowledge of singulars, this knowledge is not on a fully intellectual level, but is of lower status. In some medieval philosophies, this lack of knowledge or full knowledge of singulars is a limitation of the human mind, from which angels and God do not suffer.

The second function is to create pictures or images normally by combining or recalling them without any stimulation from the external senses. In this capacity imagination is said to be an internal sense, and it operates in dreams or when for various reasons images must be called up. As an internal sense, it is generally known as the *vis imaginativa*, or *vis phantastica* (the imaginative power).[5] The whole idea of internal senses is foreign to modern psychological thinking, but they were postulated to account for images and elementary knowledge which, although in the Aristotelian schools are ultimately due to sense experience, arise in the mind without immediate exterior stimulation. The number of internal senses varies from one to six, and includes frequently the estimative force, memory, imagination, cogitation, and common sense. The terms for these are bewilderingly confusing. Sometimes common sense or imagination (in one of its Latin forms) is used for them all. Imagination is closely linked with memory in this scheme. The confusion is due to Aristotle, who in the *De anima* allowed for only one internal sense with various functions but did not clearly distinguish between them or did not give enough detail in the matter. Ever since, the subject of the internal senses, and especially imagination, has been confused and contradictory, even as to the terms used.

But to follow Langland's use of Imaginatif, it is necessary to keep in mind the basic distinction between images created from the material of the five senses and those called up without immediate external stimulation. In the past, there has been a strong tendency (not, however, in Quirk) not to separate these two basic types of imaginative activity. As an abstractive stage in the passage of knowledge from the senses to the intellect, imagination plays an indispensable but inferior role. As an internal sense, imagination can play an inferior or a superior role depending on one's psychology or epistemology.

Now it is clear from the adjectival form of the word that Langland is using "imaginatif" as a translation of (*vis*) *imaginativa* and that he is thinking of imagination as an internal sense.[6] The problem is now to show the sources of the idea that the internal sense of imagination can give rise to true knowledge.

Before I do that, I must make the general point—which was no doubt also in Langland's mind—that "imaginatif" in any medieval psychological system would be responsible for dreams. Even if he held strictly to an Aristotelian-Thomistic low evaluation of the imagination, he would still be indebted to the faculty for the dreams which he cast into literary form, conventional though that form be. It would be proper then for the putative source of the dreams he was dreaming to be his instructor, for it was imagination (as an internal sense) which gave him the framework of his poem.

I suspect, further, that Langland, like Dante, gave imagination as an internal sense a higher rather than a lower role as a transmitter of knowledge. The manner whereby imagination could be elevated is through the medieval theory of prophecy, and it is here that the answer to our problem really lies. Without going into the whole story of this prophetic concept of the imagination, I think I can show where the answer might be found. In the particular case of Langland, I cannot but believe that an answer might be found in detail in some as yet undiscovered fourteenth-century English psychological work. To do so would require an extensive study of the numerous commentaries on the *De anima* and other psychological works which lie in European libraries, especially in England.[7]

One of the major themes of this book, although not spelled out

as such, is that Langland is a prophetic poet—a poet who felt
himself privileged to reveal to his fellow men a coming renewal
of justice and love that would transform society and through it
the individual. Like Dante, whom he certainly did not know, he
believed in and wished to hasten the day of a return to a pristine
state of justice that would regenerate Christian social life;[8] and *alta
fantasia* was an important force in enabling him to grasp and
communicate this news to his fellow men.

I do not wish to give the impression that Langland and Dante
envisaged themselves as prophets in exactly the same way. Langland is fundamentally involved in the search for Christian perfection; Dante gives us the Christian truth, the next world, against
which our present world must be measured. Langland is oriented
towards the transformation of this world; and although he no
doubt believed the same fundamental Christian truths as Dante
did, it is the quest for them in this world that is his major concern. The quest is basic to Will, Langland's hero, and on a further
quest the poem ends. The *Divine Comedy* comes to rest at the
end, and the quest is under authoritative guidance. In Dante it is
a true means to knowledge. Will's problem is to find authorities
in this world to whom he can turn and on whom he can model
himself. Christian perfection is Dante's theme; the quest for
Christian perfection is Langland's.

Although Plato had recognized certain visions as sources of
truth,[9] prophecy first became a philosophical problem with the
Arabs, because of the essential role of the prophet in the Islamic
notion of revelation, above all in Mohammed and the Koran.
Prophecy is also crucial in Judaism and Christianity, and it is discussed early in the theological writings of these religions. It became
a philosophical problem, however, only when Aristotelian psychology with its emphasis on the origin of our knowledge in sense
experience had to be rigorously applied to the problem of revelation; and inasmuch as the Arabs were the first to deal seriously
with this issue, it is only natural that they should have been the
first to elevate prophecy to a philosophical problem.[10]

In general the great Arab philosophers are more willing to
allow imagination a higher role in prophecy (and mysticism) than
the great Christian scholastics. Al-Farabi (d. 950) is the first thinker
to enhance imagination through prophetic theory, and he was

probably inspired in this matter by the Neoplatonic tradition and ancient rhetoric which tended to elevate artistic imagination.[11] These ideas, somewhat modified, probably reached the West through Maimonides, who, although he taught that God or angels effected prophecy first of all through the active intellect, nevertheless believed that the imagination of a prophet was immediately affected by the prophetic active intellect. In his *Guide for the Perplexed*, he says, "It [prophecy] is the highest degree and greatest perfection man can attain; it consists in the most perfect development of the imaginative faculty."[12]

According to Nardi, it was Albertus Magnus, who, knowing Maimonides' *Guide*, passed on this high role of the imagination in prophecy to the West.[13] Aquinas, however, like most scholastics, tended to depreciate the imagination in prophecy and in all else. He writes, "Hence it follows that the prophecy whereby a supernatural truth is seen by intellectual vision is more excellent than that in which a supernatural truth is manifested by means of the similitudes of corporeal things in the vision of the imagination."[14] This is generally the scholastic view, but all writers on prophecy had to give the imagination a place of some importance. Not all bothered to reconcile their ordinary treatment of imagination with the higher role it occupied in prophecy.

Whence all this came to Langland I do not know, but I am sure that it is in this tradition that we must put his exaltation of Imaginatif. To a prophet who is seeking the way, aware of perfection but not sure of its exact meaning, prophetic imagination would be an important guide. This line of thought, then, and not the more traditional epistemological treatment of imagination, provides the answer to our question. To Langland, Imaginatif is a vehicle of divine assurance and truth, and this is why he accords it such a high place in his poem.

The Place of the Apocalyptic View of History in the Later Middle Ages

INASMUCH as I am arguing in this book that the apocalyptic view of history, though not unique to Langland in the later Middle Ages, was especially characteristic of this author, it is legitimate to ask whether any theory of history other than the apocalyptic was possible in the Middle Ages. If one believed in Christianity, one must believe in *Heilsgeschichte* and in its culminating point, the Last Judgment. No one in the Middle Ages (or hardly anyone) could openly think otherwise. Yet we must make distinctions. It is one thing to believe in *Heilsgeschichte* and the Last Judgment, and another to think that predictions could confidently be made about it, or to be continuously concerned with it. It was also an open question whether the Last Judgment would be preceded by a millennium (as Joachim thought) or not. The Kingdom of God could be defined and conceived of in various ways. Then there was also the minor issue—except to out-and-out Joachists—whether God had completed His revelation or not.

It is also obvious that in the thirteenth and fourteenth centuries many doubted the value of speculating on the problems of Antichrist, the Millennium, and the Last Judgment.[1] The scholastics, who were committed to reason and debate as the method of attaining truth, suspected the prophetic or apocalyptic mind which stressed the historical approach and which hoped by signs to learn the truth and predict the future.[2]

To the scholastics the primary problem in perfection was to define its various meanings, to establish a norm or norms that would enable the world and human striving to be understood in a Christian way. The problem of when and how was not their main concern. To the apocalyptically minded, however, this *when* and *how* was just the crucial question. How to fit the concept of perfection into a logically ordered view of the universe would seem otiose and unnecessary—or at least secondary. Theology existed for the sake of *Heilsgeschichte* in its most concrete form; not the systematic solution but the evaluation of the historical situation was the problem to these souls. When and how is the Kingdom of God to be attained for society? Is this the time or not?

No Christian could, of course, really repudiate this emphasis on history and faith in the future end of the world, but many would prefer not to throw their intellectual energies into such millenarian speculation. On the other hand, the great mystics of the fourteenth century were primarily concerned with individual salvation and the union with God. They, too, although not theoretically opposed to a belief in the Last Judgment, were not apocalyptically oriented.

There was also a tradition of historical study going back to antiquity which emphasized the value of the subject for providing models and examples. History exists to teach us.[3] History (as well as nature) is a *speculum vitae*, a mirror of life.[4] It is a branch of rhetoric, a storehouse of *exempla* full of warning and encouragement to mankind, illustrating the ways of providence and fortune. This tradition was very much alive in the Middle Ages and was the chief justification for the study of secular history.

But to Christians who felt the reality of the Bible, who were convinced of the primary importance of history, and who took seriously the claims of the Bible to be the history not only of the Jews but of the salvation of mankind,[5] history as the source of *exempla* was not enough. Although the Greeks had not neglected history, they largely took the rhetorical point of view and in effect negated history by their preference for the cyclic view;[6] they did not expect any fundamental change for the future, in spite of the Stoic belief in *pronoia*. Myth is a-historical and more congenial to the Greek mind. But the Jews and Christians in their earliest writings had raised the question of "before" and "after,"[7] with the concomitant notion of novelty and advance in history, the fundamental requirement of historical thinking; and to some who followed, this emphasis could not be ignored. Augustine almost forced medieval thought into the historical mold.[8] The struggle of the two cities and the idea of world ages and the closely related conception of the four kingdoms and the *translatio regni* made some medieval men critical of daily events, a mood that is of the essence of apocalyptic thinking. On the other hand it must be admitted that true historical thinking in the early Middle Ages was rare because of a focus on the coming end. From the twelfth century on this attitude becomes rarer and a sense of history truly emerges,[9] for we find a new interest in facts and events and the unique. To men like Langland the signs of the coming kingdom are of supreme importance, and such men are forced into a historical viewpoint.

Another type of historical thinking that was prevalent in the Middle Ages might be called the appeal to history or origins. Medieval thinking tended to justify things and beliefs by antecedents rather than by consequences. Various movements or institutions sought justification in the past.[10] The bitter quarrels over the meaning of Christian poverty in the thirteenth and fourteenth centuries frequently turned upon the question of what kind of poverty Jesus and the Apostles practiced. The superiority of the various religious orders in the Middle Ages was often assumed to rest upon their antiquity, and much misplaced historical ingenuity was expended in substantiating claims, mostly false. This type of thinking is still widespread, of course, and we may see it in the Renaissance debate on the origins of Florence[11] and in the sixteenth- and seventeenth-century interest in the nature of the early medieval English Church (which had as a by-product the revival of Old English studies). Both Protestant and Catholic felt that by appealing to the early Church (their origins) they could substantiate or deny present claims. This type of historical thinking arose from the tradition of Jewish and Christian historical thinking. The Old Testament, for instance, justifies kindness to strangers on the grounds that the Israelites had been strangers themselves in Egypt. Unlike the Graeco-Roman festivals, most Judeo-Christian holidays were historical, going back to distinct past events that justified present rejoicing. This whole subject needs a careful study, for this kind of historical thinking was prevalent in the Middle Ages.

In a sense it is the very opposite of apocalyptic thinking, for it stresses the past rather than the future and in effect denies (or at least severely limits) novelty in history rather than affirms it. In some ways, it is anti-historical (that is, anti-progressive), but actually it is both historical and anti-historical. It is certainly, however, a way of looking at history which was common in the Middle

Ages and indeed in the modern period down to the rise of scientific historiography.

Various possibilities within the Christian scheme were thus theoretically open to a writer or thinker of the fourteenth century, and it is legitimate to point to Langland's apocalypticism as a significant element in his point of view. The apocalyptic view of history was not merely *the* Christian or medieval view; to concentrate on it wholeheartedly as Langland did represents a definite choice among possible philosophies of history. Not all fourteenth-century English thinkers or artists were so inclined—neither Occam nor Chaucer, Richard Rolle nor Bradwardine, John Gower nor Richard Bury. Langland's historical view, though not unique or original, is nevertheless a view he could have avoided but did not. He was fundamentally apocalyptically-minded in a way many of his distinguished contemporaries were not.

NOTES

ABBREVIATIONS

AFH   *Archivum franciscum historicum*
AJP   *American Journal of Philology*
ALKG   *Archiv für Literatur- und Kirchengeschichte des Mittelalters*
ARW   *Archiv für Religionswissenschaft*
CE   *College English*
CSEL   *Corpus scriptarum ecclesiasticorum latinorum*
EHR   *English Historical Review*
ELH   *Journal of English Literary History*
HTR   *Harvard Theological Review*
JEGP   *Journal of English and Germanic Philology*
JHI   *Journal of the History of Ideas*
JTS   *Journal of Theological Studies*
MARS   *Medieval and Renaissance Studies*
MLN   *Modern Language Notes*
MLQ   *Modern Language Quarterly*
MLR   *Modern Language Review*
MP   *Modern Philology*
PG   Migne, *Patrologia graeca*
PL   Migne, *Patrologia latina*
PMLA   *Publications of the Modern Language Association of America*
PQ   *Philological Quarterly*
RES   *Review of English Studies*
RHE   *Revue d'histoire écclésiastique*
RHR   *Revue d'histoire des religions*
RMAL   *Revue du moyen âge latin*
RTAM   *Recherches théologiques anciens et médiévales*
SP   *Studies in Philology*
ST   *Summa theologica*
TAPA   *Transactions of the American Philological Association*
TLS   (London) *Times Literary Supplement*
ZKG   *Zeitschrift für Kirchengeschichte*
ZKT   *Zeitschrift für katholische Theologie*
ZNTW   *Zeitschrift für neutestamentliche Wissenschaft*

NOTE TO THE PREFACE

1. See some of the penetrating remarks on this subject by Murray Krieger in his excellent article, "Recent Criticism, 'Thematics,' and the Existential Dilemma," *The Centennial Review*, IV (1960), 32–50.

NOTES FOR CHAPTER I

1. Etienne Gilson, *L'Esprit de la philosophie médiévale*, Etudes de la philosophie médiévale XXXIII, Gifford Lectures, 2nd ed. (Paris, 1944), p. 367 (my translation). See also Joseph Bonsirven, *Le Règne de Dieu*, Théologie, Etudes publiées sous la direction de la Faculté de Théologie, S.J., de Lyon-Fourvière 37 (Paris, 1957). On what Jesus may have believed about the imminence of the Kingdom of God, see W. G. Kümmel, *Promise and Fulfilment, the Eschatological Message of Jesus*, trans. from 3rd ed. 1956, Studies in Biblical Theology 23 (London, 1957). Cf. "The fundamental idea of a nascent Christianity was faith in the near inauguration of a kingdom of God which should renew the world and found therein the eternal felicity of saints," Ernest Renan, *Leaders of Christian and Antichristian Thought*, trans. W. M. Thomson (London, n.d. [1895]), p. 129. Dr. G. Hort sees, I think, this point in *Piers* when she writes, "It is not what a man is that Langland considers to be wrong, but only what he does..." (*Piers Plowman and Contemporary Religious Thought* [London, n.d.], p. 85). The phrasing, however, does not point up Langland's objective and social approach.

2. I am indebted to a former student of mine, Donald J. Gray of Indiana University, for several of the phrases in this paragraph. George W. Stone, Jr., also makes this point in "An Interpretation of the A-Text of *Piers Plowman*," *PMLA*, LIII (1938), 674.

3. Predestination is a particularly vital question to one who is exploring Christian perfection with its Pelagian overtones. If we seek for perfection, we may deny or minimize grace and hence the power of God. Langland is also motivated in this matter by the problem of love. Can the just man or righteous heathen be saved? How can we account for the apparent irrationality of God's behavior in sometimes saving sinners and damning the righteous?

4. On why Imaginatif occupies this important position, see Appendix III below.

5. See John Lawlor, "The Imaginative Unity of *Piers Plowman*," *RES*, N.S. VIII (1957), 113–126, for recognition of this point in a stimulating article.

6. Ernst H. Kantorowicz, *The King's Two Bodies: A Study in Mediaeval Political Theology* (Princeton, 1957), p. 493. See the comments by R. W. Chambers, "Robert or William Longland," *London Mediaeval Studies*, I, 3 (1948 for 1939), 442 ff. This last should be read by all believers in medieval *personae*.

7. R. W. Southern, *The Making of the Middle Ages* (London, 1953), p. 222. On some references to the pilgrimage theme in literature, see Roland M. Smith, "Three Obscure English Proverbs," *MLN*, LXV (1950), 443–447.

8. See the interesting comments on the allegorization and interiorization of the Crusades in Paul Alphandéry and Alphonse Dupront, *La Chrétienté et l'idée de Crusade*, L'Evolution de l'humanité XXXVIII bis (Paris, 1959), II, pp. 109–110.

9. A Latin translation of selections from the *Shepherd of Hermas* is to be found in Trinity College, Cambridge MS 1133 (0.2.29). It is apparently a thirteenth-century MS from a London religious house. The *Visio sancti Pauli* was very well known in the West throughout the Middle Ages.

10. Father H. Musurillo, "History and Symbol: A Study of Form in Early Christian Literature," *Theological Studies*, XVIII (1957), 366.

11. I owe this term and an awareness of this genre to Northrop Frye's *The Anatomy of Criticism* (Princeton, 1957).

12. I owe this information to Phillip W. Damon, University of California, Santa Barbara.

13. See Charles Muscatine's excellent essay, "The Emergence of Psychological Allegory in Old French Romance," *PMLA*, LXVIII (1953), 1160–1182. For the background of allegory (personification), see Jean Pépin, "Saint Augustin et la function protréptique de l'allégorie," *Recherches augustiniennes* (Supplement to *Revue des études augustiniennes*), I (1958), 243–286; C. S. Lewis, *The Allegory of Love: A Study in Medieval Tradition* (Oxford, 1936), pp. 44–111; Morton W. Bloomfield, *The Seven Deadly Sins: An Introduction to the History of a Religious Concept with Special Reference to Medieval English Literature* (East Lansing, Michigan, 1952), pp. 29–36; T. B. L. Webster, "Personification as a Mode of Greek Thought," *Journal of the Warburg and Courtauld Institutes*, XVII (1954), 10–21. See, for medieval Latin visions, C. Fritzsche in *Romanische Forschungen*, II (1886), 247–279, III (1887), 337–369; Marcus Dods, *Forerunners of Dante: An Account of Some of the More Important Visions of the Unseen World, from Earliest Times* (Edinburgh, 1903); E. J. Becker, *A Contribution to the Comparative Study of the Medieval Visions of Heaven and Hell* (Baltimore, 1899); and Max Voigt, *Beiträge zur Geschichte der Visionenliteratur im Mittelalter* (Leipzig, 1924). See also below, note 20.

In the twelfth century, the dream form was also used for moral or dogmatic instruction, as may be seen in William of Conches (?), *Moralium dogma philosophorum,* Abelard's *Dialogus inter Judaeum, philosophum et Christianum*, Godfrey of St. Victor's *Fons philosophiae*, and Henry of Settimello's *De diversitate fortunae et philosophiae consolatione* (much influenced by Boethius).

14. Dorothy L. Owen, *Piers Plowman, a Comparison with Some Earlier and Contemporary French Allegories* (London, 1912), p. 23. Cf. "The [medieval] dream setting was an acceptable way of passing out of actual life into an irresponsible world where the fancy was free to find anything whatever," J. S. P. Tatlock, *The Mind and Art of Chaucer* (Syracuse, 1950), p. 31; cf. also p. 56. Another theory of dubious validity may be seen in the explanation that the use of the dream was "a shield from the wrath of those whose anger would have been aroused by his [the author's] relentless satire," H. M. Imbert-Terry, "The Poetical Contemporaries of Chaucer," *Chaucer Memorial Lectures 1900: Read before the Royal Society of Literature*, ed. P. W. Ames (London, 1900), p. 17.

15. R. Arbesmann, "Fasting and Prophecy in Pagan and Christian Antiquity," *Traditio*, VII (1949–1951), 14. See Erich Auerbach on the "ecstatic dream," in his *Typologische Motive in der mittelalterlichen Literatur,*

Schriften und Vortrage des Petrarca-Instituts, Köln, II (Krefeld, 1953), pp. 22 ff.; and L. Th. A. Lorié, *Spiritual Terminology in the Latin Translations of the Vita Antonii* ..., Latinitas Christianorum Primaeva 11 (Nijmegen, 1955), pp. 136 ff.

16. See Chaucer, *The Squire's Tale*, v. 358. Cf. his *House of Fame*, vv. 1–65. For good summaries of medieval dream theory, see Walter Clyde Curry, *Chaucer and the Mediaeval Sciences* (New York, 1926), pp. 195–240; and George G. Fox, *The Mediaeval Sciences in the Works of John Gower* (Princeton, 1931), pp. 95 ff. On spiritual visions, see Joseph A. Mazzeo, "Dante and the Pauline Modes of Vision," *HTR*, L (1957), 275–306.

17. An English proverb; see C. Speroni, "Dante's Prophetic Morning-Dreams," *SP*, XLV (1948), 50–59; and Arbesmann, pp. 30–31. "Certiora et colatiore somniari affirmant sub extimis noctibus, quasi iam emergente animarum vigore prodacto sopore,' Tertullian, *De Anima*, 48, 1.

18. "Like all visions (a form of writing for which the Middle Ages had an unhappy partiality), the structure of 'The Vision of Piers Ploughman' is at once confused and artificial; artificial without proportion, and confused without spontaneity," "Piers Ploughman and English Life in the Fourteenth Century," *The Cornhill Magazine*, N.S. III (July-December 1897), 58.

19. I am using the term vision loosely, not strictly as in Macrobius' distinction between *somnium, visio, oraculum, insomnium,* and *visum* (in *Somnium Scipionis*, I, 3), which was widely accepted in the Middle Ages. On dream theory in the ancient Near East, see A. Leo Oppenheim, *The Interpretation of Dreams in the Ancient Near East* ..., *Transactions of the* American Philosophical Society, N.S. XLVI, 3, (1956), pp. 179–373.

20. See August Rüegg, *Die Jenseitsvorstellungen vor Dante und die übrigen literarischen Voraussetzungen der "Divina Commedia": Ein quellenkritischer Kommentar,* 2 vols. (Einsiedeln and Cologne, 1945), and Howard Rollin Patch, *The Other World According to Descriptions in Medieval Literature* (Cambridge, 1950), esp. pp. 80 ff.

21. See Wilhelm Levison, "Die Politik in den Jenseitsvisionen des frühen Mittelalters," *Festgabe Friedrich von Bezold* ... (Bonn and Leipzig, 1921), pp. 81–100.

22. *English Drama from Early Times to the Elizabethans, Its Background, Origins and Developments* (London and New York, 1950), p. 87.

23. I am much indebted in what follows to Miss Owen's analyses in her *Piers Plowman*. The French examples on which I base my comments are *Li Romans de carité* (ed. A. G. van Hamel [Paris, 1885]); *Le Songe d'Enfer* (ed. P. Lebesgue [Paris, 1908]); *La Voie de Paradis* (ed. A. Scheler, Trouvères belges [Louvain, 1876], II, 200–248); *Le Tournoiement de l'Antecrist* (ed. G. Wimmer [Marburg, 1888]); Rutebeuf's *La Voie de Paradis* (ed. P. Lebesgue [Paris, 1908]); Guillaume de Deguileville's *Le Pèlerinage de vie humaine* (ed. J. J. Sturzinger [London, 1893]); *Roman de Fauvel* (ed. A. Langfors [Paris, 1914–1919]); and Robert Grosseteste's *Chasteau d'Amour* (ed. J. Murray [Paris, 1918]). Most of these, but strictly speaking not all, are in dream form.

24. The *Romans de carité* has some features of the encyclopedic satire.

25. "The Life and Death of Longe Will," *ELH*, XVII (1950), 12.

26. See Appendix II.

27. Nevill Coghill, *The Pardon of Piers Plowman,* Sir Israel Gollancz Memorial Lecture, British Academy, 1945, *Proceedings of the British*

Academy, XXX (1944), 37 (cf. pp. 4–9 and *passim*). On *Wynnere and Wastoure*, see, besides Sir Israel Gollancz's edition, Gardiner Stillwell, "*Wynnere and Wastoure* and the Hundred Years' War," *ELH*, VIII (1941), 241–247.

28. I have been considering here allegory as a genre. Edwin Honig in "In Defense of Allegory," *The Kenyon Review*, XX (1958), 1–19, argues that it is also a style. Although he is probably using the term in a more inclusive sense than I am, more in the sense of symbolic mode, he writes interestingly enough (p. 15), "Allegory considered as a stylistic mixture of serious and comic (including the ironic) tones may accommodate, more fully than has traditionally been done, the ubiquitous elements, present in most allegories, of satire, pastoral, and the realistic or verisimilar (formerly the epic) point of view, as well as the tragic sentiment."

29. See Margaret C. Waites, "Some Aspects of the Ancient Allegorical Debate," *Studies in English and Comparative Literature by Former and Present Students at Radcliffe College Presented to Agnes Irwin*, Radcliffe College Monographs 15 (Boston and London, 1910), pp. 75–94, and "Some Features of the Allegorical Debate in Greek Literature," *Harvard Studies in Classical Philology*, XXIII (1912), 1–46; Betty Nye Hedberg, "The *Bucolics* and the Medieval Poetical Debate," *TAPA*, LXXV (1944), 47–67.

30. Stephen Gilman, *The Art of "La Celestina"* (Madison, 1956), pp. 159–160. Gilman, however, erroneously assumes that this type of debate died out in the Middle Ages. See, to take only two examples at hand, Hugh of St. Victor's *De anima et eius ad sui et ad Dei cognitionem* . . . , IV, xiii, xiv, and xv (*PL*, CLXXVII, 185 ff.), where Memoria mortis, Desiderium vitae aeternae, Timor, and the four cardinal virtues debate in the House of Animus; and Matthew of Cracow's *Dialogus conscientiae et rationis* in Leipzig University MS. 487, Heiligenkreuz, Austria, MS. 155, and various other MSS.

31. Father T. P. Dunning, *Piers Plowman: An Interpretation of the A-Text* (Dublin, 1937), pp. 169–172, has stressed the *débat* form of the Vita of the A-Text (Do-wel).

32. See Fritz Klingner, *De Boethii consolatione philosophiae*, Philologische Untersuchungen 27 (Berlin, 1921), pp. 112 ff. A recent attempt to see the influence of Boethius on *Piers* may be seen in R. H. Bowers, "*Piers Plowman* and the Literary Historians," *CE*, XXI (1959–1960), 1–4.

33. "Langland's allegory cannot long remain purely didactic; its natural movement is towards drama," Elizabeth Zeeman, "Piers Plowman and the Pilgrimage to Truth," *Essays and Studies*, N.S. XI (1958), 14. Although rightly emphasizing the dramatic element in Langland's use of personification, this statement should be qualified. For instance, it separates too distinctly the didactic and the allegorical. By its very nature, allegory must always be somewhat didactic.

34. This work and Wireker's may be found in Thomas Wright, *The Anglo-Latin Satirical Poets and Epigrammatists of the Twelfth Century*, Rolls Series I (London, 1872). The *Speculum stultorum* has recently been edited by John H. Mozley and Robert R. Raymo in the University of California, English Studies 18 (Berkeley and Los Angeles, 1960).

35. Frank W. Chandler in *The Literature of Roguery*, The Types of English Literature (Boston and New York, 1907), I, 46–47, points out Langland's numerous references to rogues but neglects to say that Will is something of a rogue himself.

36. There is a brief suggestion at the beginning of the poem of the pastoral, for Will compares his hermit clothes to those of a shepherd. But nothing more is made of this image, and the poem is not, except perhaps for the debate and *conflictus* element, which can be accounted for on other grounds, a pastoral eclogue in any fundamental way. See H. H. Glunz, *Die Literarästhetik des europäischen Mittelalters* (Bochum-Langendreer, 1937), pp. 540–541.

On "unholy of works," see Henry Morley, *Illustrations of English Religion* (London, Paris, New York, n.d.), p. 77. "He put on, not the holy garb of an anchorite in the cell, but the dress of one of the unholy hermits who go up and down and wander to and fro in the earth. . . ." Arthur Gilman, "Our Earliest Allegory," *Appleton's Journal of Literature, Science and Art*, VI (1871), 243. T. Knott and D. Fowler in their edition of the A-Text (Baltimore, 1952), p. 154, translate the phrase as "a false hermit."

37. It is even possible that Langland may have run away from a monastery and thought of himself as a kind of *gyrovagus*.

38. Besides the attacks on false hermits in the Prologue, Langland in XV, 207, says that Piers (Christ) is not among "lande-leperes hermytes" nor deceiving anchorites. Again in C, X, 188 ff., he launches a long attack on false hermits whom he calls "lollers" (v. 192) and in C, VI, 4, he refers to "lewede heremytes."

For other medieval attacks on *gyrovagi* and false hermits, see Richard Rolle's praise of the hermits and his awareness of the dangers of this profession to the soul in the *Incendium amoris*, 13–14 (ed. Margaret Deanesley [Manchester, 1915], pp. 179–187). Note the reference to "girouagi qui sunt scandalum heremitarum" (p. 183), translated in 1435 as "rynnars aboute þar ar sclaunderes of hermyts" (Early English Text Society, o.s. 106 [London, 1896], p. 32). Cf. also the early twelfth-century poem "De falsis heremitis" by Payen Bolotin, recently edited by Dom Jean Leclercq in the *Revue bénédictine*, LXVIII (1958), 52–86, and bibliographical references to eremeticism among monks, esp. pp. 85–86. For the phrase above, "anarchic eremiticism," see Leclercq, p. 67 (a phrase of B. Bligny). See also Helen Waddell, *The Wandering Scholars*, Doubleday Anchor Books (New York, 1955), pp. 175–210; Dom Louis Gougaud, *Ermites et reclus: Études sur d'anciennes formes de vie religieuse*, Moines et Monastères 5 (Liguge [Vienne], 1928), esp. pp. 42–52; and "La Theoria dans la spiritualité médiévale," *Revue d'ascétique et de mystique*, III (1922), 381–394, esp. 392 ff.

39. See my analysis of this dialogue in Chapter V.

40. Note that it is Imaginatif and Anima, both "crafts in his corps," who in Do-wel do give him the fundamental answers to his psychological questions. The psychological part of the quest leads finally to Free Will, the image of God in man, at the beginning of Do-bet. Conscience, who plays a vital role in the poem, is also a "craft" of the soul.

41. See note 38, above, where there is an allusion to C, X, 188 ff., in which false hermits are called "lolleres."

42. On Imaginatif, see Appendix III, below.

43. On Hawkin, see Stella Maguire, "The Significance of Haukyn, *Activa Vita*, in *Piers Plowman*," *RES*, XXV (1949), 97–109.

44. Besides this movement from youthful manhood to old age (and indeed death in A XII, even if the report is by John But; I suspect the very

last lines of XII should have been added to a B- or C-Text MS), we perhaps should see a movement vaguely suggested in the poem of the liturgical year, for the work opens in May, presumably after Pentecost, portrays the search for Do-wel all summer, moves to Easter at the end of Do-bet and closes at Pentecost time, the feast of the Holy Ghost and the mission of the Church. Although Dom D. Rutledge ("Langland and the Liturgical Tradition," *The Dublin Review*, CCXXVIII [1954], 405–416) does not make this particular point, he does see the liturgical tradition, the custodian of which is the monks, as the center of Langland's world of thought. To monks, of course, the liturgical is not merely a way of worship but a way of life. To support this thesis somewhat, one may point to the large number of quotations from the liturgy in the poem. See also Conrad Pepler, "The Spirituality of William Langland," *Blackfriars*, XX (1939), 848.

45. I should perhaps make reference to E. M. W. Tillyard's argument in his *The English Epic and its Background* (London, 1954), pp. 151–171, that "*Piers Plowman* emerges as the undoubted, if imperfect, English epic of the Middle Ages" (p. 171). In the sense of the word that Dr. Tillyard is using, his argument is certainly justified and indeed enlightening, but *Piers* is not an epic in the genre sense of the word, as I think he would agree. Dr. Tillyard is using the term epic as a metaphor only, as my colleague Professor Francis Utley calls Chaucer's *Troilus* a drama or, as others call it, a psychological novel. Such critical metaphors should at all times be distinguished from genre designations. Indeed I do not think that there was any sense of the epic as a literary form in the Middle Ages at all, as Dr. Tillyard himself says (p. 190). There is no question, then, of the epic in the genre background of our poem.

Glunz in his *Literarästhetik*, p. 524, points out that a gloomy ending is characteristic of the school epic since the days of Claudian (e.g., Lucan and Lucretius). However, I do not believe that the ending to *Piers* is in a fundamental sense pessimistic, as Glunz himself also seems to recognize.

46. See *European Literature and the Latin Middle Ages*, trans. W. R. Trask (London, 1953), pp. 83–85. Cf. also Gervase Mathew's reference to the "convention of literary self-caricature" in "Justice and Charity in *The Vision of Piers Plowman*," *Dominican Studies*, I (1948), 362.

47. *Complaint and Satire in Early English Literature* (Oxford, 1956), pp. 1–39, in particular. His three special examples of the Latin complaint writers—Aldhelm, Peter Damian, and Bernard of Morval (?)—are all monks. Peter does not, however, specifically tie in the complaint with the *contemptus mundi* theme. The source of the distinction between complaint and satire for Peter is a chapter heading in J. Wells' *Manual of Writings in Middle English*.

48. See his unpublished University of Florida doctoral dissertation "The Contempt of the World: A Study in the Ideology of Latin Christendom . . . ," 1954. I am indebted to this work (especially pp. 187–196) and to conversations with Dr. Howard for some of my comments in this section.

49. See Langland's specific allusion to them in XI, 11 ff.

50. See Morton W. Bloomfield, "Symbolism in Medieval Literature," *MP*, LVI (1958–1959), 73–81.

51. See Beryl Smalley, "The Biblical Scholar," *Robert Grosseteste, Scholar and Bishop: Essays in Commemoration of the Seventh Centenary of his Death*, ed. D. A. Callus (Oxford, 1955), pp. 70–97, esp. pp. 86–87.

52. The use of quotations to forward the argument is also due to the sermon form as will be seen.

53. *Literature and Pulpit in Medieval England: A Neglected Chapter in the History of English Letters and of the English* (Cambridge, England, 1933). See also Owst's earlier *Preaching in Medieval England: An Introduction to Sermon Manuscripts of the Period c. 1350–1450* (Cambridge, England, 1926), esp. Part III, pp. 222 ff. There is an extensive literature on medieval sermons and *artes predicandi* (handbooks on the art of preaching), which need not be listed here. Up to 1933 Owst provides convenient references, and other bibliographies cover the later period. For the section referred to in the next sentence, see *Literature and Pulpit*, pp. 210 ff. and also pp. 548 ff.

54. In Bernard, see, e.g., Parabola I, "De pugna spirituali...", *PL*, CLXXXIII, 757 ff., with its Castle of Sapience, *Spes* going on a journey, the moat of humility, the mountain of pride, and so forth. Cf. also Sermo VIII in *PL*, CLXXXIII, 561 ff.

55. Owst, *Preaching*, p. 247. See J. A. W. Bennett in *RES*, N.S. VIII (1957), 55.

56. *Preaching*, p. 295.

57. See J. A. Burrow, "The Audience of *Piers Plowman*," *Anglia*, LXXV (1957), 373–384, esp. pp. 379 ff. The quotation below is from p. 382. He analyzes some of the differences between the alliterative style of *Piers* and the other alliterative poems and accounts for them on the basis of a difference in audience. "They [the other alliterative poems] seem to rely on the intrinsic interest of the alliterative line and language to hold the audience's attention, as if, sometimes, the mere display of the words were enough. The sense is continually being forced to eddy back in order to include another synonym" (p. 380). J. Hulbert in "A Hypothesis Concerning the Alliterative Revival," *MP*, XXVIII (1930–1931), 405–422, admits *Piers* is not baronial in its interests, like most of the other alliterative poems. For some analyses of Langland's use of alliteration, see J. P. Oakden, *Alliterative Poetry in Middle English*, Publications of the University of Manchester CCV and CCXXXVI, 2 vols. (Manchester, 1930–1935), *passim*. Oakden must, however, be used with caution.

58. *De doctrina christiana*, IV, 20. See, e.g., Charles Sears Baldwin, *Medieval Rhetoric and Poetic (to 1400) Interpreted from Representative Works* (New York, 1928), pp. 67 ff.

59. *The Beginnings of English Literature to Skelton*, Introductions to English Literature, ed. Bonamy Dobrée, I (New York, 1940), p. 75.

60. Sister Carmeline Sullivan, *The Latin Insertions and the Macaronic Verse in Piers Plowman*, a Dissertation...Catholic University of America ...(Washington, 1932), p. vii. This work provides the basic material for a study of this feature of Langland's style.

61. This assumption is made not only in connection with specific quotations but in developing details such as the cart of Liar which transports the gang at the marriage of Meed and False to Westminster. See Alfred L. Kellogg, "Langland and two Scriptural Texts," *Traditio*, XIV (1958), 390–398. D. W. Robertson, Jr., and Bernard F. Huppé in *Piers Plowman and Scriptural Tradition* (Princeton, 1951) present valuable information on many of these quotations from scriptural commentaries.

62. See M. Ray Adams, "The Use of the Vulgate in *Piers Plowman*," *SP*, XXIV (1927), 556–566, and Hort, *Piers Plowman*..., pp. 43 ff. The source

of many of these biblical quotations may, of course, be the breviary and the missal.

63. P. Dumontier, *Saint Bernard et la Bible*, Présentation par J. M. Dechanet, Bibliothèque de Spiritualité médiévale (Paris, 1953), p. 157. On "biblical style," as the author calls it, see all of his Chapter VI (pp. 157 ff.). This point is further discussed in my next chapter.

64. Hort, *Piers Plowman* ..., p. 40.

65. A notable exception is Randolph Quirk's article, "Langland's Use of *Kind Wit* and *Inwit*," *JEGP*, LII (1953), 182–188, which shows how many meanings (from the point of view of Latin) these words had to bear in ME.

66. A phrase used of Bernard of Clairvaux's Latin style and of pre-thirteenth century medieval Latin style in general by Luigi Malagoli, "Forme dello stile mediolatino e forme dello stile volgare," *Studi letterari: Miscellanea in onore di Emilio Santini* (Palermo, 1956), pp. 57–86.

67. See Friedrich Sellert, *Das Bild in Piers the Plowman*, Inaugural Dissertation ... Universität Rostock (Rostock, 1904), for a study of Langland's imagery, which by Sellert's definition also includes his personifications. See also R. E. Kaske, "The Use of Simple Figures of Speech in *Piers Plowman* B: A Study in the Figurative Expression of Ideas and Opinions," *SP*, XLVIII (1951), 571–600.

68. "*Petrus id est Christus*: Word Play in *Piers Plowman*, the B-Text," *ELH*, XVII (1950), 163–190. See also Helmut Maisack, *William Langlands Vehältnis zum zisterziensischen Mönchtum: Eine Untersuchung der Vita imr "Piers Plowman,"* Inaugural Dissertation ... Universität Tübingen (Balingen, 1953), 120–126, for lists of repetitions, puns, antitheses, and the like in *Piers*. For a significant study of Langland's vocabulary, see Heinz Kittner, *Studien zum Wortschatz William Langlands*, Inaugural Dissertation ... Martin Luther-Universität, Halle-Wittenberg (Halle Saale, 1937).

69. "I can only record my impression that Langland's alliterative line is a very flexible medium, able not only to achieve the sententious effect to which alliteration is particularly apt [?] but to cope with sustained thought and exalted feeling." E. M. W. Tillyard, *The English Renaissance: Fact or Fiction?*, Hogarth Lectures on Literature (London, 1952), p. 92.

70. See Appendix II, below.

71. See Burrow, "Audience." Cf. "... *Piers Plowman* originated in a clerical circle, and appealed first to those who were clerks and moved in the atmosphere which had given birth to the poem. Langland dealt with the burning questions of his day, and he answered the questions that were in the minds of the more thoughtful people, be they clerical or lay," Hort, *Piers Plowman* ..., pp. 156–157. See also David Daiches, *Literature and Society* (London, 1938), pp. 66–67; and Lewis, *The Allegory of Love*, p. 159.

72. *The English Church in the Fourteenth Century*, based on the Birkbeck Lectures, 1948 (Cambridge, England, 1955), p. 233. (On p. 29, he calls him "a more or less submerged cleric.")

NOTES FOR CHAPTER II

1. See Th. Camelot, "Théologie monastique et théologie scolastique," *Revue des sciences philosophiques et théologiques*, XLII (1958), 240–253, for a good summary of the distinction between the two. See also Dom

Jean Leclercq, *L'Amour des lettres et le désir de Dieu: Initiation aux auteurs monastiques du moyen âge* (Paris, 1957), esp. pp. 179 ff.

2. Robert W. Frank, Jr., *Piers Plowman and the Scheme of Salvation*, Yale Studies in English 136 (New Haven, 1957), pp. 112 ff., stresses the importance of the reform of the friars to Langland but does not explain why. This book is an excellent study of the poem and may be highly recommended.

3. The episode is alluded to and this letter quoted in English in E. F. Jacob, "*Florida verborum venustas:* Some Early Examples of Euphuism in England," *Bulletin of the John Rylands Library*, XVII (1933), 272–273.

4. See the recent article by Father Jean Daniélou, "Terre et Paradis chez les pères de l'église," *Eranos Jahrbuch*, XXII (1953), 433–472, to which I am indebted for much of what immediately follows. See also N. A. Dahl, "Christ, Creation and the Church," *The Background of the New Testament and Its Eschatology*, ed. W. D. Davies and D. Daube (Cambridge, England, 1956), pp. 422–443. On the earthly paradise and antelapsarian man, see Antoine Slomkowski, *L'Etat primitif de l'homme dans la tradition de l'église avant Saint Augustine, Thèse ... Université de Strasbourg* (Paris, 1928).

5. See, for instance, Hugh de Fouilloi's *De claustro animae* of the twelfth century (*PL*, CLXXVI, 1017 ff.), which treats of three cloisters, the material, the spiritual (the soul), and heaven. On Fouilloi, see Henry Peltier, "Hughes de Fouilloy ... *RMAL*, II (1946), 25–44. M. Lot-Borodine calls this religious view, the theology of paradise in "*Le Conte del Graal* de Chrétien de Troyes et sa présentation symbolique," *Romania*, LXXVII (1956), 283.

6. See Louis Bouyer, *La Vie de S. Antoine: Essai sur la spiritualité du monachisme primitif*, Figures monastiques (Abbaye S. Wandrille, 1950), pp. 34–35, 67, 178, *et passim*. Clement of Alexandria writes of the Christian life, "This is the true athlete—he who in the great stadium, the fair world, is crowned for the true victory over all the passions. For He who prescribes the contest is the Almighty God, and He who awards the prize is the only-begotten Son of God. Angels and gods are spectators; and the contest, embracing all the varied exercises, is 'not against flesh and blood' [Ephesians 6:12], but against the spiritual powers of inordinate passions that work through the flesh." *Stromata*, VII, 3 (Ante-Nicene Fathers trans.).

7. On the philosophy of monasticism, although the term is not always used, see the references in Morton W. Bloomfield, "*Piers Plowman* and the Three Grades of Chastity," *Anglia*, LXXVI (1958), 228, n. 2, and the following: Edward E. Malone, *The Monk and the Martyr, the Monk as the Successor of the Martyr*, a Dissertation ... Catholic University of America ... (Washington, 1950); Kassius Hallinger, "Zur geistigen Welt der Anfänge Klunys," *Deutsches Archiv für Erforschung des Mittelalters*, X (1953–1954), 417–445; Dom Jean Leclercq, "S. Bernard et le théologie monastique de XIIᵉ siècle," *Saint Bernard théologien, Acts du Congrés de Dijon, 15–19 Septembre 1953*, Analecta sacri ordinis Cisterciensis IX (Rome, 1953), pp. 7–23; Adalbert de Vogüe, "Le Monastère, église du Christ," *Commentationes in Regulam S. Benedicti*, ed. B. Steidle, Studia anselmiana 42 (Rome, 1957), pp. 25–46; A. Mouraux, "La Vie apostolique à propos de Rupert de Deutz, †1135," *Revue liturgique et monastique*, XXI (1935–1936), 71–78, 125–141, 264–276; Dom P. Salmon, "L'Ascèse monastique et les origines de Cîteaux," *Mélanges Saint Bernard*,

*XXIVe Congrès de l'Association bourguignonne des Sociétés savantes...,
Dijon, 1953* (Dijon, n.d.), pp. 268–283; J. Didier, " 'Angelisme' ou perspectives eschatologiques," *Mélanges de science religieuse,* XI (1954), 31–48. See also note 1 above.

8. See E. Gilson, *Reason and Revelation in the Middle Ages* (New York, 1938), 87 ff.

9. See Paul de Vooght, *Les Sources de la doctrine chrétienne d'après les théologiens du XIVe siècle*... (Bruges, 1954), who deals with this issue in our period in excellent fashion.

10. See the recent work by Gordon Leff, *Bradwardine and the Pelagians: A Study of His "De causa Dei" and Its Opponents* (Cambridge, England, 1957).

11. Matthew 5:48. In the parallel dictum in Luke 6:36 the command is to be "merciful," perhaps actually Jesus' words.

12. E.g., Hebrews 2:10; 5:9; 7:19; 9:9; 10:1; 10:14; 11:40; 12:23; II Corinthians 7:1; 12:9; I John 4:17; 4:18; Galatians 3:3, etc. See Allen Wikgren, "Patterns of Perfection in the Epistle to the Hebrews," *New Testament Studies,* VI (1959–1960), 159–167.

13. See Ch. Guignebert, "Quelques Remarques sur la perfection (τελείωσις) et ses voies dans le mystère paulinien," *Revue d'histoire et de philosophie religieuses,* VIII (1928), 412–429. Arnaldo M. Lanz in the *Enciclopedia cattolica,* IX, 1173–1175, denies this suggested origin of the term and tries to trace it to the Hebrew *tam* (or *tamam*) without at the same time giving the ancient Hebrews much credit for a profound sense of religious perfection.

14. *Legum allegoria,* I, 94, and III, 159.

15. See Raffaello Morghen, *Medioevo cristiano,* Biblioteca di cultura moderna 491 (Bari, 1951), pp. 212–286.

16. Yet speculation on the perfection of man is by no means unknown in Judaism. See, e.g., the final chapters (III, 51–54) of Maimonides, *Guide for the Perplexed*; and Saadia Gaon, *The Book of Beliefs and Opinion,* V, 4, and X (trans. S. Rosenblatt [New Haven, 1948], pp. 217–218 and 357 ff.). For Islam, see Louis Massignon, "L'Homme parfait en Islam et son originalité eschatologique," *Eranos-Jahrbuch,* XV (1947), 287–314.

17. There is a very large bibliography on the idea of deification in Christian thinking. The root of the idea is probably in Plato's *Theatetus,* 176 a–c, and is certainly present in Philo and St. Irenaeus. See C. G. Rutenber, *The Doctrine of The Imitation of God in Plato,* a Dissertation... University of Pennsylvania (Philadelphia, 1946). On the Hebrew side, it lies in man's having been made in the image of God. See, on the whole concept, M. Lot-Borodine, "La Doctrine de la déification dans l'église grecque jusqu'au XIe siècle," *RHR,* CV (1932), 5–43, CVI (1932), 525–574, CVII (1933), 8–55; Jules Gross, *La Divinisation du Chrétien d'après les pères grecs: Contribution historique à la doctrine de la grace,* Thèse... Université de Strasbourg, Faculté de théologie catholique (Paris, 1938); Philip T. Wild, *The Divinization of Man According to Saint Hilary of Poitiers,* Pontificia Facultas theologica, Seminarii sanctae Mariae ad Lacum, Dissertationes ad lauream 21 (Mundelein, Illinois, 1950); Fritz Taeger, "Zur Vergottung des Menschen im Altertum," *ZKG,* LXI (1942), 3–26; Gerhart B. Ladner, "Die mittelalterliche Reform-Idee und ihr Verhältnis zur Idee der Renaissance," *Mitteilungen des Instituts für österreichische Geschichtsforschung,* LX (1952), 31 ff; Ludwig Koehler, "Die Grundstelle der Imago-Dei Lehre,

Genesis 1, 26," *Theologische Zeitschrift*, IV (1948), 16–22; Karl L. Schmidt, "Homo imago Dei im alten und neuen Testament," *Eranos-Jahrbuch*, XV (1947), 149–195; P. Hubert Merki, *ʹOMOIΩΣΙΣ ΘΕΩ von der platonischen Angleichung an Gott Gottähnlichkeit bei Gregor von Nyssa*, Paradosis VII (Freiburg in Switzerland, 1952); A. J. Festugière, *Contemplation et vie contemplative selon Plato*, 2nd ed. (Paris, 1950); Henri Crouzel, *Théologie de l'image de Dieu chez Origène*, Théologie, Etudes publiés sous la direction de la Faculté de Théologie, S.J., de Lyon-Fourvière 34 (Paris, 1956); Ludwig Baur, "Untersuchungen über die Vergöttlichungslehre in der Theologie der griechischen Väter," *Theologische Quartalschrift*, XCVIII (1916), 467–491, XCIX (1917–1918), 225–252, C (1919), 426–444, CI (1920), 28–64, 155–186; and Victorino Capánaga, "La Deificación en la soteriología augustiniana," *Augustinus Magister*, Congrès international augustinien, Paris, 21–24 Septembre 1954 (Paris 1954–1955), II, 745–754.

18. See Joseph Pascher, *ʹHBAΣΙΛΉ ΌΛΟΣ, Der Königsweg zu Wiedergeburt und Vergottung bei Philon von Alexandreia*, Studien zur Geschichte und Kultur des Altertums XVII, 3–4 (Paderborn, 1931); Walther Völker, *Fortschritt und Vollendung bei Philo von Alexandrien: Eine Studie zur Geschichte der Frömmigkeit* (Leipzig, 1938), csp. pp. 260 ff.; Erwin R. Goodenough, *By Light, Light: The Mystic Gospel of Hellenistic Judaism* (New Haven, 1935).

19. On Clement, see Walther Völker, *Der wahre Gnostiker nach Clemens Alexandrinus* (Berlin and Leipzig, 1952). On Origen, see Crouzel, *Théologie*; Walther Völker, *Die Vollkommenheitsideal des Origenes: Eine Untersuchung zur Geschichte der Frömmigkeit und zu den Anfängen christlicher Mystik* (Tübingen, 1931); Hans Windisch, *Taufe und Sünde im ältesten Christentum bis auf Origenes: Ein Beitrag zur altchristlichen Dogmengeschichte* (Tübingen, 1908); George Bürke, "Des Origenes Lehre vom Urstand des Menschen," *ŽKT*, LXXII (1950), 1–39; Hugo Rahner, "Das Menschenbild des Origenes," *Eranos Jahrbuch*, XV (1947), 197–248.

20. See Paul Wendland, " *Σωτήρ* ," *ZNTW*, V (1904), 335–353, and *Die hellenistisch-römische Kultur in ihren Beziehungen zu Judentum und Christentum*, Handbuch zum neuen Testament I, 2 (Tübingen, 1912), pp. 23 ff. *et passim*; Hans Lietzmann, "Der Weltheiland," reprinted in *Kleine Schriften*, I, Studien zu spätantiken Religionsgeschichte, ed. Kurt Aland, Texte und Untersuchungen zur Geschichte der alt-christlichen Literatur 67 (Berlin, 1958), pp. 25–62; Ernst Kornemann, "Zur Geschichte der antiken Herrscherkulte," *Klio, Beiträge zur alten Geschichte*, I (1901), 51–146; L. Cerfaux and J. Tondriau, *Un Concurrent du Christianisme: Le Culte des souverains dans la civilisation gréco-romaine*, Bibliothèque de Théologie, Série III, Vol. V (Tournai, 1957); and Johannes A. Straub, *Vom Herrscherideal, in der Spätantike* (Stuttgart, 1934). In recent years, the divine or semi-divine king idea has been extensively investigated. Here are a few of the many items that have recently appeared, besides those listed above: Aubrey R. Johnson, *Sacral Kingship in Ancient Israel* (Cardiff, 1955); Rudolf Mayer, "Der Erlöserkönig des Alten Testaments," *Münchener theologische Zeitschrift*, III (1952), 221–243; 367–384; and Fritz Taeger, *Charisma, Studien zur Geschichte des antiken Herrscherkultes*, 2 vols. (Stuttgart, 1957–1960). The classic treatment of the world saviour-emperor is in various books and articles by Franz Kampers.

21. Most authoritatively studied in Friedrich Baethgen, *Der Engelpapst, Idee und Erscheinung* (Leipzig, 1943).

22. X, 326–327. Bruno Nardi (in *Dante e la cultura medievale*, Biblioteca di cultura moderna 368 [Bari, 1942], p. 269) points out that common to Dante, Olivi, Ubertino, and all followers of the Eternal Evangel was the certainty of the advent of an envoy of God who would lead the Church back to evangelical poverty and kill the monster of the Apocalypse. Langland was also imbued with this idea.

23. On Philo, see note 18, above. On Gregory, see his *Life of Moses*, ed. J. Daniélou, Sources chrétiennes No. 1 bis, 2nd ed. (Paris, 1955), and the introduction, esp. pp. xviii–xxiv; and Hans von Balthasar, *Présence et pensée: Essai sur la philosophie religieuse de Grégoire de Nysse* (Paris, 1942).

24. Gregory of Nyssa, *Life of Moses*, ed. Daniélou, p. xix.

25. See Morton W. Bloomfield, "Some Reflections on the Medieval Idea of Perfection," *Franciscan Studies*, XVII (1957), 213–237.

26. Rahner, "Das Menschenbild...," p. 239. "Il sommo desiderio di ciascuna cosa e prima dalla Natura dato è lo ritonare al suo principio," Dante, *Convivio*, IV, 12.

27. For a good recent treatment, see René Roques, *L'Univers dionysien, structure hiérarchique du monde selon le pseudo-Denys*, Théologie, Etudes publiées sous la direction de la Faculté de Théologie, S.J., de Lyon-Fourvière 29 (Paris, 1954).

28. See Günther Müller, "Gradualismus: Eine Vorstudie zur altdeutschen Literaturgeschichte," *Deutsche Vierteljahrsschrift für Literaturwissenschaft und Geistesgeschichte*, II (1924), 681–720; and below, Chapter IV, note 11.

29. See Elias J. Bickerman, "The Name of Christians," *HTR*, XLII (1949), 109–124; but see the criticism of this interpretation and another in Harold B. Mattingly, "The Origin of the Name *Christian*," *JTS*, IX, N.S. (1958), 26–37.

30. On this whole subject, see Malone, *The Monk and the Martyr*. Cf. also E. Lohmeyer, "L'Idée du martyre dans le Judaïsme et le Christianisme primitif," *Congrès d'Histoire du Christianisme, Jubilé Alfred Loisy II, Annales d'histoire du Christianisme* (Paris, 1928), pp. 121–137; Franz Dornseiff, "Der Märtyrer: Name und Bewertung," *ARW*, XXII (1923–1924), 133–153; F. Kattenbusch, "Der Märtyrertitel," *ZNTW*, IV (1903), 111–127; Karl Holl, "Die Vorstellung vom Märtyrer und die Märtyrerakte in ihrer geschichtlichen Entwicklung," *Neue Jahrbücher für das klassische Altertum*, XXXIII (1914), 521–556; L. Gougaud, "Le Désir du martyre et le quasi-martyre," in *Dévotions et pratiques ascétiques du moyen âge*, Pax, XXI (Paris, 1925), pp. 200–219; and Marcel Viller and Karl Rahner, *Aszese und Mystik in der Väterzeit: Ein Abriss* (Freiburg im Breisgau, 1939), pp. 29–40 (pp. 41–59 deal with virginity, a second or substitute martyrdom).

31. Cf. the question, "Qui sunt perfecti," and the answer, "Quibus praecepta non sufficiunt, sed plus quam praeceptum sit faciunt, ut martyres, monachi, virgines," in the *Elucidarium*, III, 4 (c. 1105), ed. Yves Lefèvre, Bibliothèque des Ecoles françaises d'Athènes et de Rome, Fascicule 180 (Paris, 1954), p. 444. The term monk *monachos* is probably a translation of the Syriac *ihidaja* ("the unique"), one who has attained the highest stage of *ascesis*. In the West *monachus* has usually been considered equivalent to *solitarius*, but *singularis* is probably more correct. See Alfred Adam, "Grund-

begriffe des Mönchtums in sprachlicher Sicht," *ZKG*, LXV (1953–1954), 209–239. On Christ as a pilgrim, see Dom Anselme Stolz, *L'Ascèse chrétienne* (Chevetogne, 1948), pp. 82–119.

32. "The motive that drove all the chief founders of monasticism to forsake the world was the desire of perfection," R. Newton Flew, *The Idea of Perfection in Christian Theology* (London, 1934), p. 158.

33. On the importance of these two great figures in establishing the framework for and content of much of medieval ethics and spirituality, see the introduction, pp. 1–3, of Max Walther, *Pondus, Dispensatio, Dispositio, Werthistorische Untersuchungen zur Frömmigkeit Papst Gregors des Grossen*, Inaugural Dissertation . . . Universität Bern . . . (Bern?, 1941). See also Marcel Viller and Karl Rahner, *Aszese und Mystik in der Väterzeit* (Freiburg im Breisgau, 1939), pp. 247–277.

34. See Amato Masnovo, "L'Ascesa verso Dio in S. Agostino," *S. Agostino, Pubblicazione commemorativa del XV centenario della sua morte* . . . pubblicata a cura della Facoltà di Filosofia dell' Università Cattolica del Sacro Cuore, *Rivista di filosofia neo-scolastica*, Supplemento speciale al volume XXIII (Milan, 1931), pp. 31–41.

35. The best introduction to Augustine's comments on and prescriptions for monks, with an anthology of texts from his writings, is Adolar Zumkeller's *Das Mönchtum des heiligen Augustinus*, Cassiciacum XI, Reihe 1, Band 5 (Würzburg, 1950). See also his "Augustinus und das Mönchtum," *L'Année théologique augustinienne*, XIV (1954), 97–112. To these works I am much indebted. On deification and the image of God concepts in Augustine, see Capánaga, "La deificación . . ."; and Herman Somers, "Image de Dieu et illumination divine: Sources historiques et élaboration augustinienne," *Augustinus Magister* . . . , I, 450–462.

36. Gerhart B. Ladner "St. Augustine's Conception of the Reformation of Man to the Image of God," *Augustinus Magister* . . . , II, 877. "The message that the Bishop of Hippo . . . brought . . . to men is in effect that the whole world from its beginning to its end has for its only goal the establishment of a holy society; everything including the universe itself, has been made toward this end," Etienne Gilson, *Les Metamorphoses de la Cité de Dieu* (Paris, 1952), p. 36 (trans. J. Doebele). "L'idéal de saint Augustin . . . c'est l'idéal de la vie commune, telle que les apôtres à Jérusalem au lendemain de la Pentecôte l'ont pratiquée." E. Delaruelle, "Le Travail dans les règles monastiques occidentales du quatrième au neuvième siècle," *Journal de psychologie normale et pathologique*, XLI (1948), 53. For a recent treatment of Augustine's social teachings and point of view, see Hans Joachim Diesner, *Studien zur Gesellschaftslehre und sozialen Haltung Augustins* (Halle Saale, 1954).

37. In the West in general, monks kept out of ordinary parochial and ecclesiastical affairs, unlike their Eastern counterparts. Monks did, however, on occasion take over important Church and worldly offices. Yet in theory the monk in the West was concerned with his whole role in society and not merely with the state of his soul. See Philipp Hofmeister, "Mönchtum und Seelsorge bis zum 13. Jahrhundert," *Studien und Mitteilungen zum Geschichte des Benediktner Ordens und seiner Zweige*, LXV (1953–1954), 209–273.

38. See Georges Folliet, "Les Trois Catégories de chrétiens . . ." in *L'Année théologique augustinienne*, XIV (1954), 81–96; and Somers "Image de Dieu," *Augustinus Magister* . . . , II, 631–644, where references to

Augustine's works will be found. The work *De opere monachorum*, referred to above, may be found in *PL*, XL, 569 ff.

39. See *De sancta virginitate*, XLV (CSEL, XLI, 290), and *Quaestionum evangeliorum*, I, 9 (*PL*, XXXV, 1325–1326) (where the triad is, however, martyrs, virgins, and married folk). Augustine's source is probably Ambrose; see his *De viduis*, IV, 23, and XIV, 83 (*PL*, XVI, 254–255; 273–274), *Epistola*, LXIII, 40 (*PL*, XVI, 1251), and *De virginitate*, VI, 34 (*PL*, XVI, 288). Cf. Jerome, *Adversus Jovinianum*, I, 3 (*PL*, XXIII, 223) and *Epistola*, XLVIII, 3 (*PL*, XXII, 495); LXVI, 2 (*PL*, XXII, 639); and CXXIII, 9 (*PL*, XXII, 1052).

40. See Ladner, "St. Augustine's Conception of the Reformation of Man to the Image of God," pp. 867–878, and "Die mittelalterliche Reform-Idee ...." Here I am following Ladner's ideas very closely.

41. Augustine, as Dom Cuthbert Butler points out in his *Western Mysticism* ..., 2nd ed. (London, 1951, reprint of 1926), p. 130, stands somewhat apart from Cassian, Gregory the Great, and Bernard in his assessment of mysticism and monastic spirituality; Butler attributes it to his Neoplatonism.

42. On Augustine's view of history, see Giuseppe Amari, *Il Concetto di storia in Sant'Agostino* (Rome, 1951).

43. See R. T. Marshall, *Studies in the Political and Socio-religious Terminology of the "De civitate Dei,"* a Dissertation ... Catholic University of America ..., Patristic Studies LXXXVI (Washington, 1952), for many references in *De civitate Dei* to the pilgrimage metaphor. Cf. below, Chapter III, note 49. This image of venerable antiquity is discussed in Evelyn Underhill, *Mysticism: A Study in the Nature and Development of Man's Spiritual Consciousness*, 4th ed. (London, 1912), pp. 154–162. We journey horizontally and vertically towards God (or the Devil). See Hebrews 13:14; 11:10, 14, 16, etc. Philo uses the idea continually especially with an ethical significance. See above, Chapter I, note 7.

44. A metaphor found throughout Augustine's writings and also of great antiquity. See, e.g., Sermon CXXVIII, which is devoted to the battle of the soul against the concupiscence of the flesh. The ascension towards God is a continual struggle against evil and to the early monks the goal was *apatheia*. For references to the theme, mainly in pagan, Jewish, and early Christian writings, see Morton W. Bloomfield, *The Seven Deadly Sins* (East Lansing, Michigan, 1952), pp. 10, 27, 52, 59, 60, 62 ff., *et passim*.

45. The Augustinian concept of cosmic order and its reflection in the soul and in moral life has been studied by W. J. Roche in "Measure, Number, and Weight in Saint Augustine," *The New Scholasticism*, XV (1941), 350–376, whose excellent analysis I am following here and whose words I occasionally use. See also Walther, *Pondus, Dispensatio, Dispositio ...*, pp. 57 ff.

46. See Cicero's *De officiis* I, 27–42, on temperance, which he equates with propriety and decorum and modesty. He implies, at least in I, 45, that after wisdom it is the most important of the virtues. Of course, to Augustine as a Christian, temperance meant much more, above all, comprising restraint of and conquest over concupiscence.

47. See Dom Olegario María Porcel, *La Doctrina monástica de San Gregorio Magno y la "Regula monachorum,"* a Dissertation ... Catholic University of America ..., Studies in Sacred Theology, Second Series No. 60 (Washington, 1951), p. 61. Besides this work and relevant sections

in the large standard works on Gregory like that of F. H. Dudden, on Gregory's thought, see Leonhard Weber, *Hauptfragen der Moraltheologie Gregors des Grossen: Ein Bild altchristlicher Lebensführung*, Paradosis I (Freiburg in Switzerland, 1947), (with an excellent bibliography); and Dom Cuthbert Butler, *Western Mysticism*, pp. 65–92. A large collection of material in periodicals is alluded to in Weber (up to 1946). See also Dom Jean Leclercq, *L'Amour des lettres et le désir de Dieu* . . . , pp. 30–39.

48. Porcel, *La Doctrina monástica*, pp. 99 ff. and 109 ff.

49. See *Moralia*, XXXII, 20 (*PL*, LXXVI, 657).

50. See Bloomfield, *The Seven Deadly Sins*, pp. 72 ff.

51. On this paragraph, see Walther's valuable and interesting dissertation, *Pondus, Dispensatio, Dispositio*. . . . We also find there a study of the concept of *pondus* in antiquity, pp. 40 ff.

52. ". . . le monastère n'est pas *une* Eglise particulière, mais plutôt la pointe et l'avant-garde de l'Eglise entière," Vogüé, "Le Monastère, église du Christ," p. 43.

53. In "Zur geistigen Welt der Anfänge Klunys . . . ," pp. 417–445. See also Rose Graham, "The Relation of Cluny to Some Other Movements of Monastic Reform," *JTS*, XV (1914), 179–195.

54. Hans Frhr. von Campenhausen, *Die asketische Heimatlosigkeit im altkirchlichen und frühmittelalterlichen Mönchtum* (Tübingen, 1930), p. 8. See this whole book for the idea of homelessness on earth in early monasticism, a force which drove many of the Irish saints to go wandering on the seas without a definite goal.

55. For a brief history of the rise of chronicles and annals in the West, see G. N. Garmonsway's introduction to his translation of the *Anglo-Saxon Chronicle* in Everyman's Library (London and New York, 1953), pp. xix ff.

56. See, however, Enrico de' Negri, "The Legendary Style of the Decameron," *Romanic Review*, XLIII (1952), 166–189, for an interesting study of saints' lives or legends as models for medieval narrative, and Boccaccio's *Decameron* in particular. On other monastic genres, see Leclercq, *L'Amour des lettres*, pp. 145–178. Leclercq also refers to florilegia, letters, and monastic sermons.

57. The most elaborate attempt (although marred at times by special pleading and an attempt to find too much autobiography in the poem) to relate *Piers* to Bernard and the Cistercian tradition may be found in Helmut Maisack, *William Langlands Verhältnis zum zisterziensischen Mönchtum* . . . , Inaugural Dissertation . . . Universität . . . Tübingen . . . (Balingen, 1953). E. Talbot Donaldson, *Piers Plowman: The C-Text and Its Poet*, Yale Studies in English 113 (New Haven, 1949), also makes considerable use of Bernard to explain the poem.

58. See Morton W. Bloomfield, "Joachim of Flora: A Critical Survey of his Canon, Teachings, Sources, Biography and Influence," *Traditio*, XII (1957), 247–311.

59. See Appendix III, below.

60. See Philippe Delhaye, *Le Problème de la conscience morale chez S. Bernard, Etudié dans ses oeuvres et dans ses sources*, Analecta mediaevalia namurcensia 9 (Namur, Louvain, and Lille, 1957).

61 See Dumontier's *Saint Bernard et la Bible*, Présentation par J. M. Dechanet, Bibliothèque de Spiritualité médiévale (Paris, 1953), pp. 157 ff. On similarity of linguistic style between Langland and Bernard, see Maisack, *William Langlands Verhältnis*, pp. 120 ff. On Bernard's literary style in

general, see Luigi Negri, "Appunti sulla personalità letteraria di S. Bernardo," *Humanitas*, IX (1954), 625–637 (the quotation above is translated from Negri, p. 636); and Jean Leclercq, "Aspects littéraires de l'oeuvre de Saint Bernard," *Cahiers de civilisation médiévale*, I (1958), 425–450. This subject has been briefly discussed in Chapter I above.

62 "In Augustine's thought, religious perfection is possible at every point of the course of history after Christ; in Joachim's thought only in a definite period at a definite juncture. To Augustine the Christian truth is revealed in one single event, to Joachim in a succession of dispensations," Karl Löwith, *Meaning in History: The Theological Implications of the Philosophy of History* (Chicago, 1949), p. 156.

63. See E. Benz, "La Messianità di San Benedetto: Contributo alla filosofia della storia di Gioacchino da Fiore," *Ricerche religiose*, VII (1931), 336–353.

64. On the evidence for assuming a knowledge of Joachim in England, see Appendix I, below.

NOTES FOR CHAPTER III

1. "Was William Langland a Benedictine Monk?" *MLQ*, IV (1943), 57–61.

2. There were many more of these than is commonly realized: "But many of those who were ordained in the Middle Ages were clerks in minor orders, below the rank of deacon, and often they did not advance any further, but practically lived as laymen." A. Abram, *English Life and Manners in the Middle Ages* (London, 1913), p. 51. See also the figures Abram gives of William of Wykeham's ordinations, pp. 51–52. See also E. Talbot Donaldson, *Piers Plowman: The C-Text and Its Poet*, Yale Studies in English 113 (New Haven, 1949), pp. 202 ff.

3. This awareness of the symbolic significance of the cloister for Langland is discussed later in the chapter.

4. On hermits and anchorites, see F. D. S. Darwin, *The English Mediaeval Recluse* (London, n.d.), pp. 1–5; Rotha Mary Clay, *The Hermits and Anchorites of England* (London, 1914); Dom Paul Piolin, "Note sur la réclusion religieuse," *Bulletin monumental*, XLV (1879), 449–480, XLVI (1880), 518–550; and J. J. Jusserand, *English Wayfaring Life in the Middle Ages (XIVth Century)*, trans., 4th ed. (London, 1892), pp. 137–143. On wandering religious and clerics in the Middle Ages generally, see Martin Bechthum, *Beweggründe und Bedeutung des Vagantentums in der lateinischen Kirche des Mittelalters*, Beiträge zur mittelalterlichen, neueren und allgemeinen Geschichte 14 (Jena, 1941).

5. See *Speculum inclusorum, auctore anonymo anglico saeculi XIV*, ed. P. Livario Oliger, Lateranum, N.S. IV, 1 (Rome, 1938), pp. 9–12 and 41. "The desire for a solitary life in later Medieval England was widespread," Dom Hugh Farmer, "The Meditations of the Monk of Farne," *Analecta monastica*, 4th Series, Studia anselmiana 41 (1957), p. 142. See also Peter F. Anson, *The Quest of Solitude* (London and Toronto, 1932), pp. 223–249.

6. See W. A. Pantin, "Some Medieval English Treatises on the Origins of Monasticism," *Medieval Studies Presented to Rose Graham*, ed. Veronica Ruffer and A. J. Taylor (Oxford, 1950), p. 191, where a section "De anachoretis vel heremitis" in a monastic treatise of the fourteenth century is referred to.

7. "Ex quibus concluditur quod unus laicus, ab hominibus in eremo sequestratus, aequaliter et plus potest mereri sicut episcopus vel papa bonus," Duns Scotus (?), *De perfectione statuum* (ed. Vives, *Opera omnia*, XXVI, p. 553).

8. As also suggested above, in Chapter I, some of this self-deprecation may be due to the traditional *trepidatio* of the literary prologue.

9. Cf. the attack on *sarabaites*, the other type of evil monk attacked in the Rule—those under no rule—in XIII, 285–286. On Will's role as a hermit "unholy of works," see above, Chapter I.

10. See, e.g., Thomas Docking's *questio* in his *Quaestiones in Job* in Bibliothèque nationale, Paris, latin 3183, fols. 181[b]–182[a], on whether working with the hands is nobler and more perfect than begging (cf. Bibliothèque nationale, Paris, latin 3183, fols. 147[b]–152[a]); Wilton's *questio*, "Utrum viri ad corporales labores validi . . . ," which is preserved in a number of MSS (Bodley 52, fols. 140[b]–146; 158, fols. 147–152[b]; Bodley, Digby 75, fols. 122[a]–124[b]; and Lambeth Library, London, 357); and Richard Maidstone's *Protectorium paupertatis*, ed. A. Williams in *Carmelus*, V (1958), 132–180. The monkish point of view may be seen in Uthred of Boldon's *Contra fratrum mendicitatem* (Bibliothèque nationale, Paris, latin 3183, fols. 160[b] ff.). Fitzralph, the great enemy of the friars in the fourteenth century, denies any biblical authority for mendicancy again and again. Guillaume de Saint-Amour in his famous quarrel with the friars in Paris in 1256 and following years had raised the question of the validity of begging and stressed the importance of manual labor.

11. Langland does at times praise begging and mendicancy, but I think he is in these cases thinking of the virtue of spiritual recklessness, throwing oneself on God (*Sorgenlosigkeit*), as St. Francis recommended. One must become a minstrel of God, a "ioculator Dei." On the relation between the Franciscans and minstrelsy, see F. Baethgen, "Franziskanische Studien," *Historische Zeitschrift*, CXXXI (1925), 427 ff. For this whole subject, see Donaldson, *Piers Plowman: The C-Text*, pp. 170 ff. (on recklessness) and 129 ff. (136 ff. on minstrels). It is the C author who seems more willing than B to allow deserving beggars, especially "ioculatores Dei," their rights (p. 135) Donaldson might also have pointed to Langland's favorable treatment of mendicants in the long discussion (only in C) at the beginning of XIV, 1–100, where the messengers who travel light ("the mendinans") are contrasted favorably with the merchants (the rich) who travel heavy towards heaven. The proper solution of the problem of begging is a crucial issue for Langland, as we may see at the end of the poem, for Conscience, in searching for Piers, desires that the friars may have "a fyndyng" (provisions).

12. Dom David Knowles, *The Religious Orders in England*, 3 vols. (Cambridge, England, 1948–1959), II, 111.

13. The history of the concept is treated at some length in Dom Jean Leclercq, *La Vie parfaite: Points de vue sur l'essence de l'état religieux*, Tradition monastique 1 (Turnhout and Paris, 1948), pp. 164 ff. See also Morton W. Bloomfield, "*Piers Plowman* and the Three Grades of Chastity," *Anglia*, LXXVI (1958), 229, n. 1 (note especially the reference to Thomas Brinton's sermon), and "Joachim of Flora: A Critical Survey of his Canon, Teachings, Sources, Biography and Influence," *Traditio*, XIII (1957), 281, n. 136; R. E. Kaske, "Langland and the *Paradisus claustralis*," *MLN*, LXXII (1957), 481–483. Rodulfus Tortarius, d. 1122, compares the cloister of Cluny to paradise in his *Elogium cluniacum*, 85 ff. *et passim* (ed. M. B.

Ogle and D. M. Schullian [Rome, 1933], pp. 451–452). See also Denis the Carthusian on Psalm 132:3 in *Opera omnia* (Montreuil, 1898), VI, 620 (I am indebted to Dr. Kaske for this reference). He speaks there of charity making the cloister a paradise and the monks angels, just as hate makes of it, hell, and them, devils. The root of the notion lies probably in the oriental and ancient Hebraic idea that the earthly temple is a copy or reflection of the heavenly temple.

14. Pantin, "Some Medieval English Treatises," pp. 189–215. We find in an attached *questio* to this treatise the very same point made: True dependency on God requires an intelligent appraisal of one's needs. In pushing back monasticism historically, the Benedictine Uthred of Boldon, Langland's contemporary, even claims Adam and Eve led the monastic life before the fall; see Knowles, *The Religious Orders in England*, II, 53.

15. See, e.g., the Commentary of Bernard Aiglerius (Bernardus I, Abbot of Monte Cassino, d. 1282) on the Benedictine Rule on St. Benedict's words, "Si autem necessitas loci . . . ," which both appeals to history and emphasizes manual labor (ed. Dom Anselm M. Caplet, p. 315). A MS of this work from Norwich Cathedral Priory is preserved in Cambridge University Library MS Kk ii, 21. Wyclif, *Sermones*, IV, 6 (ed. J. Loserth, IV, 51–52), and *Dialogus* 25 (ed. A. W. Pollard, p. 52), accuses the friars of not working with their hands. It is, of course, a commonplace in Christian tradition (see e.g., Jerome, *Epistola* 125, 7, Cassian, *Institutes*, I, 1 and 2, Isidore of Seville, *De ecclesiae officiis*, II, 16, 1 [*PL*, LXXXIII, 794]) that certain Old Testament figures like Elijah and Elisha were monks and founders of monasticism.

16. Langland had a highly ambivalent attitude towards the friars. In this very passage, he admits that the Austins had a long history and allows their claim that they were founded by St. Paul, the first hermit (XV, 284). This claim apparently was widely accepted in the fourteenth century. See, e.g., Pantin, "Some Medieval English Treatises," pp. 193–194.

17. On the Longinus legend, see R. J. Peebles, *The Legend of Longinus in Ecclesiastical Tradition and in English Literature . . .*, a Dissertation presented to . . . Bryn Mawr (Baltimore, 1911).

18. Sermon 37 (*Sermons*, ed. M. A. Devlin, Camden Society, 3rd Series LXXXV–LXXXVI [London, 1954], trans. William Brandt, in typescript.

19. On Rymington, see J. McNulty, "William of Rymyngton," *Yorkshire Archaeological Journal*, XXX (1931), 231 ff.; and Arta Fruth Johnson, "A Critical Text and Translation of the 'Meditaciones Anachoritam ad quendam monachum anachoritam' of William Rymyngton," a Dissertation . . . of the Ohio State University, 1951 (typewritten). On Easton, see W. A. Pantin, "The *Defensorium* of Adam Easton," *EHR*, LI (1936), 675–680; and *The English Church in the Fourteenth Century* (Cambridge, England, 1955), pp. 175–181 and *passim*. On Brinton (or Brunton), see Pantin, *English Church*, pp. 182 ff.; Sister M. A. Devlin, "Bishop Brunton and his Sermons," *Speculum*, XIV (1939), 324–344; F. A. Gasquet, "A Forgotten English Preacher," *The Old English Bible and Other Essays*, 2nd ed. (London, 1908), 54–86; and *Sermons*, ed. Devlin. On Uthred, see Pantin, *English Church*, pp. 165 ff., and "Two Treatises of Uthred of Boldon on the Monastic Life," *Studies in Medieval History Presented to F. M. Powicke*, ed. R. W. Hunt, W. A. Pantin, and R. W. Southern (Oxford, 1948), pp. 363–385; M. E. Marcett, *Uthred de Boldon, Friar William Jordan and "Piers Plowman"* (New York, 1938); Dom D. Knowles, "The Censured Opinions

of Uthred of Boldon," *Proceedings of the British Academy*, XXXVII (1951), 305–342; and Dom Hugh Farmer, "The *Meditacio devota* of Uthred of Boldon," *Analecta monastica*, 5th Series, Studia anselmiana XLIII (Rome, 1958), pp. 187–206.

20. E. H. Kellogg, "Bishop Brunton and the Fable of the Rats," *PMLA*, L (1935), 57 ff., and G. R. Owst, "The 'Angel' and the 'Goliardeys' of Langland's Prologue," *MLR*, XX (1925), 270 ff. (cf. C. Brett in *MLR*, XXII [1927], 260 ff.). In Sermon 44 (ed. Devlin, I, 197) Brinton praises the poverty of those in religious orders and compares them to angels, another well-known metaphor of monastic philosophy.

21. Marcett, *Uhtred de Boldon*. Perhaps Langland's thought comes closest to Uthred's in his liberal view of salvation for the unbaptized and in his theological naturalism, although these views are by no means unique to Uthred. Indeed, however, Langland definitely differs with Uthred on monastic rights of property and the role of the state in supervising them.

22. "*Piers Plowman* and the Three Grades of Chastity," 227–253.

23. "Quia nemo saluatur nisi continentiam coniugalem, uidualem aut virginalem seruuando," John Purvey (?), Commentary on Apocalypse 14:4 (edited by Luther and printed Wittenberg, 1528, p. 126ᵃ), written 1390 in England.

24. See *Anglia*, LXXVI (1958), Plate I and pp. 245 ff., for the details of this arboreal image and its background.

25. Fol. 70ᵇ of the edition of 1519. See also "Spiritus sanctus qui operatur specialius in ordine monachorum" (*Concordia*, V, 48 [fol. 83ᵃ]); *Expositio in Apocalypsim, Liber introductorius*, 5 (fol. 18ᵇ B of the edition of 1577); and *De vita sancti Benedicti et de officio divino secundum eius doctrinam*, ed. C. Baraut in *Analecta sacra tarraconensia*, XXIV (1951), p. 77. See also below, note 27.

26. Collectio XXII, 16.

27. See Morton W. Bloomfield, "*Piers Plowman* and the Three Grades of Chastity," *Anglia*, LXXVI (1958), 251–252, n. 2, where various possible identifications are discussed. Januensis may be a corruption of Joachim, as B. Hirsch-Reich suggests in a review of my article in *RTAM*, XXVI (1959), 136. She also points to Tavola XIII of the Joachite *Liber figurarum* (ed. L. Tondelli, M. Reeves, and B. Hirsch-Reich [Turin, 1953], II), where the same parallels are made.

28. There was a remarkable efflorescence and growth of Charterhouses in the later Middle Ages, but although rooted in monastic spirituality, Carthusian spirituality is extremely individualistic. See E. Margaret Thompson, *The Carthusian Order in England* (London, 1930). It should be considered as part of late medieval mysticism and spirituality, which flourished especially, but not exclusively, on the Continent. See W. A. Pantin, "English Monks before the Suppression of the Monasteries," *The Dublin Review*, CCI (1937), 250–270.

29. Quotation from Charles Trinkaus, "Petrarch's Views on the Individual and His Society," *Osiris*, XI (1954), 168. "It is difficult to exaggerate the importance of this neo-Augustinianism in England at this time [fourteenth century] ...," R. R. Betts, "The Influence of Realist Philosophy on Jan Hus and his Predecessors in Bohemia," *The Slavonic and East European Review*, XXIX (1951), 407.

30. "At present, the intellectual life of the period [fourteenth century] is everywhere still largely veiled in mists," Gordon Leff, *Bradwardine and*

the Pelagians: *A Study of His "De causa Dei" and Its Opponents*, Cambridge Studies in Medieval Life and Thought, ed. Dom. D. Knowles, N.S. 5 (Cambridge, England, 1957), p. 1.

31. See Appendix II, below.

32. Besides the general works of Pantin and Knowles, we have some more or less specialized histories, such as A. Gwynn, *The English Austin Friars in the Time of Wyclif* (Oxford, 1940); A. Hamilton Thompson, *The Abbey of St. Mary of the Meadows Leicester*, The Leicestershire Archaeological Society (Leicester, 1949); Douglas Jones, *The Church in Chester, 1300–1540*, The Chetham Society, 3rd Series VII (Manchester, 1957); K. L. Wood-Legh, *Studies in Church Life in England under Edward III* (Cambridge, England, 1934); and J. R. H. Moorman, *The Grey Friars in Cambridge, 1225–1538* (Cambridge, England, 1952). There are a number of studies of economic life and monasticism and of course a large number of articles and works of various types and value on Wyclif and the Lollards. W. W. Capes, *The English Church in the Fourteenth and Fifteenth Centuries*, (London, 1909), still has, in spite of its age and strong Protestant bias, some things of value. A mass of material for the history of the Benedictine monks in the later Middle Ages in England, scarcely as yet exploited, is now available in *Documents Illustrating the Activities of the General and Provincial Chapters of the English Black Monks, 1215–1540*, ed. W. A. Pantin, 3 vols. Camden Society, 3rd Series XLV, XLVII, and LIV (London, 1931–1937).

33. "By the fourteenth century chronicle writing was the poor sister of scholastic studies...," John Taylor, "Fourteenth Century Chronicle Writing in the Diocese of York," *Proceedings of the Leeds Philosophical and Literary Society*, Literary and Historical Section VIII, 1 (1956), 55.

34. See A. G. Little, "Cistercian Students at Oxford in the Thirteenth Century," *EHR*, VIII (1893), 83–85; and C. H. Lawrence, "Stephen of Lexington and Cistercian University Studies in the Thirteenth Century," *Journal of Ecclesiastical History*, XI (1960), 164–178.

35. *Répertoire des maîtres en théologie de Paris au XIIIᵉ siècle*, 2 vols. (Paris, 1933–1934).

36. On Fitzralph and his attack on "poverty" as a spiritual good and on fraternal claims in general, see Pantin, *English Church*, pp. 151–165; John J. Greaney, "Richard Fitzralph of Armagh and the Franciscans (1349–1360)," *The Catholic University Bulletin*, XI (1905), I, 68–74, and II, 195–245; Aubrey Gwynn, "Two Sermons of Primate Richard Fitzralph, Preached before the Provincial Councils of Armagh on 7 February 1352 and 5 February 1355." *Archivium Hibernicum (Irish Historical Records)*, XIV (1949), 50–65, and a series of articles in *Studies*, XXII (1933), 389–405, 591–607, XXIII (1934), 395–411, XXIV (1935), 25–42, 558–572, XXV (1936), 81–96; and R. R. Betts, "Richard Fitzralph, Archbishop of Armagh, and the Doctrine of Dominion," *Essays In British and Irish History in Honour of James Eadie Todd*, ed. H. A. Crome, et al. (London, 1949), pp. 46–60; and L. L. Hammerich, *The Beginnings of the Strife Between Richard Fitzralph and the Mendicants...*, Det Kgl. Danske videnskabernes Selskab, Historisk-filologiske Meddelelser XXVI, 3 (Copenhagen, 1938). For the general secular attack against friars in this century in England, see Jean L. Copeland, "The Relations between the Secular Clergy and the Mendicant Friars in England during the Century after the Issue of the Bull 'Super Cathedram' (1300)," M.A. Thesis, University of London, 1938 (unpub-

lished); and Arnold Williams, "Chaucer and the Friars," *Speculum*, XXVIII (1953), 499–513.

37. See Pantin, ed., *Documents*, III, 255. Wyclif refers to these disputes between monks and friars as to their *status* when he writes "non enim sustinuerunt monachi quo status fratrum foret suo perfeccior" in *Sermones*, III, 37 (ed. J. Loserth, III, 311–312).

38. See V. H. Galbraith, *Historical Research in Medieval England*, The Creighton Lecture in History, 1949 (London, 1951); and Hans Wolter, *Ordericus Vitalis: Ein Beitrag zur kluniazensische Geschichtsschreibung*, Veröffentlichungen des Instituts für europäische Geschichte, Mainz, 7 (Wiesbaden, 1955), pp. 72–78.

39. See Pantin, "Some Medieval English Treatises," pp. 203–204, as in British Museum, Cotton, Claudius E. IV (from St. Albans), fol. 326^b.

40. See W. Wattenbach, "Über erfundene Briefe in Handschriften des Mittelalters, besonders Teufelsbrief," *Sitzungsberichte der Königlich-preussischen Akademie der Wissenschaften zu Berlin*, 11 February 1892, I, 9, pp. 91–123; Paul Lehmann, *Die Parodie in Mittelalter* (Munich, 1922), pp. 85–101; and Gianni Zippel, "La Lettera del diavolo al clero, dal secolo XII alla Riforma," *Bullettino dell'Istituto storico italiano per il medio evo e Archivio muratoriano*, LXX (1958), 125–179.

41. The document is printed in V. H. Galbraith, "Articles Laid before the Parliament of 1371," *EHR*, XXXIV (1919), 579–582, under the monastic rubric "Articuli maliciose."

42. Langland is no doubt here thinking of texts from these authors referred to by the scholastics in discussing the common good. See I. Th. Eschmann, "A Thomistic Glossary on the Principle of the Pre-eminence of a Common Good," *Mediaeval Studies*, V (1943), 123–165; and "Bonum commune melius est quam bonum unius: Eine Studie über den Wertvorrang des Personalen bei Thomas Aquinas," *Mediaeval Studies*, VI (1944), 62–120, where Thomas' teachings on the principle are given with material from Cicero, Seneca, and others.

43. See Pantin, *English Church*, pp. 175–176.

44. This chronicle, with a few slight differences, is also to be found in University College, Oxford MS 97, fols. 348^b–349^a. A reference to the Abbey of Battle in both MSS probably indicates the affiliation of the author, unless this is another misfortune. The University College MS comes from Westminster Abbey.

45. See note 14, above. Parts of this treatise have been printed, for instance at the end of Anthony Hall's edition of the chronicle of Trivet and Adam of Murimuth (Oxford, 1722), pp. 157–192.

46. A similar list is to be found in the *Eulogium historiarum*, III, 127 (Rolls Series I, 436 ff.). The inclusion of the friars indicates that they too are monks in a way to some, and, as I argue, to Langland also. Other forms of the treatise contain other lists and sections—on monastic missionaries, writers, etc.

47. Pantin, "Some Medieval English Treatises," pp. 212–214.

48. Edited by Dom Cipriano Baraut in *Analecta sacra tarraconensia*, XXIV (1951), 33–122. The reference below is from p. 37. Cf. Joachim's *Concordia*, V, 48.

49. Baraut, p. 77. See also Yves-Marie-Joseph Congar, "Eglise et Cité de Dieu chez quelques auteurs cisterciens...," *Mélanges offerts à Etienne Gilson*, Etudes de philosophie médiévale, Hors série (Toronto and Paris,

1959), pp. 173–202, on the idea of monasticism as the pilgrim part of the City of God on earth in the twelfth century. Cf. above, Chapter II, note 43.

50. Vatican, Reg. Lat. 127, fol. 171ª (second column).

51. *Ibid.*, fols. 171ᵇ–172ª.

52. See E. Benz, "La Messianità di San Benedetto," *Ricerche religiose,* VII (1931), 336–353. The source of some of this in the monk of Bury St. Edmunds' treatise is given as a Januensis in *Libro questionum de antichristo.* See, above, note 27.

53. Printed in W. A. Pantin, "A Sermon for a General Chapter," *The Downside Review,* LI (1933), 291–308.

54. For this quarrel and Uthred's opinions, see Dom David Knowles, "The Censured Opinions of Uthred of Boldon," *Proceedings of the British Academy,* XXXVII (1951), 305–342.

55. This concern with the righteous heathen was a preoccupation of fourteenth-century theologians, owing perhaps to a greater knowledge of non-Christians then current. See Dom David Knowles, "The Censured Opinions of Uthred of Boldon," p. 315. See also Walter Burley's *questio* printed by S. Harrison Thomson in "An Unnoticed *Questio theologica* of Walter Burley," *Medievalia et Humanistica,* VI (1950), 84–88, where with much qualification Burley seems to say that man can be saved by natural law alone. I say "seems" because the *questio* may be' incomplete; only the *sic* side is given, and all the author claims is that such a man is saved from extreme misery ("miseria extrema"), which may only envisage a kind of Dantesque Limbo for him. In any case the *questio* is revelatory of fourteenth-century concerns. See also some of Thomas Buckingham's *questiones,* in M. D. Chenu, "Les *Quaestiones* de Thomas de Buckingham," *Studia Mediaevalia in honorem . . . Raymundi Josephi Martin . . .* (Bruges, n.d.), pp. 229–241. See also Nicholas of Lyra's *questiones* in Franz Pelster, "Quodlibeta und Quaestiones des Nikolaus von Lyra OFM (1349)," *Mélanges Joseph de Ghellinck, S.J.,* Museum Lessianum, Section historique No.14 (Gembloux, 1951), II, 956.

56. "Two Treatises of Uthred of Boldon on the Monastic Life," *Studies in Medieval History Presented to Frederick Maurice Powicke,* ed. R. W. Hunt, *et al.,* pp. 363–385.

57. Recently edited by Dom Hugh Farmer, "*The Meditacio devota* of Uthred of Boldon."

58. Rymington's meditations (*Meditaciones ad quendam monachum anachoritam*) have been edited by Mrs. Arta Fruth Johnson in a dissertation presented to the Ohio State University in 1951 for the degree of Doctor of Philosophy, and the meditations of the Monk of Farne, by Dom Hugh Farmer in "The Meditations of the Monk of Farne."

59. General introduction to his edition of the *Kirkstall Abbey Chronicles,* The Publications of the Thoresby Society XLII (Leeds, 1952), p. 3. On the St. Albans school of historians, see V. H. Galbraith, *Roger Wendover and Matthew Paris, Being the Eleventh Lecture on the David Murray Foundation in the University of Glasgow . . .* (Glasgow, 1944).

60. Ed. Edward Maunde Thompson (Oxford, 1889). The reference to *De semine* is to be found on pp. 173–174. "Political prophecies abound in the fourteenth century [historical] writing," Taylor, *Kirkstall Abbey Chronicles,* p. 14. Cf. also p. 40.

61. This pseudo-Joachite writing was well known in England. See Bloomfield, "Joachim of Flora," p. 303, n. 236.

62. Such as Thomas Sprott, ed. T. Hearne (Oxford, 1719), the various versions of *The Brut*, Henry Knighton, John Reading (a monk of Westminster Abbey), Thomas Walsingham, Ranulf Higden, and Bartholomew Cotton. John of Reading's *Chronicle* (ed. James Tait [Manchester, 1914]) is, for example, very prejudiced against the friars and records under 1354 the burning at Avignon of some friars (the event actually took place in 1355)—apparently as part of his anti-mendicant campaign.

63. Ed. Frank Scott Haydon for the Rolls Series, 3 vols. (London, 1858–1863). The title of the work is itself significant for my argument.

64. *Eulogium*, ed. Haydon, I, 419. The second prophecy is to be found on p. 420. The lunar phenomena referred to below are found in *Eulogium* III, 240–241.

65. See Eulogium, ed. Haydon, I, 436–438.

66. *Preaching in Medieval England* (Cambridge, England, 1926), Appendix V (pp. 360–362). The sermon was edited by K. F. Sundén, *A Famous Middle English Sermon (MS. Hatton 57, Bodleian Library)* (Göteburg, 1925) —unfortunately from only one manuscript. Langland himself uses this biblical text in C, X, 274, to attack negligent bishops.

67. For some of these attempts, see O. Cargill, "The Date of the A-Text of Piers the Ploughman," *PMLA*, XLVII (1932), 354–362; B. F. Huppé, "The A-Text of *Piers Plowman* and the Norman Wars," *PMLA*, LIV (1939), 37–64, "The Date of the B-Text of *Piers Plowman*," *SP*, XXXVIII (1941), 34–44, and *"Piers Plowman*: The Date of the B-Text Reconsidered," *SP*, XLVI (1949), 6–13; J. A. W. Bennett, "The Date of the A-Text of *Piers Plowman*," *PMLA*, LVIII (1943), 566–572, and "The Date of the B Text of *Piers Plowman*," *Medium Aevum*, XII (1943), 55–64; A. Gwynn, "The Date of the B-Text of *Piers Plowman*," *RES*, XIX (1943), 1–24.

68. See letter to *TLS*, March 11, 1939 (Vol. XXXVIII, 149–150).

69. It must be admitted that "this" is only in the Vernon MS of the A-Text, which is, however, the earliest one extant. Still such a word could have been used only of a fairly recent event and only needs to have been used once. It should be pointed out that Professor Kane in his recent edition of the A-Text (London, 1960) does not accept the reading "this" but rather "the." In any case, my argument for the early date of A does not depend on this particular reading.

70. "Two Notes on Piers Plowman," *Medium Aevum*, IV (1935), 83–89.

71. The choice may also have been dictated by Langland's acquaintance with Oxford, for this Abbey is in its vicinity. It is possible Langland was at Oxford; see Appendix II, below.

72. See Sister May Aquinas Devlin, "The Date of the C Version of *Piers the Plowman*," *Abstracts of Theses*, Humanistic Series, University of Chicago, IV (1928), 317 ff.

73. On prophecy in the later Middle Ages, especially in England, see Rupert Taylor, *The Political Prophecy in England* (New York, 1911); Reinhard Haferkorn, *When Rom is Removed into England: Eine politische Prophezeiung des 14. Jahrhunderts . . .*, Beiträge zur englische Philologie XIX (Leipzig, 1932); J. Rawson Lumby, *Bernardus de cura rei familiaris, With some Early Scottish Prophecies Etc . . .*, Early English Text Society 42 (London, 1870); Lynn Thorndike, *A History of Magic and Experimental Science*, III, Fourteenth and Fifteenth Centuries (New York, 1934), *passim* (mainly astrological prophecies); Sister Helen Margaret Peck, "The Prophecy of John of Bridlington," a Dissertation . . . for the Degree of Doctor of

Philosophy, The University of Chicago, 1930 (typewritten manuscript); Paul Zumthor, *Merlin le prophète: Un Thème de la littérature polémique de l'historiographie et des romans* (Lausanne and Geneva, 1943); and Lucy Allen Paton, *Les Prophecies de Merlin . . .*, The Modern Language Association of America, Monograph Series I, 2 vols. (New York and London, 1926–1927). For a French prophet of the mid-fourteenth century who was very influential in England, see Jeanne Bignami-Odier, *Etudes sur Jean de Roquetaillade (Johannes de Rupescissa)* (Paris, 1952).

74. See Appendix IV, below.

75. Printed by M. R. James in "The Catalogue of the Library of the Augustinian Friars at York, Now First Edited from the Manuscript at Trinity College, Dublin," *Fasciculus Ioanni Willis Clark dicatus* (Cambridge, England, 1909), pp. 2–96 (actual text pp. 19–83). The fact that of some 646 codices only 5 are known today to have survived gives us an idea of how many manuscripts must have been destroyed at the Reformation. On Erghome, besides Sister Helen Margaret Peck's dissertation, "The Prophecy of John of Bridlington," see A. Gwynn, *The English Austin Friars* (Oxford, 1940), pp. 129 ff.

76. One version is printed by T. Wright in *Political Poems*, I, 123–215. Some of the twenty-three manuscripts of the work do not have the commentary.

77. I am in general following Mme Bignami-Odier's summaries (see her *Jean de Roquetaillade*), although most of these dates and the further ones mentioned below have been checked in the texts themselves. For another recent study, see E. F. Jacob, "John of Roquetaillade," *Bulletin of the John Rylands Library*, XXXIX (1956–1957), 75–96.

78. In his commentary (written 1354–1355) on *Veh mundo in centum annis*, a work of Arnold of Villanova's, Jean de Roquetaillade, following Arnold, places the advent of Antichrist in 1388 (although Arnold apparently favored 1378).

79. See Bignami-Odier, *Jean de Roquetaillade*, pp. 201–202; Heinrich Finke, *Aus den Tagen Bonifaz VIII, Funde und Forschungen*, Vorreformations-geschichtliche Forschungen II (Münster i. W., 1902), pp. 209 ff.; Paul Diepgen, *Arnold von Villanova als Politiker und Laientheologe*, Abhandlungen zur mittleren und neueren Geschichte 9 (Berlin and Leipzig, 1909), pp. 16 ff. *et passim*. For speculation in the fourteenth century on the date of Antichrist, see Richard Salomon, *Opicinus de Canistris, Weltbild und Bekenntnisse eines avignonesischen Klerikers des 14. Jahrhunderts*, Studies of the Warburg Institute IA (London, 1936), I, 125–129; on p. 127 we find 1365 and 1367 mentioned (for Opicinus, earlier ·in the century, 1335 was the crucial date). The Czech Milicius (d. 1374) also chose 1365 as the year of Antichrist; see Matthias of Janov, *Regulae veteris et novi Testamenti*, ed. V. Kybal and O. Odlozilik, 5 vols. (Innsbruck and Prague, 1908), III, 372 ff. Matthias of Janov (d. 1394) wrote an immense work on every aspect of Antichrist in the 1380's and preserved earlier speculations on the subject. On Jewish speculation on the coming of the Messiah and the corresponding millennium, see Joseph Sarachek, *The Doctrine of the Messiah in Medieval Jewish Literature* (New York, 1932), pp. 37–41, 59–60, 78, 99, 144 ff., 173 ff., 315 ff. The year 1358 was a favorite Jewish date. The great Italian jurist Giovanni da Legnano in his *De jure belli*, quinta causa, written in 1360, refers to 1365 as a crucial date (ed. Thomas E. Holland [Washington, 1917], pp. 77–78).

80. For example, this prophecy is in British Museum Royal 8. C. IV and Cotton, Vespasian, E. VII; Bodley, Ashmole 393 and Digby 218; Corpus Christi, Cambridge 138; apparently in the National Library of Wales, Peniarth 50; and on the Continent in Riccardiana, Florence, 688 and Bibliothèque nationale, Paris, français 902. See Morton W. Bloomfield and Marjorie Reeves, "The Penetration of Joachism into Northern Europe," *Speculum*, XXIX (1954), 788.

81. See, e.g., the "Cum fuerunt anni transacti" prophecy on Antichrist discussed in Bloomfield and Reeves, "The Penetration of Joachism," pp. 787–788, and the different versions of the Letter of Toledo prophecy discussed in Moses Gaster, "The Letter of Toledo," *Studies and Texts in Folklore, Magic, Mediaeval Romance, Hebrew Apocrypha and Samaritan Archaeology*, 3 vols. (London, 1925–1928), II, 985–1004 (reprinted from *Folklore*, 1902).

82. See Thorndike, *History of Magic*, III, 294 ff. I am indebted to this work for much of what immediately follows. Brinton in Sermons 44 and 45 (ed. Devlin, I, 198 and 202) attacks those who think current misfortunes are due to Saturn rather than to sin.

83. Thorndike, *History of Magic*, III, 325–346. Eschenden's views can be best seen in Bodley, Ashmole 393 (and a seventeenth-century transcription of it in Ashmole 192).

84. Any prophecy in order to gain attention likes, of course, to make predictions about the foreseeable future. A "prophet" must always be torn between being proved wrong or out of date.

85. On this affair, see John R. H. Moorman, *The Grey Friars in Cambridge, 1225–1538*, The Birkbeck Lectures, 1948–1949 (Cambridge, England, 1952), pp. 95 ff. On Henry de Costesy, see P. Arduin Kleinhans, "Heinrich von Cossey O.F.M.: Ein Psalmen-Erklärer des 14. Jahrhunderts," *Miscellanea Biblica et Orientalia R.P. Athanasio Miller Oblata*, Studia anselmiana 27–28 (Rome, 1951), pp. 239–253. Costesy's commentary on the Apocalypse in Bodley MS Laud Misc. 85 quotes extensively from Joachim of Flora. On heresy in fourteenth-century England, see H. G. Richardson, "Heresy and the Lay Power under Richard II," *EHR*, LI (1936), 1–28, and John Rea Bacher, *The Prosecution of Heretics in Mediaeval England*, an essential portion of a Dissertation . . . University of Pennsylvania (Philadelphia, 1942). Chapter I deals with some fourteenth-century cases before Richard II's reign. Bodley 158 (S.C. 1997), fols. 142ᵇ–145ᵃ, contains some documents concerning a Friar Richard Helmyslay O.P. in Newcastle in 1380, who was involved in heresy. In general, as all authorities agree, England was remarkably free of heresy until the time of the Lollards.

86. Printed in 1471 at Nuremberg (Hain, 8993). The copy I have studied is in the Rare Book Room of the Library of Congress. As for Ubertino da Casale, I am thinking of his masterpiece *Arbor vitae crucifixae*, with its stress on devotion to the human side of Christ.

87. See Ch. V. Langlois, "Hugo de Novocastro or de Castronovo, Frater Minor," *Essays in Medieval History Presented to Thomas Frederick Tout*, ed. A. G. Little and F. M. Powicke (Manchester, 1925), pp. 269–275; and P. Leo Amoros, "Hugo von Novo Castro O.F.M., und sein Kommentar zum ersten Buch der Sentenzen," *Franziskanische Studien*, XX (1933), 177–222.

88. The references are to II, 24, 25, and 26.

89. Although G. G. Coulton admits that Spirituals and their influence were rare in England (*Medieval Panorama* [New York and Cambridge, England, 1938], pp. 521 and 551), he professes to find an allusion to the Spirituals in XX, 60, where it is related that only fools do not come out of the friars' Convent to welcome Antichrist. These fools may well be only the few upright friars Langland allowed in the orders.

90. See Appendix II, below.

NOTES FOR CHAPTER IV

1. Although I believe K. Burdach tends to exaggerate the importance of the Adamite sects and *Adammystik* (both of which are left historically vague) in *Der Dichter des Ackermann aus Böhmen und seine Zeit*, Vom Mittelalter zur Reformation III, 2, in 2 vols. (Berlin, 1926–1932), pp. 131 ff. and esp. pp. 140–142, nevertheless his work should be consulted for valuable comments on this phenomenon, which sometimes manifested itself in a stress on the pre-lapsarian Adam, as the perfect man. See also H. Grundmann, "Der Typus des Ketzers in mittelalterlicher Anschauung," *Kultur und Universalgeschichte Walter Goetz zu seinem 60. Geburtstage* ... (Leipzig and Berlin, 1927), pp. 91–107. The Adamites of Bohemia are a rather unimportant group and concerned with special doctrines. See Ernst Werner's essay in T. Büttner and E. Werner, *Circumcellionen und Adamiten, Zwei Formen mittelalterlicher Haeresie,* Forschungen zur mittelalterlichen Geschichte 2 (Berlin, 1959), pp. 73 ff. On late medieval historical thinking, see the recent work by Hanno Helbling, *Saeculum humanum, Ansätze zu einen Versuch über spätmittelalterliches Geschichtsdenken*, Istituto italiano per gli studi storici 11 (Naples, 1958). For the point in the following sentence, see p. 7.

2. My translation from *Super quatuor Evangelia*, ed. E. Buonaiuti (Rome, 1930), p. 43. Cf. also the similar sentiment in Joachim's *Expositio in Apocalypsim* quoted in the footnote on the same page. Cf. Ernest H. Kantorowicz, *The King's Two Bodies* (Princeton, 1957), p. 144 n., where he writes "I do not believe that any mediaeval political theory could work without some fiction or some 'metaphor of perfection.'"; and "Est verum quod Hildegardis et Abbas Joachim sonant quasi finem mundi et adventum antichristi precessure sint una vel plures reformaciones ecclesie seu reduciones in statum primitive sanctitatis," from Henry of Hassia's *Epistola quedam consolatorice, c.* 1384, printed in *Historische Jahrbuch*, XXX (1909), 306. Henry's main point in this letter is that the Church must suffer before a reformation could be expected. See also the quotation from the *Liber memorandorum Ecclesie de Bernewelle* in G. G. Coulton, *A Medieval Garner* (London, 1910), pp. 444–445.

3. See Ray C. Petry, in "Social Responsibility and the late Medieval Mystics," *Church History*, XXI (1952), 3–19, who defends the mystics against the charge that they had no sense of social responsibility.

4. The fourteenth-century Alvarius Pelagius in *De planctu ecclesie*, printed in *Bibliotheca maxima pontificia* (Rome, 1698), III, 424, argues that Franciscans are the main contenders against Antichrist.

5. Conrad Pepler, "The Spirituality of William Langland," *Blackfriars*, XX (1939), 853. J. A. Burrow just recently (in *Neophilologus*, XLIII [1959], 128) has made the same point in comparing the Old English *Dream of the*

Rood with *Piers Plowman*. The Crucifixion is treated in *Piers* with "little of pathos or passivity." Moreover, we do not find much emphasis on Mary or Mariology in the poem.

6. On the Greek view of history, see B. A. Van Groningen, *In the Grip of the Past: Essay on an Aspect of Greek Thought*, Philosophia Antiqua VI (Leiden, 1953), who denies that the Greeks had no sense of history.

7. For some recent studies on world ages, see J. Daniélou, "La Typologie millénariste de la semaine dans le Christianisme primitif," *Vigiliae Christianae*, II (1948), 1–16; J. H. J. Van der Pot, *De Periodisering der Geschiedenis: Een Overzicht der Theorieën* (The Hague, 1951); V. Grumel, "Les Premières Eres mondiales," *Revue des études byzantines*, X (1952), 93–108; Roderich Schmidt, "Aetates mundi, Die Weltalter als Gliederungsprinzip der Geschichte," *ZKG*, LXVII (1955–1956), 288–317; Michael Landmann, *Das Zeitalter als Schicksal: Die geistesgeschichtliche Kategorie der Epoche*, Philosophische Forschungen N.F., ed. K. Jaspers 7 ed. (Basel, 1956); Anna-Dorothee v. den Brincken, "Weltären,' *Archiv für Kulturgeschichte*, XXXIX (1957), 133–149; Max Förster, "Die Weltzeitalter bei den Angelsachsen," *Neusprachliche Studien, Festgabe Karl Luick*...Die neueren Sprachen, Beiheft 6 (Marburg, 1925), pp. 183–203; and Morton W. Bloomfield, "Joachim of Flora," *Traditio*, XIII (1957), 275, n. 115.

8. Even in the Middle Ages, we can find Utopianism in some thinkers, and in the quest of alchemy.

9. It is largely irrelevant, although at times Langland certainly seems to allow power of spiritual correction, not under Church guidance, to the state. He is, however, unlike Wyclif, rather guarded in this attitude.

10. Possibly if George Dumézil is right (*Les Dieux des indoeuropéens*, Mythes et Religions, ed. P. L. Couchoud [Paris, 1952]), this view may go back to the times of Indo-European unity.

11. On medieval hierarchical thinking, see the early part of Günther Müller, "Gradualismus: Eine Vorstudie zur altdeutschen Literaturgeschichte," *Deutsche Vierteljahrsschrift für Literaturwissenschaft und Geistesgeschichte*, II (1924), 681 ff., esp. 694 ff. For social *status* in the Middle Ages, see Ruth Mohl, *The Three Estates in Medieval and Renaissance Literature*, Columbia University Studies in English and Comparative Literature 114 (New York, 1933); Sylvia Thrupp, *The Merchant Class of Medieval London* (Chicago, 1948), pp. 288 ff.; J. Huizinga, *The Waning of the Middle Ages* (1924) (Anchor Reprint, New York, 1954), Chapter III (pp. 56–67), Maria Wickert, *Studien zu John Gower* (Cologne, 1953), pp. 110 ff.; Luise Manz, *Der Ordo Gedanke: Ein Beitrag zur Frage des mittelalterlichen Ständegedankes*, Beiheft 33 zur *Vierteljahrschrift für Sozial- und Wirtschaftsgeschichte* (Stuttgart and Berlin, 1937); and E. Lousse, "Les Caractères essentiels de l'état corporatif médiéval," *Les Etudes classiques*, VI (1937), 203–223. For Langland and this subject, see Rufus William Rauch, "Langland and Mediaeval Functionalism," *The Review of Politics*, V (1943), 441–461.

12. See below, note 63.

13. *The Rise of the Novel* (Berkeley and Los Angeles, 1957), p. 270.

14. Maurice Keen, "Robin Hood: A Peasant Hero," *History Today*, VIII (1958), 689.

15. "Behind all his [Langland's] social doctrine lies a definition of justice first popularized by St. Ambrose—the unswerving determination to

give to each man that which is his due." Gervase Mathew, "Justice and Charity in *The Vision of Piers Plowman*," *Dominican Studies*, I (1948), 363.

16. F. M. Powicke calls the poem an "apocalyptic challenge to authority" in *Three Lectures Given in the Hall of Balliol College, Oxford, in May 1947* (London, 1947), p. 60.

17. On the plurality of Antichrists, see below, note 70. The very notion of more than one Antichrist implies an awareness of continual (or at least many) crises and of the fact that the world would not necessarily end soon, an attitude very different from that of the very early Middle Ages. The "redeeming" and "cleansing" function of Antichrist is recognized in that pseudo-Joachite work, *De seminibus scripturarum*, known in England in the fourteenth century. See Franz Kampers, "Zur *Notitia saeculi* des Alexander de Roes," *Festgabe Karl Theodor von Heigel* (Munich, 1903), p. 108.

18. "In that strange last passus the author depicts once more the four-teenth-century field-of-folk." H. W. Troyer, "Who is Piers Plowman?" *PMLA*, XLVII (1932), 383. I disagree with Professor Kaske (and others) who say that Piers "is vitally concerned with the inner development of man in his quest for salvation," *SP*, XLVIII (1951), 590. Father T. P. Dunning in "The Structure of the B-Text of Piers Plowman," *RES*, N.S. VII (1956), 226, makes my point neatly: "From the beginning, Langland shows that his subject is Christian Society, or the Church; and that his concern is with the reform of society" (cf. also p. 237). I would perhaps allow that Langland gives a little more autonomy to secular society than Father Dunning at least implies, although in the last analysis, society in a Christian world is the Church, and Christ is the head of the *regnum* as well as the *sacer-dotium*. Father Dunning, however, makes the Vita revolve around the spiritual progress of the individual (pp. 233 and 236) in spite of having quite correctly pointed to the social emphasis in *Piers*. Will in Do-wel is, at least in part, searching himself but in order to find the psychological basis for perfection which can be complete only in a social setting.

19. See E. Zeeman, "Piers Plowman and the Pilgrimage to Truth," *Essays and Studies*, N.S. XI (1958), 1–16. E.g., "...he [Piers] becomes a symbol of the operation of the divine upon the human...."

20. See D. W. Robertson and B. F. Huppé, *Piers Plowman and Scriptural Tradition* (Princeton, 1951), p. 105, who recognize the relation of the three "Do's" to states of perfection.

21. See Robertson and Huppé, *Piers Plowman*, pp. 245 ff. On Piers as a symbol, see H. Troyer, "Who is Piers Plowman?", pp. 368–384, as well as comments *passim* by almost all *Piers Plowman* scholars.

22. See Yves Congar, "Ecclesia ab Abel," *Abhandlungen über Theologie und Kirche, Festschrift für Karl Adam*, ed. M. Reding (Düsseldorf, 1952), pp. 79–108. I am not making any distinction here between the pastoral and the agricultural, as no doubt the original story did.

23. See J. Daniélou, "La Charrue, symbole de la Croix (Irénée, *Adv. haer.* IV, 34, 4)," *Recherches de science religieuse*, XLII (1954), 193–203, for texts on the plow and harvest in the early Fathers. In Thomas Brinton's Ser-mon 20 (ed. M. A. Devlin) the plow is taken as the symbol of penance.

24. Cf. Augustine, Sermon 259, in *PL*, XXXVIII, 1197 ff. Cf. "No man, having put his hand to the plow, and looking back, is fit for the kingdom of God" (Luke 9:62).

25. See Augustine, *In Psalmos*, XXXVI, 4 (*PL*, XXXVI, 358).

26. G. R. Owst, *Literature and Pulpit in Medieval England* (Cambridge, England, 1933), pp. 549 ff. See also Wyclif in *Select English Works*, ed. T. Arnold (Oxford, 1871), III, p. 512.

27. "Piers Plowman ist Urbild und Vorbild des Apostels Petrus und seiner päpstlichen Nachfolger, gleichzeitig des Typus des kommenden Königs der Liebe und des Friedens, der die Kirche in den biblischen Stand zurückführen (reformieren) wird, drittens aber und hauptsächlich der Vertreter des armen, arbeitenden, schaffenden Volkes, das durch Redlichkeit und Treue sich den gebührenden Lohn verdient." Burdach, *Der Dichter des Ackerman*, p. 189. Peter is interpreted as the symbol of mankind in the *Glossa ordinaria* on Luke 22:32 (*PL*, CXIV, 339) (I am indebted to Dr. William Palmer of Morningside College for this reference). Professor Kaske says of Piers as a symbol, "A triumph in the expression of the inexpressible," *SP*, XLVIII (1951), 600.

28. See Dom Jean Leclercq, "Aspects littéraires de l'oeuvre de Saint Bernard," *Cahiers de civilisation médiévale*, I (1958), 447–449. Cf. also the anonymous poem "De abbatibus mitris utentibus et deliciose viventibus," printed in T. Wright, *The Anglo-Latin Satirical Poets*, Rolls Series (London, 1872), II, 230–231. For a very recent treatment of some references to food in *Piers*, see A. C. Spearing, "The Development of a Theme in *Piers Plowman*," *RES*, N.S. XI (1960), 241–253.

29. See Henri de Lubac, "La Rencontre de *Superadditum* et *Supernaturale* dans la théologie médiévale," *Revue du moyen âge latin*, I (1945), 27–34. See also for the subject in general, George Fenwick Jones, "Sartorial Symbols in Mediaeval Literature," *Medium Aevum*, XXV (1956–1957), 63–70; Jean Pépin, "Saint Augustin et le symbolisme néoplatonicien de la vêture," *Augustinus Magister, Congrès international augustinien, Paris, 21–24 Septembre 1954* (Paris [1954–1955]), I, 293–306; Philippus Oppenheim, *Das Mönchskleid im christlicher Altertum*, Römische Quartalschrift 28, Supplementheft (Freiburg in Breisgau, 1931), and *Symbolik und religiöse Wertung des Mönchskleides im christlichen Altertum, vornehmlich nach Zeugnissen christlicher Schriftsteller der Ostkirche*, Theologie des christlichen Ostens, Texte und Untersuchungen 2 (Münster i.W., 1932); Joseph Pascher, ʽΗ ΒΑΣΙΛΙΚΗ ΟΔΟΣ: *Der Königsweg zu Wiedergeburt und Vergottung bei Philon von Alexandreia*, Studien zur Geschichte und Kultur des Altertums XVII, 3–4 (Paderborn, 1931), pp. 48 ff.; and Erik Peterson, "Theologie des Kleides," *Benediktinische Monatschrift*, XVI (1934), 347–356; Johannes Quasten, "A Pythagorean Idea in Jerome," *AJP*, LXIII (1942), 207–215. On the primitive significance of changing clothes to fool evil spirits, see Appendix to J. G. Frazer, "On Certain Burial Customs as Illustrative of the Primitive Theory of the Soul," *Journal of the Anthropological Institute of Great Britain and Ireland*, XV (1886), 98–101.

30. "So ist das Mönchskleid nicht nur Standeskleid, sondern auch heiliges Kleid, das sich der Hochschätzung nicht bloss seiner Träger, sondern auch vieler ausserhalb des Mönchtums erfreut. Es ist das heilige Kleid, in dem der Mönch Christus anzieht und ein Engelsleben führt, das ihm in manchen Dingen ein besonderer Schutz ist und das seine Kraft oftmals durch Wunder bewiesen hat." P. Oppenheim, *Symbolik und religiöse Wertung*, pp. 145–146. Cf. Wyclif, *Sermones*, III, 15 (ed. J. Loserth, III, pp. 114 ff.), on the thirteen garments necessary for the Christian *viator*.

31. The tower is also a symbol of chastity and virginity (equivalent to heaven); see Erwin Panofsky, *Early Netherlandish Painting, Its Origins and Character* (Cambridge, 1953), I, 132. Langland may have this monkish point in mind here. Cf. the tower, symbol of the Church (i.e., heaven on earth), in the *Shepherd of Hermas*, second century apocalypse, Vis. III (ed. Kirsopp Lake, pp. 30 ff.).

32. E. Talbot Donaldson, *Piers Plowman: The C-Text and Its Poet*, Yale Studies in English 113 (New Haven, 1949), pp. 93 ff. The word also has other connotations, but at this date it is unlikely to mean the House of Commons.

33. This poem may have been the creation of Langland, but I doubt it, for I have found it in Lambeth MS 61, fol. 147ᵇ. The MS is of the fourteenth century, although the poem may be in a later hand. It is also in Bibliothèque nationale, Paris, latin 5178, fol. 69Aᵃ (of the fifteenth century), although there it differs considerably from the Langland version. Closely related is a version in an English Latin poem on the truce of 1347 printed in T. Wright, *Political Poems and Songs*, Rolls Series (London, 1859–1861), I, 56–57 (but it is not exactly the same as the one in *Piers*). Langland may, of course, have composed the poem here with others of the same type in mind.

34. See J. Balogh, " 'Rex a recte regendo,' " *Speculum*, III (1928), 580–582. Grosseteste refers to this etymological commonplace ("cum rex a recto dicatur regimine") in his letter (ed. H. Luard, Rolls Series, p. 308) to Henry III. In Westminster Abbey MS 27 on the top of fol. 33ᵃ we find written "O rex si rex es rege te vel eris sine re rex/ nomen habes sine re te nisi recte regis," the formulation of which may have been influenced by *Piers*. Cf. also Trinity, Cambridge MS 723, British Museum, Harley 200, and Bodley, Douce 128. The Harley item is printed by Thomas Hearne in *Roberti de Avesbury: Historia de Mirabilibus Gestis Edvardi III* (Oxford, 1720), p. 257. Cf. also Wright, *Political Poems*, I, 278; in Thomas Brinton, Sermon 38 (ed. M. A. Devlin).

35. From Ecclesiastes 10:16. Widely quoted in the Middle Ages and earlier against the dangers of a regency. See Wyclif, *De potestate Pape*, XII (ed. J. Loserth, p. 376), quoting Jerome, Homily XI. Cf. "Whanne child is king; and cherl bissop; and þral alderman þanne is þe fole wo" from Ipswich Museum MS 6 (see M. R. James, *On the Abbey of S. Edmund at Bury*, Cambridge Antiquary Society [Cambridge, 1895], p. 106). The phrase is applied to Richard II by Adam of Usk in his *Chronicon*, ed. E. Maunde Thompson, p. 3, under the year 1382 and written *c.* 1394. Cf. Salimbene, *Cronica*, ed. F. Bernini, Scrittori d'Italia 187, I, 91–93.

36. For a recent treatment with a bibliography of the "Good Parliament" of 1376 and indeed fourteenth-century constitutional history, see B. Wilkinson, *Constitutional History of Medieval England* (London, New York, Toronto, 1948–1958), II. For the Good Parliament, see pp. 52 ff. and 204 ff.

37. In fourteenth-century England, there were written, in Latin, the *De speculo Regis Edwardi III* (ed. Joseph Moisant [Paris, 1891], in two versions *c.* 1337 and *c.* 1345, and Wyclif's *De officio regis*. See also Wickert, *Studien zu John Gower*, pp. 110 ff.; and Wilhelm Kleineke, *Englische Fürstenspiegel vom Policraticus Johannes von Salisbury bis zum Basilikon Doron König Jakobs I*, Studien zur englischen Philologie, XC (Halle / Saale, 1937). Kleineke, p. 127, recognizes that Langland's advice to kings hardly

fits the "Fürstenspiegel" tradition. See also J. T. Durkin, "Kingship in the Vision of Piers Plowman," *Thought*, XIV (1939), 413–421 (to be used with caution).

38. On superfluity and the problems it raises, see P. Hermengildus Lio, *Determinatio "Superflui" in doctrina Alexandri Halensis eiusque scholae,* Spicilegium Pontificii Athenaei Antoniani 6 (Rome, 1953); R. P. Léon Bouvier, *Le Précepte de l'aumône chez Saint Thomas d'Aquin*, Studia Collegii Maximi Immaculatae Conceptionis I (Montreal, 1935); René Brouillard, "La Doctrine catholique de l'aumône," *Nouvelle revue théologique,* LIV (1927), 5–36; P. Goreux, "L'Aumône et le régime des biens," *Nouvelle revue théologique*, LIX (1932), 117–131, 240–254; Cornelius Damen, "De recto usu bonorum superfluorum," *Miscellanea Vermeersch*, Analecta gregoriana IX and X, 2 vols. (Rome, 1935), I, 63–79; N. Noguer, "La Propriedad de lo superfluo," *Razón y Fe*, LVII (1920), 5–23, and "La Propriedad privada y la necesidad extrema," *Razón y Fe*, VII (1920), 137–154. For further items, see Lio, *Determinatio "Superflui,"* in notes. The basic issue is how to measure superfluity in various classes, for all are agreed, following Jesus' commandment (e.g., Luke 11:41—"quod superest, date elemosynam"), that all that is superfluous must be given to the poor. Cf. I Timothy 6:7–8. The danger of wealth is that one may keep instead of giving away all genuine superfluity. The issue of superfluity in *Piers* is discussed fully in the next chapter.

39. *Piers Plowman*, p. 227, points out that need is the "regulating principle of temperance" (and hence the determinant of superfluity). Temperance fuses both self-control in its many senses and the practice of charity. Robertson and Huppé do not, however, link temperance and need with the problem of superfluity.

40. On Lady Meed, see A. G. Mitchell, *Lady Meed and the Art of "Piers Plowman,"* The Third Chambers Memorial Lecture, delivered 27 February 1956 (London, 1956).

41. *William Langlands "Piers Plowman" (Eine Interpretation des C-Texts)* (Heidelberg, 1957), pp. 60–63. "Et dicunt aliqui synderesim esse conscientium vel conscientiae judicium," Pseudo-Gerson, *Compendium theologiae*, VIII (Gerson, *Opera omnia* [Antwerp, 1706], I, 365). Thomas says, *ST*, I, q. 17, a. 13, that "conscience" can be used of "synderesis," for the cause may often be called by the effect.

42. In spite of diligent search among the many prophecies of the fourteenth century current in Europe, I have not yet been able to find an exact or even close parallel to this puzzling prediction. The suns seem to refer to ages, and it was commonly believed in millenarian circles in the later Middle Ages that the seventh (last) age of the Church was about to begin. There are nine suns in the Tiburtine Sibyl prophecy and seven in the apocryphal Irish *Tenga Bithnua*, but specifically six, I have been able to find nowhere. The reference is, however, probably to the sixth age, which is drawing to a close. We find a folklore motif of a plurality of suns, but it is mostly confined to the Far East and America. See Gudmund Hatt, *Asiatic Influences in American Folklore*, Det Kgl. Danske videnskabernes Selskab, Historisk-filologiske Meddelelser XXXI, 6 (Copenhagen, 1949), pp. 73 ff.

The moon has associations with Antichrist and the Day of Judgment. Roger Bacon speaks of the *lex lune* as the religion of Antichrist, of the law of Saturn as Judaism, and of the law of Mercury as Christianity (in *De viciis contractis in studio theologie*, ed. R. Steele, Opera hactenus inedita

Rogeri Bacon I (Oxford [909]), pp. 43–44 and 49–50). The moon's age or conjunction is to be the time of Antichrist according to an astrological treatise by Franciscus Florentinus discussed and quoted in L. Thorndike, "Franciscus Florentinus or Paduanus," *Mélanges Mandonnet*, Bibliothèque Thomiste XIV (Paris, 1930), II, 353 ff., esp. 359. The Arabic astronomer Masala says that part of the moon is turned against the Jews, in the text in Vatican, lat. urb. 1398. (See W. Gundel, "Religionsgeschichtliche Lesefrüchte aus lateinischen Astrologenhandschriften," *Mélanges Franz Cumont*, Annuaire de l'Institut de Philologie et d'Histoire orientales et slaves, Université Libre de Bruxelles, IV [Brussels, 1936], p. 230). The *Elucidarium*, III, 50, tells us that the Last Judgment will take place at midnight ("myddel of a mone"?). On moon symbolism in general, although not helpful as far as I can see for this passage, see H. Rahner, "Mysterium Lunae: Ein Beitrag zur Kirchentheologie der Väterzeit," *ZKT*, LXIII (1939), 311–349, 428–442, LXIV (1940), 61–80, 121–131; and Mircea Eliade, *Patterns in Comparative Religion*, trans. R. Sheed (London and New York, 1958), pp. 154–187.

The arrows suggest the zodiacal sign of Sagittarius, and Robert Holcot (d. 1349) in his famous Commentary on the Book of Wisdom (lectio LXI) says the present age is that of the Archer, which began with the Donation of Constantine. Holcot explains contemporary attacks on the Church by this theory. In Merlin's Prophecy by Geoffrey of Monmouth and commentaries thereon, the moon, virgins, and archers in common, although I have found no exact parallel to Langland's prophecies. Whatever the prophecy may mean in detail, it is clear, I think, that it does refer to a new or final apocalyptic age.

43. The other two major prophecies in *Piers* equally hard to crack are to be found in VI, 322 ff. (part of this dire prediction of hunger and famine is easy enough to interpret, but the last part on the two monks' heads and multiplying by eight has never been explained), and XIII, 152 ff. (where the "myddel of the mone" comes in again). Saturn, with his baleful astrological power, appears in both. Jan van Ruysbroeck in his *Book of Twelve Beguins* writes that on the Day of Judgment Saturn will be in the ascendant (see E. Colledge, "The Equatorium of the Planets," *Blackfriars* XXXVI [1955], 282).

In the first prophecy, we find the general Sibylline idea of the reign of the woman (or virgin) in the last days. See H. Jeanmaire, "Le Règne de la Femme des derniers jours et le rajeunissement du monde: Quelques remarques sur le texte de Oracula Sibyllina VIII 190–212," *Mélanges Franz Cumont* (note 42, above), pp. 297–304. Cf. also Dante, *De monarchia*, I, 11; and Virgil, *Eclogues*, IV. See also H. Bradley, "Some Cruces in Piers Plowman," *MLR*, V (1910), 340–342, on these obscure Langland prophecies. (On Virgilian prophecy, see Jérome Carcopino, *Virgile et le mystère de la IVe eclogue* [Paris, 1930]; Joseph B. Mayor, W. Warde Fowler, and R. S. Conway, *Virgil's Messianic Eclogue, Its Meaning, Occasion & Sources...* [London, 1907].)

44. I cannot follow Rupert Taylor's assumption in his *The Political Prophecy in England* (New York, 1911), p. 127, that Langland's dark prophecies are parodies. Such an interpretation is completely incompatible with Langland's apocalypticism and inconsistent with his general attitude.

45. See Arthur B. Ferguson, "The Problem of Counsel in *Mum and the Sothsegger*," *Studies in the Renaissance*, II (1955), 67–83. In *Piers* counsel

is both the gift and the council of trusted advisers, a double meaning Middle English spelling makes easy to indicate. See also Atcheson L. Hench, "The Allegorical Motif of Conscience and Reason, Counsellors," *English Studies in Honor of James Southall Wilson*, University of Virginia Studies IV (Charlottesville, 1951), pp. 193–201. On *consilium, deliberatio,* and *discreto*, see Gervais Dumeige, *Richard de Saint-Victor et l'idée chrétienne de l'amour* (Paris, 1952), p. 46 n. and pp. 62 ff. In Letter 106 (April-May 1175) of Arnulf of Lisieux (ed. Frank Barlow, Camden Society, 3rd Series, LXI [London, 1939], pp. 166–168) we find a disquisition on *consilium* quoting Ecclesiasticus 32:24.

46. See Father T. P. Dunning's analysis of this part of the poem, although confined to the A-text, in his *Piers Plowman: An Interpretation of the A-Text* (Dublin, 1937), pp. 68–112. As Father Dunning points out, the exposure of Meed (avarice and cupidity) grows out of the discussion with Holy Church on the problem of superfluity (although he does not use this term) and charity. On Scotus' view of the relation of conscience (and synderesis) and reason to the will (and hence moral act), see Joseph Klein, "Intellekt und Wille als die nächsten Quellen der sittlichen Akte nach Johannes Duns Skotus," *Franziskanische Studien*, III (1916), 309–338; VI (1919), 107–122; VII (1920), 118–134; VIII (1921), 260–282; esp. III, 323–338.

47. This idea, of course, is to be found in the Gospels. For example, in Matthew 5:10–12 in the Sermon on the Mount, Jesus says, "Blessed are they which are persecuted for righteousness' sake: for theirs is the kingdom of heaven. . . ." Bonaventure speaks of the persecutions and tribulations of the saints until the end of the world in his *Lignum vitae (Opera omnia,* ed. Quaracchi, VIII, 83).

48. It is to be found in the Chronicle of John of Reading (ed. James Tait [Manchester, 1914], pp. 150–151); The *Brut* (ed. Brie, Early English Text Society, o.s., 131 and 136 [1906–1908], p. 315); the British Museum, Harley 2261 (continuation to Higden's *Polychronicon*, Rolls Series VIII [London, 1882], p. 435). Stanzas or brief references to it may also be seen in British Museum, Cotton, Titus D. XIX, fol. 118ᵇ; Westminster Abbey 26, fols. 15ᵃ and 33ᵃ; University College, Oxford 97 Magdalen, Oxford 147; Westminster Abbey 25 (at end); Christ Church, Canterbury Cathedral 56 (C. 13); and in the Chronicle from the Grey Friars at Lynn (ed. Antonia Gransden in *EHR*, LXXII [1957], 275).

49. On the pardon, see R. W. Chambers, "*Piers Plowman*: A Comparative Study" in *Man's Unconquerable Mind* (London, 1939), pp. 117–121, and "Incoherencies in the A- and B-Texts of *Piers Plowman* and Their Bearing on the Authorship," *London Mediaeval Studies*, I, i (1937), 27–30; Nevill Coghill, "The Pardon of Piers Plowman," Sir Israel Gollancz Memorial Lecture, British Academy, 1945, *Proceedings of the British Academy*, XXX (1944), esp. 16–20 (of separate reprint); John Lawlor, "*Piers Plowman*: The Pardon Reconsidered," *MLR*, XLV (1950), 449–458; and R. W. Frank, Jr., "The Pardon Scene in *Piers Plowman*," *Speculum*, XXVI (1951), 317–331.

50. See, e.g., Archbishop Thoresby's Catechism 1357 in the original Latin, printed in *The Lay Folks' Catechism*, ed. T. F. Simmons and H. E. Nolloth, Early English Text Society, o.s., 118 (London, 1901), p. 30, under C. lines 66–67; the Coghill reference may be found p. 19, n. 2.

51. To many commentators, the priest's repudiation is taken as Will's repudiation of natural law (although why Piers and the priest should continue to fight is not explained); yet it should be pointed out that the

principle of post-mortem rewards and punishment is by no means universally accepted as part of natural law. Duns Scotus, for instance, argues that "reason does not know naturally that there is a judge who acts according to retributive and punitive laws" (D. E. Sharp, *Franciscan Philosophy at Oxford in the Thirteenth Century* [London, 1930], p. 317, referring to *Opus oxoniense* IV, d. 43, q. 2, n. 17 ff., and *Reportata parisiensa* IV, d. 43, q. 2, n. 13 ff.). In other words, this principle need not be a natural law principle at all.

One further point, when the priest says to Piers that he might preach as an interpreter in divinity, with *dixit insipiens* as his theme, it may be he is accusing him of being an atheist because he seemed to have ignored the clergy in speaking of his education. See Psalm 13:1 (Vulgate), where the words following *dixit insipiens* are *Non est Deus*.

52. In VII, 132, Piers says, "Abstinence the abbesse myne a.b.c. me tau3te," a possible reference to monastic discipline.

53. See S. S. Hussey, "Langland, Hilton and the Three Lives," *RES*, N.S. VII (1956), 132–150; and R. W. Frank, Jr., *"Piers Plowman" and the Scheme of Salvation* (New Haven, 1957), pp. 34 ff. (who sums up the problem effectively and who believes the division is not fundamental—"The poet ... used the triad Dowel, Dobet, and Dobest, not as a set of terms, but as a literary device to elaborate his meaning," p. 37). Piers does not appear in Do-wel and in the Visio seems the embodiment of Do-wel. After the priest impugns the pardon, Piers says he will cease sowing and not work so hard and concentrate on prayers and penance (vv. 117–120). This may mean he has moved to Do-bet and explains his absence in Do-wel, for Piers has already gone through this state. Piers is again active in Do-best. This interpretation, which was in part suggested to me by my pupil James A. Odom, Jr., would seem to support, for Piers at least, the equating of the three Do's with the active, contemplative, and mixed lives.

54. G. Kane, *Middle English Literature* (London, 1951), pp. 240–241; and J. A. W. Bennett, "William Langland's World of Visions," *The Listener*, XLIII (1950), 381. See also Father Dunning, "The Structure of the B-Text," pp. 232–237, wherein he distinguishes two types of definition of the three Do's.

55. See Appendix III, below.

56. See, e.g., Wyclif, *Sermones*, IV, 48 (ed. J. Loserth, IV, 387; cf. II, 147); and *The Cloud of Unknowing*, Chapter 21 (ed. Phyllis Hodgson, Early English Text Society, o.s., 218 [London, 1944], pp. 52–55).

57. Frank, *"Piers Plowman,"* p. 18 n. The text of Abbot Abbo referred to above may be found in *PL*, CXXXIX, 446 ff.

58. *Piers Plowman: The C-Text*, pp. 196–197.

59. Chambers, *Man's Unconquerable Mind*, pp. 129–131.

60. See Morton W. Bloomfield, *"Piers Plowman* and the Three Grades of Chastity," *Anglia*, LXXVI (1958), 227–253.

61. Langland is not totally clear here (VIII, 98–106) as to who chooses the king. He first says Do-wel and Do-bet choose a king to keep them in order if they should act against Do-best, and then immediately says all three chose such a king.

62. The three grades of chastity, a perfection metaphor of great antiquity, are definitely to be found in XII, 31 ff., where they are linked with faith, hope, and charity, and in XVI, where we find the Tree of Perfection or

Charity. See Bloomfield, *"Piers Plowman* and the Three Grades of Chastity."

63. The remarks in parentheses are my own. They are not paraphrasing Clergy's remarks. Cf. Alvarius Pelagius, in *De planctu ecclesiae,* I, 65 (written in 1330–1332), in *Biblioteca maxima pontificia* (Rome, 1698), III, 227, who speaks of three grades of innocence—not to do evil, not to approve of those who do, and to correct the sinner. The *De triplici ecclesia,* a pseudo-Wyclifian work, possibly by Hus (printed by Thomson in *Speculum,* III [1928], 387–391), makes the point that of the three *regulae vivendi,* the highest is that of the clerics whose job is to teach others (p. 388). It seems that the role of corrector and teacher was considered in the fourteenth century the highest earthly task, a point Langland makes in defining Do-best more than once. Aquinas, in *De caritate,* a. 11, ad 6 um (*Quaestiones disputatae*), says that the summit of perfection lies in prelates or preachers "qui procurandae saluti aliorum insistunt." See Martin Grabmann, "Katholisches Priestertum und christliches Vollkommenheitsideal nach der Lehre des hl. Thomas von Aquin," *Zeitschrift für Aszese und Mystik,* II (1927), 189–209.

64. *Regulae pastorales,* II, 4. A text much used in the fourteenth century (and at other times) against negligent and evil priests. See, e.g., *Chronicle of St. Albans,* ed. E. Maunde Thompson, Rolls Series (London, 1874), pp. 104–105; Brinton (quoted in F. A. Gasquet, "A Forgotten English Preacher," *The Old English Bible and Other Essays,* 2nd edition [London, 1908], p. 67); and John Bromyard in his great *Summa predicantium,* A XXVII, lviii ad fin. (Yale University Library copy) (I owe this last reference to the kindness of Professor A. L. Kellogg). See A. L. Kellogg, "Langland and the 'canes muti'," *Essays in Literary History, Presented to J. Milton French,* ed. R. Kirk and C. F. Main (New Brunswick, 1960), pp. 25–35.

65. Where the Bible tells this, I do not know. It sounds more like the *Oracula sibyllina* or some apocryphal work. The pristine status to which monks should return is a phrase used for the fundamental reform of the orders and world in the later Middle Ages. We return in order to progress. In a spurious prophecy (*Prophecia Domini Roberti de Grostest*) attributed to Grosseteste in Bodley, Digby 196, fol. 28 (fifteenth century) printed in S. Harrison Thomson, *The Writings of Robert Grosseteste, Bishop of Lincoln, 1235–1253* [Cambridge, England, 1940], p. 260, we find a reference to this pristine state to which the "strong eagle," raging, will renew the holy places. Even more striking, however, is the reference in the *Eulogium historiarum sive temporis* by a monk of Malmesbury roughly contemporary with our poet. In III, 120 (Rolls Series edition I, 417 ff.), the author is discussing a prophecy (Incipit—"Ter tria lustra tenent cum semi tempora sexti . . ." also found in Westminster Abbey MS 27; Corpus Christi, Cambridge 138; and British Museum, Cotton, Vespasian E. VII 726) often applied to Edward III's reign. He speaks in his commentary on it of a just king "debellando, inimicos suos superando" (echoing Virgil), who will reduce "clerum in statum pristinum et privilegia ecclesiastica renovabit, quae prius fuerant subpeditata" (p. 419).

66. See R. W. Frank, "The Conclusion of *Piers Plowman*" in *JEGP,* XLIX (1950), 312 and n., and the discussion in Chap. V below.

67. See Morton W. Bloomfield, *"Piers Plowman* and the Three Grades of Chastity."

68. In C XIX, 1, *Liberium arbitrium* is the guide, and the owner of the land is *Cor-hominis*.

To us, today, free will is a metaphysical problem; to the Middle Ages, it was a psychological one. See, e.g., Pierre Michaud Quantin, "Die Psychologie bei Radulfus Ardens," *Münchener theologische Zeitschrift*, IX (1958), 81 ff. (Ardens says the soul has four basic *potentiae: ratio, concupiscibilitas/irascibilitas, potestas,* and *libertas*). Langland in his exploration of the soul in Do-wel, finally, at the beginning of Do-bet, arrives at Free Will, the ground of the soul and the best evidence of God's grace and charity, as Scotism, the dominant philosophy of fourteenth-century England, teaches. The whole emphasis on the eminence of free will (stressed even more in C than in B where he takes over as guide from Anima) is highly Scotistic. Free will is the most divine element in our souls, the part closest to God (even in St. Bernard; see his *De gratia et libero arbitrio*, 9) and closely related to the Holy Ghost. Hence, free will logically leads us (and Will) to the Godhead and the Trinity—and this is what follows the Tree of Perfection scene. We now witness God's supreme grace as manifested in his Son (and the rest of Do-bet is concerned with Him and the theological virtues and Do-best with the activities of Holy Ghost, the continuing guarantee of God's love for man and His Church). Do-bet deals with the various aspects of Jesus' life, with the preparation for Him in Abraham (Faith) and Moses (Hope), and culminates after a strange discussion of the Trinity (Passus XVII) in the story of the Passion and in the Harrowing of Hell.

69. Abraham as the symbol of faith is well established in the tradition, to be seen even as early as Philo and the New Testament itself; but Moses as hope is rare or unknown. I suppose one could argue thus: The prophets of Israel are the bearers of hope to the world in the dark period before the Incarnation and symbolize hope (which is the virtue of the future). To the Middle Ages, Moses was the greatest of the prophets (see, e.g., Aquinas, *De veritate*, q. XII, a. 14) and hence the best symbol of hope. Deuteronomy 32, for instance, is traditionally interpreted as foretelling Jesus as directly as are the better-known christological passages in Isaiah.

It is possible that Abraham and Moses represent the first two Joachite ages. Cf., e.g., "Quis mysterice Abrae pertinent proprie utiam diximus ad primum statum et quasi ad deum patrum," Joachim, *Concordia*, V, 47, fol. 81^b (ed. of 1519) (yet here he goes on to parallel Isaac and Jacob, not Moses, with the next two ages), and "Ordo secundi status designatur in Moyse," *Concordia*, III, 14, fol. 32^a. Jesus, who comes next, as charity, in *Piers*, can surprisingly enough symbolize the Holy Ghost in Joachim's system ("Habraam significat deum patrem, Isaac filius; Jacob spiritum sanctum et nihilominus. Zacharius pater Joannis significat deum patrem; Joannes baptista filium; homo christus Jesus spiritum sanctum," *Concordia*, II, tractatus I, c. 3, fol. 8^a). These three figures then, Abraham, Moses, and Jesus, can be made in Joachim's system to equal the three persons of the Trinity. See Francis A. R. Carnegy, *The Relations Between the Social and Divine Order in William Langland's "Vision of William concerning Piers the Plowman,"* Sprache und Kultur der germanischen und romanischen Völker, Anglistische Reihe XII (Breslau, 1934), pp. 36–38.

70. Langland believed in periods of Antichrist. Langland did not think that the end of the world was near; rather he thought that the world was suffering from the incursions of an Antichrist (*mysticus*), not the final one (*ultimus*), which would be the prelude to a new or reformed age or just a

reconstitution of the Church in its primal purity. On the idea of plurality of Antichrists, found also in the New Testament, see Morton W. Bloomfield, "Joachim of Flora," *Traditio*, XIII (1957), 265, n. 71. Cf. also Wyclif, *De potestate Pape*, XII and IX (ed. J. Loserth, pp. 328, 217–218). See above, note 17.

71. Henry Wells recognized this point, although he did not analyze it in any detail himself. "The more serious view of the poem hangs upon the interpretation of its last few pages." "The Philosophy of *Piers Plowman*," *PMLA*, LIII (1938), 348.

72. "And at the end, the crucifixion is not only the supreme showing-forth of *caritas*; it enables the claims of Truth and Righteousness to be satisfied—for that is the inner meaning of the wonderful colloquy between the four daughters of God—Mercy and Truth, Peace and Righteousness—in the eighteenth passus." J. A. W. Bennett, "William Langland's World of Visions," *The Listener*, XLIII (1950), 382. See also Erzgräber, *William Langlands "Piers Plowman,"* pp. 185 ff.

73. On the kingship or sovereignty of Christ in the Middle Ages, see, e.g., J. Leclercq, "L'Idée de la royauté du Christ au XIVe siècle," *Miscellanea Pio Paschini*, Lateranum, N.S. XIV (Rome, 1948), I, 405–425; "L'Idée de la seigneurie du Christ au moyen âge," *RHE*, LIII (1958), 57–68; and *The Kingship of Jesus Christ,* trans. (Paterson, N.J., 1944). This question had important political implications, especially in Langland's century.

74. See Bonaventure, *In Lucam*, IX, 34 (ed. Quaracchi, VII, 226–227).

75. This touches upon the medieval *triduum* problem—whether Jesus was still a man while He lay in the tomb. In the fourteenth century, Wyclif (*De benedicta incarnacione*, ed. E. Harris, IV, 57 ff. etc.) argued that he was.

76. See Gervase Mathew, "Justice and Charity in *The Vision of Piers Plowman*," *Dominican Studies*, I (1948), 366. On the place of the apocalyptic view of history in the later Middle Ages, see Appendix IV, below.

NOTES FOR CHAPTER V

1. See the same parallel in Wimbledon's sermon discussed in Chapter III, above.

2. On Langland's view of Conscience, see below, Appendix II.

The B-Text (XIX, 12) reads: these (Piers' figure) are "Pieres armes" followed by "ac he that cometh so blody/ is Cryst" (vv. 13–14), whereas C (XXII, 12) as this point reads: these are "Cristes armes" followed by "and he that cometh so blody, Hit is Crist," (vv. 13–14). E. Talbot Donaldson in *Piers Plowman: The C-Text and Its Poet*, Yale Studies in English 113 (New Haven, 1949), pp. 243–244, argues that this is an error by C, but I think the "ac" and "and" make all the difference. The B and C readings are merely two different ways of saying the same thing. In general this point supports Donaldson's argument that C preserves better readings than B when both are approximately saying the same thing, for this reading in his opinion was an exception.

3. This problem must have bothered others in Langland's time. Wyclif, in his *Sermones*, I, 6 (ed. J. Loserth [London, 1887–1890], I, 38–39), asks why believers in Jesus are called Christians instead of Jesuans; and, although aware of the meaning of "anointed one," he answers that it is because Christ is a common noun, unlike Jesus.

Just as it is difficult to determine exactly where Do-bet begins, so also it is difficult to separate Do-best and Do-bet. The three "lives" run into each other, and I think deliberately.

4. R. W. Frank, Jr., *"Piers Plowman" and the Scheme of Salvation* (New Haven, 1957), pp. 100–101.

5. Brinton, in Sermons 35, 44, 87, and 90, makes the point that all are free in Christ; see also M. A. Devlin's introduction to her edition of Brinton, I, xxii–xxiii.

6. The "lesson" of Do-wel. Cf. Wyclif's remark about the soldier of Christ "qui paciendo vincit totum mundum, carnem et totum exercitum demonum" in *Sermones*, IV, 32 (ed. J. Loserth, IV, 280).

7. Langland was probably aware that the name meant anointed one, but inasmuch as only rulers were anointed, the term could be considered equivalent to king or ruler. Nicholas of Lyra on Luke 2:11 (ed. Venice, 1487) writes "Christus grece idem est quod unctus latine. Antiquitus atque in vetere lege ungebantur tamen reges et pontifices. Christus autem rex est et pontifex."

8. Although I have not specifically made the point, Langland at the beginning of Passus XVIII in conceiving the Incarnation and Passion of Jesus as a joust is emphasizing there too Christ's royalty. In this matter in particular Langland is Scotistic, I think, although in general the stress on the kingship of Christ is monastic.

9. In his Sermon I in *Epiphania* (IX, 145–151 [Quaracchi ed.]), Bonaventure makes the point that Jesus was revealed as King for the first time to the Magi. This is probably a theological commonplace.

Usually the gold represents royalty; the frankincense, godhead; and the myrrh, death. On legends and portrayals of the Magi, see Hugo Kehrer, *Die Heiligen drei Könige in Literatur und Kunst*, 2 vols. (Leipzig 1908–1909).

10. Angels and archangels came to His empty tomb before daybreak and sang "Christus resurgens" (Romans 6:9), words that are sung in the liturgy on Wednesday and Saturday and the fourth Sunday after Easter. This scene in the poem follows after Easter at the end of the Harrowing of Hell passus.

11. The idea, of course, is found in many places in the Old and New Testaments and in the works of the Fathers and scholastics.

12. Father Gervase Mathew is one of the few to recognize Langland's stress on justice and its close relationship to love. See his "Justice and Charity in *The Vision of Piers Plowman*," *Dominican Studies*, I (1948), 360–361.

13. Manly could not see the relevance of lines 236–237 in Sloth's confession in A and assumed they really belonged to the confession of Robert the Robber, which follows it. He accounted for this apparent confusion by his famous hypothesis of the missing leaf (in "The Lost Leaf of *Piers the Plowman*," *MP*, III [1906], 359 ff.). These lines, however, which may be translated as, "And yet I will give back, if I am able, all that I wickedly gained since I [first] had intelligence," refer to the neglect of the religious duty of restitution. Sloth comprises all such sins of negligence. To Langland, of course, making restitution would be one of the more important of these religious requirements. However, in B, the passage devoted to restitution is enormously expanded and put under the confessions of Avarice and Robert the Robber. (In C, Robert the Robber is portrayed as a type of avarice.) Langland, by the time he came to rewrite A, was no doubt much more

aware of the heinousness of the neglect of restitution. Yet neglect of restitution is not only the sin of avarice but also the sin of sloth. Sloth is also, as Langland makes clear, the sin of neglecting to pay servants and pay back debts (V, 429–435).

14. *"Piers Plowman,"* pp. 106 ff.

15. On the high medieval theory of satisfaction, see Joseph A. Spitzig, *Sacramental Penance in the Twelfth and Thirteenth Centuries,* a Dissertation submitted to ... the Catholic University of America ... Studies in Sacred Theology, 2nd Series, No. 6 (Washington, 1947). See also Rosalind Hill, "Public Penance: Some Problems of a Thirteenth-Century Bishop," *History,* N.S. XXXVI (1951), 217. Although restitution presupposes contrition in some respects, it may also be looked on as a part of the last division of the Sacrament of Penance—satisfaction. See the *questiones* on satisfaction in Thomas' *Summa,* III, Supplement, 12–15. Thomas Brinton in his Sermon 31 seems to consider restitution a part of satisfaction. See also below, note 68.

16. See, e.g., Benjamin N. Nelson, "The Usurer and the Merchant Prince: Italian Business Men and the Ecclesiastical Law of Restitution, 1100–1550," *The Tasks of Economic History,* Supplement VII to *The Journal of Economic History,* VII (1947), 104–122; and Florence Edler de Roover, "Restitution in Renaissance Florence," *Studi in onore di Armando Sapori* (Milan, 1957), II, 773–789. See Guy Terrena's (d. 1342) *questio* on whether the Pope can absolve the sin of usury without restitution (the answer is no). The text of this *questio* (*Quodlibet,* IV, q. 11) is printed in Fr. B. F. M. Xiberta, *Guiu Terrena, Carmelita de Perpinyà,* Estudis Universitaris Catalans, Serie Monogràfica II (Barcelona, 1932), pp. 319–320.

17. *Reportata parisiensa,* IV, dist. 15, q. 4 (ed. Vives, XXIV, p. 242).

18. See Brinton's Sermons 22, 31, 35, *et passim*; and for Fitzralph, see Aubrey Gwynn, "Richard Fitzralph, Archbishop of Armagh," Part VI, *Studies,* XXV (1936), 83, and "The Black Death in Ireland," *Studies,* XXIV (1935), 31; and L. L. Hammerich, "The Beginning of the Strife Between Richard Fitzralph and the Mendicants," *Det Kgl. Danske videnskabernes Selskab,* Historisk-filologiske Meddelelser XXVI, 3 (Copenhagen, 1938), p. 28.

19. "Again and again in the late thirteenth and early fourteenth centuries, Franciscans ... are accused, among other things, now of absolving outstandingly wealthy usurers without requiring restitution ... ," Nelson, "The Usurer," p. 112.

20. Lib. I, corol. 28. Cf. also Wyclif, *Trialogus,* IV, 23 (ed. G. Lechler [Oxford, 1869], pp. 326–328), where he hardly mentions restitution or satisfaction in his discussion of the Sacrament of Penance.

21. *"Piers Plowman,"* p. 108.

22. *Summa contra Gentiles,* I, 93. See also *ST,* II, II, q. 58, a. 1 (a. 2 argues for the essentially social nature of justice—e.g., "Therefore justice is concerned only about our dealings with others"). See also his comments in *De veritate,* q. 23, a. 6 ad 3.

23. In the Preface to his *Tractatus de vitiis et virtutibus,* printed in Jordani de Saxonia, *Liber vitasfratrum,* ed. R. Arbesmann and W. Hümpfner, Cassiciacum I (American Series) (New York, 1943), pp. XXXIV–XXXV. He continues, "Et subdit: *Nemini quidquam debeatis, nisi ut invicem diligatis, qui enim diliget proximum, legem implevit. In hoc igitur quod*

unicuique debitum suum reddimus, omnem iustitiam implemus, secundum quod iustitia includet in se omne bonum et excludit omne malum...."

24. See Augustine, *Ennarrationes in Psalmos*, 132, 2 and 6 (*PL*, XXXVII, 1729 and 1736).

25. No mention is made of the wind (Acts 2:2). Perhaps Langland is thinking of Joachim of Flora's belief that the Holy Ghost comes as a dove in the first age, as a wind in the second, and as fire in the third; see his *Expositio in Apocalypsim* (Venice, 1527), fol. 124 (and *Romania*, LVI [1930], 548 n.). The Pentecost described in *Piers* is the first pentecost, every pentecost, and the ideal and future pentecost. The Joachite point, if there is one, would apply only to the latter.

26. For fourteenth-century associations of these terms, see H. A. Oberman, *Archbishop Thomas Bradwardine, a Fourteenth Century Augustinian: A Study of His Theology in Its Historical Context* (Utrecht, 1957), pp. 135 ff., esp. pp. 130–137.

27. But note no friars.

28. See D. W. Robertson and Bernard F. Huppé, *Piers Plowman and Scriptural Tradition* (Princeton, 1951), pp. 221–222 and the references there.

29. To Joachim, John is the symbol of the contemplative or monastic life, and is finally to replace Peter.

30. "Of þe four cardinal vertues speken moche þe olde philosofres, but þe Holy Gost 3euþ hem moche bettre and techeþ hem an hundred so wel," *The Book of Vices and Virtues, a Fourteenth Century English Translation of the Somme le Roi...*, ed. W. Nelson Francis, Early English Text Society, o.s., 217 (London, 1942), p. 122. The fact that Langland names these virtues with the prefix spiritus—i.e., *spiritus iusticie*, etc.—would also argue for the same point. The early scholastics were agreed that the cardinal virtues were infused for Christians; see D. Odon Lottin, *Psychologie et morale aux XIIe et XIIIe siècles*, III (Louvain and Gembloux, 1942 ff.), III, 184 and 199 ff. The problem had its complexities, and there was later much debate over these infused virtues; see Lottin, III, 459–535, and IV, 739–807; and Gabriel Bullet, *Vertus morales infuses et vertus morales acquises selon Saint Thomas d'Aquin*, Studia friburgensia, N.S. 23 (Fribourg, 1958). By the fourteenth century the possibility of the infusion of moral virtues seems to have been generally accepted.

31. A possible reference to the War of Eight Saints between Gregory XI and the Florentines in 1376–1378; see Christopher Dawson, "The Vision of Piers Plowman," reprinted in *Medieval Essays* (London and New York, 1953), p. 259 n. This would, if the date of B is correct, put Langland very *au courant* with contemporary history. No particular deed is really needed in view of medieval papal history in general.

32. "Sed quare non providet Deus homini sine omni solicitudine sicut avibus et vegetabilibus? Secundam theologiam est respondum quod in statu innocentie fuit provisum homini de victu et vestitu sine omni solicitudine." So the fourteenth-century English Carmelite John Baconthorpe in his Postilla on Matthew 6:28, quoted in B. Smalley, "John Baconthorpe's Postilla on St. Matthew," *MARS*, IV (1958), 115. Cf. the argument by the Monk of Bury St. Edmunds in the *questio* on whether mendicants or possessioners are more perfect, that if we renounce all necessities, we must seek with great solicitude other ways to satisfy our basic needs, for we cannot think or understand if we are hungry, thirsty, cold, or hot. To avoid this solicitude about worldly matters, it is better, the monk argues, to have some posses-

sions in common and to labor with one's hands than to beg (ed. W. A. Pantin, "Some Medieval English Treatises on the Origins of Monasticism," *Medieval Studies Presented to Rose Graham*, ed. V. Ruffer and A. J. Taylor [Oxford, 1950], p. 213). Need is arguing here as the monk is—that only by the recognition and satisfaction of genuine need can one truly throw oneself on God and be "sorglos" as Jesus commanded ("Take no heed for the morrow . . ." etc.). This is essentially Augustine's argument. See below, note 82. This subject is to be discussed in greater detail below.

33. The same argument occurs in Anima's speech in Passus XV, as discussed above in Chapter III.

34. *ST*, II, II, q. 186, a. 3 ad 3. On the same problem in connection with virginity, see *ST*, II, II, q. 152, a. 2 ad 2, where the issue is dealt with in similar fashion. I am quoting from the translation by the English Dominican Fathers.

35. *ST*, II, II, q. 66, a. 7. A. Gwynn, "Richard Fitzralph, Archbishop of Armagh," Part VI, *Studies*, XXV (1936), 93.

36. *ST*, II, II, q. 141, a. 8 ad 3. Justice occasionally takes first place, as for instance in the early thirteenth-century English treatise on the powers of the soul published by Father D. Callus in *RTAM*, XIX (1952), 161. In Plato, of course, justice is the crown of all the cardinal virtues, but it is especially linked with temperance.

37. Ed. J. Holmberg (Uppsala, 1929), pp. 52–53.

38. On temperance in classical antiquity, see Arnold Stein, *Heroic Knowledge, an Interpretation of "Paradise Regained" and "Samson Agonistes"* (Minneapolis, 1957), pp. 17–35. The reference below is to pp. 34 ff. See also the unpublished dissertation by Helen North, "The Concept of Sophrosyne in Greek Literature from Homer to Aristotle," Cornell University, 1946.

39. Macrobius in his *Commentary on Scipio's Dream*, I, viii, 7, specifically refers to "political temperance," thus assuming a wider meaning for the term.

40. This concept of the mean is so widely assumed and referred to in Thomas Aquinas that many references could be given. See, e.g., "virtus ipsa est quaedum medietas inter duas malitias et inter duos habitus vitioses," Commentary on the *Nicomachean Ethics*, II, lectio VII, 324.

41. *ST*, II, II, q. 141, a. 2.

42. Ed. Francis, p. 288.

43. See Aristotle, *Physics*, III, 6 (207a) and *De anima*, II, iv, 416a. See also Morton W. Bloomfield, "Perfection . . . ," *Franciscan Studies*, XVII (1957), 220–221.

44. I, q. 2, ed. H. Kühle, C. Feckes, B. Geyer, and W. Kübel in *Opera omnia*, XXVIII (Münster i.W., 1951).

45. Not all scholastics treat the matter as Albertus does; see, e.g., Friedrich Stegmüller, "Der Traktat des Robert Kilwardby O.P., De imagine et vestigio Trinitatis," *Archives d'histoire doctrinale et littéraire du moyen âge*, X and XI (1935–1936), 324–407; and Alexander of Hales, *Glossa in quatuor libros sententiarum Petri Lombardi*, Biblioteca franciscana scholastica medii aevi XIII and XIV [Quaracchi, 1952–1954], II, dist. III (Vol. XIII, pp. 29 ff.). Alexander, referring to Augustine (the exact reference the editor cannot find), does say, however, that *mensura* is equivalent to the "distributio bonorum Spiritus sancti," in spite of differing on most points from Albertus. The confusion is at least partially due to Augustine's rather confused treat-

ment of the subject. See W. J. Roche in *New Scholasticism*, XV (1941), 350–376.

46. *Legum allegoria*, I, 70–72.

47. *Reportata parisiensa*, III, dist. 34, n. 7 (ed. Vives, XXIII, 526). See, e.g., "Temperantia est nihil appetere paenitendum, in nullo legem moderationis excedere, sub jugo rationis cupiditatem domare," Alexander of Hales, *Summa de virtutibus* (part of his *Summa theologica*), Collatio 90, art. 1.

48. See, e.g., *Opus oxoniense*, III, d. 34, 15 ff. The third book of Albertus' *De bono* discusses temperance.

49. Patience is often, as in Thomas Aquinas, for instance, considered a branch of fortitude rather than of temperance. I suspect that Langland assimilated this virtue to humility and meekness, which are the monastic equivalents, and these are branches of temperance. In Tertullian's *De patientia*, 13, bodily patience includes humility, poverty, chastity, martyrdom, etc. Similar ideas are to be found in Cyprian's *De bono patientiae* and Augustine's *De patientia*, wherein humility and patience are on occasion equated.

50. Gulielmus Peraldus, *Summa virtutum*, "De patientia" (ed. Lyons, 1668, I, 268). Peraldus makes no essential distinction between humility and patience. Cf. "et in humilitate tua patientiam habe," Ecclesiasticus 2:4. "Humilitas enim est quasi area temperata in qua oportet omnia plantaria aliarum virtutum inseri . . . ," Wyclif, *Sermones*, IV, 28 (ed. Loserth, IV, 24).

51. Revelation 3:10. See the "Spiritual" Peter John Olivi's comments on this verse in his famous *postillae* on the Apocalypse and quoted in the extracts from this work published by Etienne Baluze in his *Miscellanea novo ordine digesta* . . . (Lucca, 1761), II, 261, wherein poverty, humility, and patience are stressed as the virtues of this, the sixth age of the Church.

52. *Concordia*, V, c. 51. See also his *Tractatus super Quatuor Evangelia* (ed. E. Buonaiuti, pp. 68, 115, 242 ff.) and *Expositio in Apocalypsim*, II (ed. Venice, 1527, p. 111c). On this subject, see E. Benz, "Joachim-Studien. I. Die Kategorien der religiösen Geschichtsdeutung Joachims," *ZKG*, L (1931), 83.

53. See Etienne Gilson, *La Théologie mystique de Saint Bernard*, Etudes de philosophie médiévale XX (Paris, 1947), pp. 93–97. For humility in the Middle Ages, see R. A. Gauthier, *Magnanimité: L'Idéal de la grandeur dans la philosophie païenne et dans la théologie chrétienne*, Bibliothèque thomiste XXVIII (Paris, 1951), pp. 375 ff., 418 ff., and 460 ff. Cf. "Summa virtus monachi humilitas," Isidore of Seville, *Sententiae*, III, 19 (*PL*, LXXXIII, 694).

54. Cf., e.g., "Verbum enim Dei in sublimi constitutum ut ad nos descenderet, prior humilitas invitavit," St. Bernard of Clairvaux, *Epistola*, 469, 2 (*PL*, CLXXXII, 674).

55. See Francis D. S. Darwin, *The English Mediaeval Recluse* (London, n.d. [1944]), pp. 35 ff.

56. *ST*, II, II, p. 161, a. 5 ad 2. I have related poverty and chastity, two of the three monastic vows, to temperance; and one can also relate the third, obedience, to this same virtue. Although in Thomas Aquinas, it is a branch of justice, in some monastic treatises (see, e.g., the Cistercian Commentary on the Benedictine Rule printed in part by C. H. Talbot in *Analecta monastica*, 5th Series, Studia anselmiana XLIII [Rome, 1958], pp. 133–134), obedience is considered a type of humility and hence of temperance.

57. Aquinas, *ST*, II, II, q. 118 a. 1 (English Dominican Fathers translation).

In the early Renaissance we find the reintroduction of the more secular and classical concept of temperance, which soon became dominant. In fact, in Renaissance thinking temperance in this sense came to occupy an even more important role in aretology than in the Middle Ages. For temperance in Petrarch, who regarded it as one of Virtus' chief weapons, above all against pride, see Klaus Heitmann, *Fortuna und Virtus: Eine Studie zu Petrarcas Lebensweisheit*, Studi italiani 1 (Cologne and Graz, 1958), pp. 157 ff.

58. See above, Chapter IV, note 38, for some bibliographical references.

59. Especially in the long speech of Anima in XV.

60. See *Piers Plowman: The C-Text*, pp. 169 ff. The quotation below is from p. 171.

61. Ed. A. J. Perry in Early English Text Society, o.s., 167 (London, 1925), pp. 1–38. The quotation is from p. 23.

62. The reference to Fitzralph is to his *Defensio curatorum* in English translated by Trevisa (printed in A. J. Perry edition [London, 1925], pp. 76–77). In Fitzralph's sermon *Nemo vos seducat* preached at St. Paul in 1356 Fitzralph says the greatest cause of sin is superfluous riches (British Museum, Lansdowne 343, fol. 129*b*). Nicholas of Lyra in his *Questio de usu paupere* writes among other things that "usus superfluus est indecens clericis," printed in Franz Pelster, "Nikolaus von Lyra und seine Quaestio de usu paupere," *AFH*, XLVI (1953), 244. The Wyclifian argument may be seen in *Dialogus*, 30 (ed. A. W. Pollard [London, 1886], pp. 65 ff.) and *Responsiones ad argumenta Radulfi Strode* (in *Opera minora*, ed. J. Loserth [London, 1913], pp. 182–183).

63. As a type, he is appropriate enough to be Pride's helper, but he may also be a particular lord who has not yet been identified.

64. Cf. the saying attributed to St. Francis, "Dixit mihi Dominus quod volebat quod ego essem unus novellus pazzus in mundo," and "Crist chese to his discyples þe foolys of þis world"; and pseudo-Wyclif, "Of Antecrist and his Meynee," ed. J. H. Todd in *Three Treatises by John Wycklyffe O.D.* (Dublin, 1851), p. cli. See Natalino Sapegno, "La *Santa Pazzia* di Frate Jacopone e le dottrine dei mistici medievali," *Archivum Romanicum*, VII (1923), 349–372. Although some Franciscans especially cultivated spiritual recklessness and holy madness in the later Middle Ages, actually the virtue is very old and based on the New Testament. We must finally throw ourselves on God. See also Gervais Dumeige, *Richard de Saint-Victor et l'idée chrétienne de l'amour* (Paris, 1952), and especially Richard's *Tractatus de quatuor gradibus violentae charitatis* (PL, CXCVI, 1211 ff.).

65. Henri Stegemeier, in *The Dance of Death in Folksong, with an Introduction on the History of the Dance of Death* (Chicago, 1939), takes these lines as evidence for the presence of the Dance of Death motif in the fourteenth century.

66. Probably matrimony as the first grade of charity (perfection) and hence layfolk.

67. Belief probably in the finality and stability of life.

68. Here Unity must in some sense correspond to satisfaction and *redde quod debes*. In spite of Aquinas and Scotus, Langland must regard restitution as part (at least) of satisfaction in the Sacrament of Penance. This is an older view. See, e.g., Bartholomew of Exeter, *Penitential*, X and XI (ed.

Dom Adrian Morey in *Bartholomew of Exeter, Bishop and Canonist: A Study in the Twelfth Century* [Cambridge, England, 1937], pp. 181–183). See above, note 15.

69. See, e.g., Oscar Cargill, "The Langland Myth," *PMLA*, L (1935), 36 ff.

70. "Infernus latus est sine mensura," Hugh of St. Victor, *De anima . . . ,* XIII (*PL*, CLXXVII, 186). Cf. also Aquinas in his commentary on Job 10:22 (c. X, lectio 3). This biblical verse is frequently used to justify describing hell as being without boundaries—complete immoderateness and chaos. Wyclif, in one of his English works (ed. Matthews, Early English Text Society, 74 [London, 1880], p. 478), writes ". . . fendis wanten ordre in helle."

71. In spite of Langland's own threats about secular lords who will dispossess the rich religious, no doubt in the last analysis he would agree with the monk of Oxford (Uthred of Boldon?) mentioned by Wyclif (*De civili dominio,* II, 3, ed. J. Loserth [London, 1884–1904], II, 23–24), who argued that the lords' taking goods from the Church is a violation of the commandment, "Non concupisces rem proximi tui," which Langland himself quotes here too (v. 277).

72. See Bloomfield, "Perfection," 219 ff., and references there. On Plato in particular, see n. 9. For Aristotle, see *Physics* III, 6, 207a, and for Plotinus, *Enneads,* VI, 6.

73. *De principiis,* II, 9, 1. See Charles Bigg, *The Christian Platonists of Alexandria,* Bampton Lectures, 1886 (Oxford, 1886), pp. 158–162.

74. *De divinis nominibus,* IV, 4; and *De Genesi ad litteram,* IV, 3, 4, 5 (*PL*, XXXIV, 299–300).

75. *Metalogicon,* II, 20 (trans. Daniel D. McGarry [Berkeley and Los Angeles, 1955], pp. 132–133). This whole chapter deals with this subject in relation to the problem of universals. John, like all medieval thinkers who were concerned with the principle of limit, was concerned with saving the rationality of the universe.

76. Ed. A. J. Perry, Early English Text Society, o.s., 167 (London, 1925), pp. 59–60. In Fitzralph's defense, it should be pointed out that the misunderstanding of the meaning of metaphysics which the use of this argument reveals was widespread in the fourteenth century and is indeed an evidence of the breaking down of scholasticism. See for a similar misuse of metaphysical argument, the protest of the Cistercian abbots against what they thought was an encroachment on their powers by the new constitution of the order issued by Pope Benedict XII (1334–1342), "Fulgens sicut stella," printed as an appendix to Jean-Berthold Mahn, *Le Pape Benoît XII et les Cisterciens,* Bibliothèque de l'Ecole des Hautes Etudes, Fasc. 295 (Paris, 1949). They do not hesitate (pp. 101 ff.) to use the pseudo-Dionysian metaphysical principle of hierarchy to argue that the lower (i.e., the monks) must be subordinated to the higher (i.e., the abbots). The new constitution violates the order of the universe. Even with this in mind, however, it is still hard to excuse a metaphysician and philosopher of the stature of Fitzralph from this misuse of metaphysics. Frank, *"Piers Plowman,"* p. 110, n. 6, has also pointed out the similarity of Fitzralph's and Langland's charges against the multiplication of the friars. See him for some further contemporary references. The same point about the friars is made in "Jack Upland," printed in T. Wright, *Political Poems,* Rolls Series (London, 1859–1861), II, 30-31 (see the answer in "Reply to Friar Daw Topias," II, 104 ff.).

77. II, ed. M. H. Dziewicki (London, 1889), p. 42. Cf. also Wyclif's *Trialogus*, Supplementum (ed. Lechler, p. 432), in which he says these new orders sin against the Trinity in number, weight, and measure. In *Dialogus*, 25 (ed. A. W. Pollard, p. 52) he writes "in fratribus superfluis." Cf. also *Sermones*, III, 29 (ed. Loserth, III, 230–231).
78. On why the pilgrimage is given up, see Donaldson, *Piers Plowman: The C-Text*, pp. 165–166; and D. C. Fowler, "The 'Forgotten' Pilgrimage in *Piers the Plowman*," *MLN*, LXVII (1952), 524–526.
79. See, e.g., XVI, 223.
80. The only medieval reference I know of to the Holy Ghost killing Antichrist occurs in *King Solomon's Book of Wisdom* (before 1400), vv. 295–296 (Early English Text Society 69 [London, 1878], p. 90), where we read:

Atte last schal come þe holi gost: in fourme of swerd al[i]3t,
& Anticrist to deþ smyte: þorou3 his swete mi3t.

81. Cf. "Who art thou? Thou art the high priest, the sovereign pontiff. Thou art the prince of bishops and the inheritor of the Apostles. Thou art like Abel, the ancestor, like Noah the pilot, like Abraham, the patriarch. Thou representest the order of Melchizedek, the dignity of Aaron, the authority of Moses, the jurisdiction of Samuel, the power of Peter and the Messiahship of Jesus Christ," St. Bernard to Pope Eugenius III in *De consideratione*, II, 8 (15) (my translation). The whole of Book II of this work is full of vineyard, harvest, and worker imagery.
82. ". . . paupertas que habet vite necessaria, non appetens aliena, videtur esse perfeccior," in W. A. Pantin, "Some Medieval English Treatises," p. 213. Fitzralph in his *Defensio curatorum*, p. 60 (ed. A. J. Perry), makes briefly the same point: ". . . beggers compelled by nede most leve þe seruise [of God] & go abegged ofte tyme." Neither they nor Langland would have agreed with the Franciscan position as put by, say, Peckham in his questio on the subject of poverty (ed. P. Livarius Oliger in *Franziskanische Studien*, IV [1917], 127–176) that absolute poverty equals the perfect love of God. The monk of Bury St. Edmunds, Fitzralph, and Langland are all following here Augustine's *De opere monachorum*, 34–35, which points out that spiritual lack of solicitude which Jesus Himself commanded is not inconsistent with monastic labor for the necessities of life. "He [Jesus] says this [Matt. 6:25], not to forbid the procuring of what the monks need in order to live respectably, but so that they may not fix their attention on these commodities and, with them in mind, do whatever they are ordered in preaching the gospel" (trans. Sister Mary Sarah Muldowney in The Fathers of the Church XVI [New York, 1952], p. 380).
83. "The Imaginative Unity of Piers Plowman," *RES*, N.S. VIII (1957), 126.
84. See Leo Spitzer, "Des Guillemets qui changent le climat poétique . . . ," *PMLA*, LIX (1944), 336–338.
85. On medieval minstrels, see Anton E. Schönbach, "Studien zur Geschichte der altdeutschen Predigt," Part II in *Sitzungsberichte der philosophisch-historischen Klasse der Kaiserlichen Akademie der Wissenschaften*, Vienna, CXLII (1900), 7, pp. 56–89. (Based on the sermons of Berthold von Regensburg); Arthur K. Moore, "Sir Thopas as Criticism of Fourteenth-Century Minstrelsy," *JEGP*, LIII (1954), 532–545; Clair C. Olson, "The Minstrels at the Court of Edward III," *PMLA*, LVI (1941),

601–612; Wilhelm Grossmann, *Frühmittelenglische Zeugnisse über Minstrels* (*circa 1100 bis circa 1400*), Inaugural Dissertation ... Friedrich-Wilhelms-Universität zu Berlin (Brandenburg a. H., 1906); and Edmond Faral, *Les Jongleurs en France au moyen âge*, Bibliothèque de l'Ecole des Hautes Etudes, publiés sous les auspices du Ministère de l'Instruction publique: Sciences historiques et philologiques 187 (Paris, 1910).

86. *Piers Plowman: The C-Text*, pp. 136–155.

87. From the Middle English (late fourteenth century) Commentary on *Bonum est confiteri Domino*, ed. Bjorn Wallner, Lund Studies in English XXIII (Lund and Copenhagen, 1954), p. 59.

NOTES FOR APPENDIX I

1. See, e.g., *Piers Plowman, A Contribution to the History of English Mysticism*, trans. M. E. R., revised and enlarged by the Author (London, 1894), p. 195.

2. H. B. Workman in his great biography of Wyclif makes the point that the reformer could not have known Joachim at first hand as there were no manuscripts of his work in England in the fourteenth century. (*John Wyclif*, 2 vols. [Oxford, 1926], II, 99 n.). Although there are references to Joachim in Wyclif's writings, most of them were of a conventional sort and of the type that could easily have come from secondary sources. I agree with Workman that Wyclif's references to Joachim are conventional; however, there can be little doubt that Joachim's writings were available in the original. Joachim was widely and directly known in England in this period, as the kind of comment frequently made about him and the number of the manuscripts of his works then available reveal. Workman's point about the absence of Joachite MSS in England has been again made recently by R. Freyhan, "Joachism and the English Apocalypse," *Journal of the Warburg and Courtauld Institutes*, XVIII (1955), 214.

Allusions to Joachim in Wyclif may be found in his *Opus evangelicum*, III, 58 (ed. J. Loserth [London, 1895–1896], II, p. 216); *Tractatus de apostasia* (ed. M. H. Dziewicki [London, 1889], pp. 68–69); *Sermones* (ed. J. Loserth [London, 1887–1890], I, 85); *Super Matthei*, XXIV, 7, in *Opera minora* (ed. J. Loserth [London, 1913], p. 375); *De veritate Sacrae Scripturae* (ed. R. Buddensieg [London, 1905–1907], I, 140–141); *De eucharistia* (ed. J. Loserth [London, 1892], p. 278); *De dominio divino*, I, 12 (ed. R. L. Poole [London, 1890], p. 94).

3. See, for example, manuscripts like Corpus Christi, Cambridge 404; Gonville and Caius, Cambridge 388/608; Trinity College, Dublin 347; British Museum, Cotton, Vespasian E. VII. One of these pseudo-Joachite prophecies, the *De concordanciis*, has been discussed above, in Chapter IV. The pseudo-Joachite *De semine Scripturarum*, for instance, was well known in England and probably was known directly to Wyclif. In 1356 a work which is in part a translation into English of the *De semine* (although I have not collated the two) and which is entitled by its modern editor *The Last Age of the Church* (ed. James H. Todd [Dublin, 1840]) made its appearance. The pseudo-Joachite *Noticia seculi* was also known to the author of the *Last Age* and Wyclif (in Supplement to the *Trialogus* [ed. G. Lechler, Oxford, 1869, pp. 453 ff.]). Both of these works were assumed in the fourteenth century to be by Joachim himself.

4. I include them because they are relatively early and although not by Joachim are certainly full of genuine Joachism. Part of the Isaiah *Commentary* circulated as a separate work in England and elsewhere and was known as *De oneribus prophetarum*.

5. On English property owned by the Florensians, see D. Mauro Cassoni, "La Badia Ninfana di S. Angelo o del Monte Mirteto nei Volsci fondata da Gregorio IX," *Rivista storica benedettina*, XIV (1923), 185; and Filippo Caraffa, *Il Monastero Florense di S. Maria della Gloria presso Anagni ...* (Rome, 1940), pp. 43, 60–64, 69.

6. MSS now in England definitely known to be of foreign provenance are not mentioned. I am indebted to Dr. A. I. Doyle of the University of Durham for his expert opinion on the origin of some of these MSS. I have not been strict about the dates, since dating MSS is in general hazardous. Even if the date is of the fifteenth century, we can assume in most cases that the manuscript was copied from an exemplar in England.

7. This is a composite MS made up of several originally separate MSS bound together. N. R. Ker, *Medieval Libraries of Great Britain: A List of Surviving Books*, Royal Historical Society Guides and Handbooks No. 3 (London, 1941), lists the parts as coming from Battle Abbey; the Benedictine abbey and Cathedral Priory, Ely; Exeter Cathedral; Glastonbury Abbey; and the Cathedral Priory, Winchester. But his references omit this portion of the MS with either deliberate or accidental intent. It is hence impossible to say whence this part of the MS comes, but considering its style and its neighbors, it is probably of English origin.

8. There are a number of thirteenth-century references which I omit but which clearly argue for a knowledge of Joachim in the preceding century.

9. "John Russel OFM," *RTAM*, XXIII (1956), 300–304. In a recent letter, Dr. Smalley speaks of a further example of his influence on John Lathbury O.F.M. (d. 1362) in his commentary on Lamentations. See her "Flaccianus *De visionibus Sibyllae*," *Mélanges offerts à Etienne Gilson*, Etudes de philosophie médiévale, hors série (Toronto and Paris, 1959), pp. 547–562, esp. p. 552.

10. See Morton W. Bloomfield, "Joachim of Flora," *Traditio*, XIII (1957), 302 and nn. 233 and 234, for references. See also B. Hirsch-Reich, "Heinrichs von Harclay Polemik gegen die Berechnung der zweiten Ankunft Christi," *RTAM*, XX (1953), 148.

11. Referred to in W. D. Macray, "Sermons for the Festivals of St. Thomas Becket etc., Probably by Archbishop Stratford," *EHR*, VIII (1893), 89.

12. Discussed above in Chapter IV.

13. There is also no reason to doubt that Peter John Olivi, the foremost Franciscan Spiritual, was also known in England in this period. John Bale (d. 1563) possessed a copy of his Postilla on the Apocalypse and on Genesis, although this work may have been purchased on the Continent (see Honor McCusker, *John Bale Dramatist and Antiquary* [Bryn Mawr, 1942], p. 44). There are some MSS of his works in English libraries, and one in the Vatican (Urb. lat. 480) is of English provenance. Syon Monastery possessed some of his works (see Bateson, *Catalogue of the Library of Syon Monastery*, pp. 59 and 76). Duns Scotus certainly knew his purely philosophical works in spite of not, as was customary when referring to contemporaries, mentioning his name. William Butler, regent master of the

Franciscans at Oxford, in his "determination" against the lawfulness of translating the Bible into the vernacular quotes Olivi with discrimination (see Margaret Deanesley, *The Lollard Bible and Other Medieval Biblical Versions*, Cambridge Studies in Medieval Life and Thought [Cambridge, England, 1920], p. 404).

NOTES FOR APPENDIX II

1. Popular piety and mysticism also flourished in the fourteenth century in England and, as has occasionally been indicated in the notes, left their mark on *Piers*; but, since I consider this piety and mysticism to be less important in their influence on our poem than monastic philosophy and scholasticism, it does not need any extended treatment on my part. Perhaps it may be best seen in Langland's continual reliance on and use of biblical texts, but this is also a characteristic of monkish philosophy and above all of Bernard of Clairvaux. Monasticism in fourteenth-century England was not unaffected by his mysticism, as its fondness for the *meditatio* shows (see W. A. Pantin, "The Monk-Solitary of Farne: A Fourteenth-Century English Mystic," *EHR*, LIX [1944], 162–186).

2. Mother Catherine Elizabeth Maguire, R.S.C.J., in her unpublished dissertation "Franciscan Elements in the Thought of Piers Plowman" (Fordham University, 1950), has made a good start in relating the thought of *Piers* to Duns Scotus, Occam, and Bonaventure in particular. Although I do not agree with her in every detail, I feel that this is a noteworthy contribution to the subject, one which I hope will soon be published. G. Hort, *Piers Plowman and Contemporary Religious Thought* (London, n.d.), and Willi Erzgräber, *William Langlands "Piers Plowman" (Eine Interpretation des C-Textes)*, Frankfurter Arbeiten aus dem Gebiete der Anglistik und der Amerika-Studien, Heft 3 (Heidelberg, 1957), both have valuable things to say on this subject. Hort is, however, not always accurate in her knowledge of scholastic thought, and Erzgräber is not careful enough about parallels; and both overrate the influence of Thomas. In order to prove influence it is not sufficient to find a parallel. See my review of Erzgräber in *Anglia*, LXXVI (1958), 550–554.

3. This statement does not mean that Langland was in every respect in agreement with the English Franciscan thought. It must also be remembered that there were differences within the latter "school."

4. "Present State of *Piers Plowman* Studies," *Speculum*, XIV (1939), 232. See also Gertrud Görnemann, *Zur Verfasserschaft und Entstehungsgeschichte von "Piers the Plowman,"* Anglistische Forschungen, Heft 48 (Heidelberg, 1916), pp. 138–139.

5. J. J. Jusserand, *Piers Plowman*, trans. M. E. R. (London, 1894), p. 81; and Jan Ten Brink, *Early English Literature (to Wyclif)*, trans. H. M. Kennedy (London, 1883), p. 352. E. M. Hopkins is probably the source of the idea that Langland was basically an ignoramus; see his "The Education of William Langland," *Princeton College Bulletin*, VIII (1895), 41–45, where he sets out to refute Ten Brink's and Jusserand's theories that Langland had a university training.

6. "Franciscan Elements," pp. 34 ff. She also suggests, p. 44, that the meeting of Will with the two Franciscans, the first of his teachers in the Vita when he sets out to seek Do-wel, may be an autobiographical reference.

7. See G. G. Coulton, "Theological Schools in Medieval England," *Church Quarterly Review*, CXVIII (1934), 98–101. Coulton, however, does not seem to subscribe to the view that Langland had some sort of higher education.

8. VIII, 20; X, 345; and XII, 278.

9. See, e.g., B. L. Ullman, "Some Aspects of the Origin of Italian Humanism," *PQ*, XX (1941), 212 ff.

10. Cf. the C title (XVII between 297–298), "Distinctio caritatis."

11. See Konstanty Michalski, *Le Problème de la volonté à Oxford et à Paris au XIVᵉ siècle* (Leopoli, 1937), pp. 260 ff. There is a large bibliography on this subject, of which I shall mention only two items: P. Agostino Fioravanti, "La Distinzione tra l'anima e le sue facoltà nella dottrina del Ven. G. Duns Scoto," *Studi francescani*, I (1914), 235–244; and P. Celestino Piana, "La Controversia della distinzione fra anima e potenze ai primordi della scuola scotista (1310–1330c)," *Miscellanea del Centro di Studi medievali*, Serie prima, Pubblicazioni dell'Università cattolica del S. Cuore, N.S. LVIII (Milan, 1956), 65–168.

12. See, e.g., *Quaestiones in Librum sententiarum*, IV, d. 15, q. 15.

13. Many other individual terms or rare ideas could be used to bolster the case I am arguing here, but I limit myself to two, the second one being below.

14. In *JEGP*, LII (1953), 182–188.

15. On this problem in the fourteenth century, see Paul de Vooght, *Les Sources de la doctrine chrétienne d'après les théologiens du XIVᵉ siècle et du début du XVᵉ* ... (Bruges, 1954).

16. *ST*, I, q. 79, a. 13.

17. Unless (as some do) we take kind wit as synderesis, but I myself do not.

18. On all this, see Endre von Ivánka, "Byzantinische Theologumena und hellenische Philosophumena im Zisterziensisch-Bernhardinischen Denken," *Bernhard von Clairvaux* ... Internationaler Bernhardkongress, Mainz, 1953, ed. J. Lortz, Veröffentlichungen des Instituts für europäische Geschichte, Mainz, 6 (Wiesbaden, 1955), pp. 168–175; and "Apex mentis, Wanderung und Wandlung eines stoischen Terminus," *ZKT*, LXXII (1950), 129–176; and Hans Hof, *Scintilla animae: Eine Studie zu einem Grundbegriff in Meister Eckharts Philosophie* ... (Lund and Bonn, 1952), esp. pp. 198 ff.

19. *De veritate*, q. 16.

20. In Chapter VIII (Gerson's *Opera omnia* [Antwerp, 1706], I, 365).

21. Modern theologians (as for instance René Carpentier in his article on "Conscience" in the *Dictionnaire de Spiritualité*) usually distinguish only the moral from the spiritual (or mystical) conscience, yet Langland's view of conscience in the Vita does not exactly correspond to either, although it is perhaps nearer the spiritual. I cannot investigate the history of this concept, but Langland after the Visio conceives of conscience as a kind of social moral force, related to *Heilsgeschichte*, within us.

22. *PL*, CLXXXIV, 507–552; the quotation is my translation of a passage found in column 517.

23. See Philippe Delhaye, *Le Problème de la conscience morale chez S. Bernard, etudié dans ses oeuvres et dans ses sources*, Analecta mediaevalia namurcensia 9 (Namur, Louvain, and Lille, 1957), pp. 99 ff. and 100 n., for these two references.

NOTES FOR APPENDIX III

1. "Of all the psychological personifications encountered by Will, Imaginative is the one who comes to grips most directly with the rebellious ideas expressed by Will at the end of Passus X" (and I would add "and throughout XI"), R. E. Kaske, "The Use of Simple Figures of Speech in *Piers Plowman*, B: A Study in the Figurative Expression of Ideas and Opinions," *SP*, XLVIII (1951), 588–589.

2. Omitting the mass of primary material, among analyses of the subject I have found useful for the medieval side of the subject, the following may be mentioned: R. P. S. Belmond, "Le Mécanisme de la connaissance d'après Pierre Olieu, dit Olivi," *La France franciscaine*, XII (1929), 291–323; 463–487; George P. Klubertanz, *The Discursive Power, Sources and Doctrine of the "Vis cogitativa" According to St. Thomas Aquinas* (St. Louis, 1952); Harry Austryn Wolfson, "The Internal Senses in Latin, Arabic and Hebrew Philosophical Texts," *HTR*, XXVIII (1935), 69–133; D. E. Sharp, "Thomas of Sutton O.P., His Place in Scholasticism and an Account of His Psychology," *Revue néoscolastique de philosophie*, XXXVI (1934), 332–354; F. Rahman, *Avicenna's Psychology* (London, 1952); Paulo Tochowicz, *Joannis Duns Scoti de cognitionis doctrina*, Studia friburgensia (Freiburg, Paderborn, and Paris, 1926); Edmund Joseph Ryan, *The Role of the "Sensus Communis" in the Psychology of St. Thomas Aquinas*, a Dissertation submitted to ... St. Louis University ... (Carthagena, Ohio, 1951); Robert Edward Brennan, "The Thomistic Concept of the Imagination," *The New Scholasticism*, XV (1941), 149–161; Edmund G. Gardner, "Imagination and Memory in the Psychology of Dante," *A Miscellany of Studies in Romance Languages and Literatures, Presented to Leon E. Kastner*, ed. M. Williams and James A. de Rothschild (Cambridge, England, 1932), pp. 275–282; Abelardo Lobato, O.P., "Avicena y Santo Tomás: Presencia del filósofo árabe en las primeras obras del aquinatense," *Estudios filosóficos*, IV (1955), 45–80, and V (1956), 83–130; and Murray Wright Bundy, *The Theory of Imagination in Classical and Mediaeval Thought*, University of Illinois, Studies in Language and Literature XII, 2–3 (Urbana, 1927).

3. H. S. V. Jones, "Imaginatif in Piers Plowman," *JEGP*, XIII (1914), 583–588; and Randolph Quirk, "Vis Imaginativa," *JEGP*, LIII (1954), 81–83.

4. Alhazen (d. 1039?) in his *Perspectiva* or *Optica*, II, 66, seems, surprisingly enough, to allow universals in the imagination. This concession is extremely rare. See Hans Bauer, *Die Psychologie Alhazens*, Beiträge zur Geschichte der Philosophie des Mittelalters X, 5 (Münster i. W., 1911), p. 63.

5. Although not always. Sometimes *imaginatio* or *vis imaginativa* is used as the term to describe all of the internal senses. Sometimes *phantasia* is used for either function, as described above, or the internal senses as a whole. The confusion of the terminology is incredible.

6. John Peckham in his *Tractatus de anima*, X (ed. G. Melani, Biblioteca di Studi francescani I [Florence, 1948], p. 35), distinguishes following Avicenna, among the internal "vires," the *imaginatio* (a kind of receptacle) from the *vis imaginativa*. The latter operates when we are awake and asleep, and can receive impressions from above in dreams. *Phantasia* is equivalent to the *sensus communis* in this system.

7. Occam, for instance, stressed the power and spontaneity of the imagination. See Franz Federhofer, "Die Philosophie des Wilhelm von Ockham

im Rahmen seiner Zeit," *Franziskanische Studien,* XII (1925), 277.

8. See Bruno Nardi, *Dante e la cultura medievale: Nuovi saggi di filoso-fia dantesca,* Biblioteca di cultura moderna 368 (Bari, 1942), Chapter IX (pp. 258–334), entitled "Dante Profeta."

9. See, e.g., *The Republic,* IX, 571c–572a; *Timaeus,* 72a; and *Phaedrus,* 248c–d.

10. A major problem among Christian thinkers of late antiquity and the early Middle Ages was how to distinguish true from false prophecies. They all agreed that spiritual beings—angels, demons, and God—could give us visions in the imagination, but the problem was how we can distinguish them. The philosophical problem is a psychological one—how can we account for suprasensuous knowledge on the basis of our knowledge of the soul? The psychology of mysticism is also a related issue. Some thinkers, like the Victorines, recognized, largely for mystical purposes, the importance of imagination even before the Arab-Jewish theory of prophecy reached the West, but it was still a rather low source of knowledge.

11. See the important article by R. Walzer, "Al-Farabi's Theory of Prophecy and Divination," *The Journal of Hellenic Studies,* LXXVII (1957), 142–148. On early prophetic theory among medieval Jews and Arabs and its Hellenistic sources, see A. Altmann and S. M. Stern, *Isaac Israeli, a Neoplatonic Philosopher of the Early Tenth Century,* Scripta Judaica I (London, 1958), pp. 140–145, 209–217, and R. Walzer, "Platonism in Islamic Philosophy," *Recherches sur la tradition platonicienne,* Sept exposés ... Fondation Hardt, Entretiens sur l'antiquité classique III (Vandoeuvres-Geneva, 1955), pp. 213 ff.

12. *Guide for the Perplexed,* trans. M. Friedländer, 2nd ed. (London, 1936), p. 225 (II, 36).

13. *Dante e la cultura medievale,* pp. 286 ff.

14. *ST,* II, II, q. 174, a. 2 (English Dominican translation). Cf. *De veritate,* XII, a. 12, where he makes substantially the same point.

NOTES FOR APPENDIX IV

1. For this debate—and especially the views of Henry Harclay, Hugh of Newcastle, John Eshenden, and Wyclif, all Englishmen of the fourteenth century—see Morton W. Bloomfield, "Joachim of Flora," *Traditio,* XIII (1957), 302 n. 234. David of Augsburg, a Franciscan who died in 1272, complains of the excessive number of prophecies concerning the advent of Antichrist in his *De septem processibus religiosorum,* quoted in Dagobert Stockerl, *Bruder David von Augsburg...,* Veröffentlichungen aus dem kirchenhistorischen Seminar, München, IV, 4 (Munich, 1914), pp. 179–180.

2. See Silvio Vismara, *Il Concetto della storia nel pensiero scolastico,* Pubblicazione dell'Università cattolica del Sacro Cuore, Serie V, Vol. II (Milan, 1924). For the impact of Aristotelianism on Christian eschatology and the difficulties it created, see Tullio Gregory, "L'Escatologia cristiana nell'aristotelismo latino del XIII secolo," *Ricerche di storia religiosa,* I (1954–1957), 108–119.

3. See D. T. Starnes, "Purpose in the Writing of History," *MP,* XX (1922–1923), 281–300; Robert W. Ayers, "Medieval History, Moral Purpose, and the Structure of Lydgate's *Siege of Thebes,*" *PMLA,* LXXIII (1958), 463–474; Eva Matthews Sanford, "The Study of Ancient History in the

Middle Ages," *JHI*, V (1944), 21–43, esp. 28 ff. Hugh of St. Victor also allows, besides the didactic value of history, that studying history trains the memory. See preface to his *De tribus maximis circumstantiis gestorum*, ed. W. M. Green in *Speculum*, XVIII (1943), 484 ff.

4. So says the compiler of the *Historia regum francorum* in the early thirteenth century, quoted by Laura Hibbard Loomis in *Speculum*, XXXIII (1958), 251.

5. See Clement C. J. Webb, *The Historical Element in Religion*, Lewis Fry Lectures delivered at the University of Bristol, 1934 (London, 1935), pp. 36–37.

6. See B. A. Van Groningen, *In the Grip of the Past, Essay on an Aspect of Greek Thought*, Philosophia antiqua VI (Leiden, 1953), esp. pp. 109 ff.

7. See Jean Daniélou, "The Conception of History in the Christian Tradition," *The Journal of Religion*, XXX (1950), 171–179.

8. See Giuseppe Amari, *Il Concetto di storia in Sant' Agostino* (Rome, 1951); and W. Lipgens, "Die Bekenntnisse Augustins als Beitrag zur christlichen Geschichtsauffassung," *Münchener theologische Zeitschrift*, II (1951), 164–177—to take only two recent treatments of this subject.

9. See M.-D. Chenu, "Conscience de l'histoire et théologie au XIIIᵉ siècle," *Archives d'histoire doctrinale et littéraire du moyen âge*, XXIX (1954), 107–133; Morton W. Bloomfield, "Chaucer's Sense of History," *JEGP*, LI (1952), 301–313; and Otto Herding, "Geschichtsschreibung und Geschichtsdenken im Mittelalter," *Theologische Quartalschrift*, CXXX (1950), 129–144.

10. This tendency to "antiquify" things also was extended to literature; so Paul Lehmann, *Pseudo-antike Literatur des Mittelalters*, Studien der Bibliothek Warburg XIII (Leipzig and Berlin, 1927). This habit of mind is also, of course, found in antiquity.

11. See Hans Baron, *The Crisis of the Early Italian Renaissance: Civic Humanism and Republican Liberty in an Age of Classicism and Tyranny* (Princeton, 1955), I, 38–63. On this general view of history, see Herding, "Geschichtsschreibung ...," p. 142, where he writes that the medieval historian, not less than the medieval emperor, felt himself the continuer of antiquity.

INDEX